Pehr Osbeck, Johann Reinhold Forster

A Voyage to China and the East Indies

Vol. I

Pehr Osbeck, Johann Reinhold Forster

A Voyage to China and the East Indies
Vol. I

ISBN/EAN: 9783743385276

Manufactured in Europe, USA, Canada, Australia, Japa

Cover: Foto ©Andreas Hilbeck / pixelio.de

Manufactured and distributed by brebook publishing software (www.brebook.com)

Pehr Osbeck, Johann Reinhold Forster

A Voyage to China and the East Indies

VOYAGE

TO

CHINA AND THE EAST INDIES,

By PETER OSBECK,
RECTOR of HASLOEF and WOXTORP,
Member of the ACADEMY of STOCKHOLM, and of the
SOCIETY of UPSAL.

Together with A VOYAGE TO SURATTE,
By OLOF TOREEN,
Chaplain of the GOTHIC LION EAST INDIAMAN.

AND

An Account of the CHINESE HUSBANDRY,
By Captain CHARLES GUSTAVUS ECKEBERG.

Tranflated from the GERMAN,
By JOHN REINHOLD FORSTER, F.A.S.

To which are added,

A FAUNULA and FLORA SINENSIS.

IN TWO VOLUMES.

VOL. I.

LONDON,
Printed for BENJAMIN WHITE,
at Horace's Head, in Fleet-ftreet.
M DCC LXXI.

TO

THOMAS PENNANT, Esq;

OF

DOWNING, in FLINTSHIRE.

DEAR SIR,

THE peculiar obligations your goodness has laid me under, have left me no room to hesitate one moment in the choice of a patron for this publication.

THIS work was undertaken with your approbation, enriched by you with many important additions, and has often been the subject of our conversation.

BUT my obligations to you are not confined to the assistance you have afforded me in this present work: by your favour, I, who was an utter stranger to this

this country, have been introduced to a number of munificent and worthy friends, whoſe acquaintance is both my honour and my happineſs.

THE ſimilitude of our ſtudies was what firſt recommended me to your notice; but your humanity was engaged to receive me to a nearer intimacy from a circumſtance, which too frequently would have been the cauſe of neglect: the diſtreſſes I labour under affected your heart, and excited you to remove them in a moſt tender and benevolent manner.

HAVING no other way to expreſs the ſtrong impreſſions it has made on me, I beg leave to prefix your name to theſe Voyages; and thus publicly to acknowledge your great and moſt ſeaſonable favours. But I will ſay no more on this ſubject; well knowing, that thanks are often leaſt pleaſing where they are moſt due. Permit me, however, to offer up the moſt ſincere and earneſt wiſhes of a

grateful

grateful heart for your happiness. May you and your family long enjoy, in full measure, all the blessings of life; and may these be heightened by the continuance of every intellectual and moral pleasure. And while you are distinguished even amongst foreigners, as a patron and promoter of learning, especially of natural history; may you continue to have in your own country the honour and pleasure of being a father to the afflicted and necessitous.

I am,

with the truest regard,

Dear Sir,

Your most obedient

humble servant,

John Reinhold Forster.

Warrington,
Dec. 1, 1770.

THE

EDITOR's PREFACE.

TO a nation fo enlightened as the *Englifh*, the following tranflation can hardly be unacceptable, and therefore I might well have been excufed the common appendage of a preface; but as there are many particulars relative to the author, which may contribute to ftamp a value on this work, I fhall briefly ftate them without any farther apology.

THE author, Mr. OSBECK, chaplain to an *Eaft India* fhip of *Sweden* (his native country),

was

was a pupil of the great LINNÆUS, whose name alone is a sufficient encomium. He followed punctually and literally the rules prescribed by his excellent tutor in his *Instructio Peregrinatoris*. Nothing escaped the attention of Mr. OSBECK. The history, the antiquities, the religion, the manners, the dress, the character, the policy, the government, the military and civil establishments of the country, were equally objects of his attention; and what is very remarkable, and will of course prejudice this nation in favour of our author, is, that we find the judgment of Lord ANSON about the *Chinese* confirmed and justified in his observations on the character of that nation.

THE merchant will find a minute and accurate account of many commodities brought from the East, with an exact delineation of the whole commerce of *China*. The œconomist and husbandman will find many useful and agreeable remarks in Mr. OSBECK's and Mr. ECKEBERG's accounts, which might be considered as good hints even in this country,
where

where agriculture and hufbandry have been improved both in theory and in practice, to the great emolument of the inhabitants; while many facts here related are applicable to the *Englifh* colonies and plantations. In fhort, the reader will find many remarks in the courfe of this work, that will affift him in the ftudy of medicine, hiftory, geography, and almoft every other branch of learning.

But the natural hiftorian will find the richeft treafures in this ufeful performance; and as a tafte for this branch of knowledge begins very juftly to attract the attention of this nation, and to fpread fo univerfally that it even finds the protection of perfons of the higheft quality, and the patronage of the fairer fex: I thought my leifure hours could not be better beftowed, than on a tranflation of a work of fo general utility.

Hasselquist's journey to *Egypt* and *Palestine* has very defervedly had the approbation of the nation, in its *Englifh* drefs; and confirmed the high opinion which the public had

had before conceived of Profeſſor LINNÆUS and his pupils; and it may be hoped, this performance will recommend itſelf equally to the reader, from the uncommon variety of objects deſcribed, and the uſefulneſs of the author's remarks.

A WORD or two I muſt ſay in regard to the tranſlation, which is made from the *German*, and not from the original *Swediſh*; but as Mr. OSBECK not only reviſed the *German* tranſlation, but alſo made ſome additions to it which are not found in the original *Swediſh* edition, it is rather an advantage to the work than a prejudice. It was tranſlated into *German* by Mr. J. GODLIEB GEORGI, under the direction of Dr. DANIEL SCHREBER [a], who both underſtood the *Swediſh* language perfectly well, having ſtudied at *Upſal* for many years. The latter was a pupil and friend of LINNÆUS, and well known for many uſeful publications in œconomy, huſbandry, and natural

---

[a] Dr. *Schreber* has enriched this work with ſeveral remarks, which are marked at the end with D. S. and thoſe of the editor with an F.

EDITOR'S PREFACE.

hiſtory, and particularly a botanical and œconomical deſcription of graſſes [b].

As I have met with great encouragement and generous aſſiſtance in the tranſlation of this work, from many gentlemen of great worth, whoſe names would be an ornament, was I permitted to mention them; I take this opportunity to acknowledge in a public manner the great obligations I feel myſelf under; and that the remembrance of them will not be obliterated, but will ever fill my heart with the warmeſt ſentiments of gratitude.

[b] The firſt part of this work, already publiſhed, contains twenty coloured plates, and twenty-ſeven different graſſes, with a large introduction to the ſtudy of this branch of botany: and very accurate deſcriptions of each kind, together with remarks on the cultivation, uſes, and ſoil proper for each ſpecies.

PREFACE

PREFACE

OF

Mr. OSBECK.

IN the year 1750 I was chosen by the *Swedish East India* company, to perform the functions of a chaplain to a ship going to the *East Indies*; that is, to read prayers in the morning and evening, to confess the people, to administer the Lord's supper, to catechise, to visit the sick, to bury the dead, and to preach on *Sundays* and Holidays.

So tedious a voyage required some amusement: during all intermissions from our ordinary

nary bufinefs. Every one chofe fomething adapted to his tafte; for my part I found nothing that could entertain more innocently both myfelf during the voyage, and my friends after my return, than natural hiftory.

The inftruction I drew from the lectures which I had attended in this fcience at *Upfal*, obliged me to be grateful. I returned without any money; more of which I could have employed during my voyage in the gratification of my thirft after knowledge: for I knew that to fo learned a man, as Linnæus, I could no how exprefs my obligations fo well as by fpecimens of natural hiftory.

I kept for my own amufement a journal of every thing worthy of obfervation during my voyage; from this I gave him fome defcriptions of new plants found in *Spain*, *China*, and other places, which were immediately incorporated into that capital botanical book then printing under the title of *Species Plantarum*, and with which my names of plants agree [c].

[c] The author's animals are alfo admitted into the *Syftema Naturæ*, edit. 12; and where *Linn.* though't proper to alter the genus, his names are quoted as fynonyms

AUTHOR'S PREFACE.

In his letters from time to time he put me in mind of publishing the account of my voyage; but I always oppofed it, as believing that fuch defcriptions could only pleafe naturalifts, or lovers of natural hiftory; but all my objections were furmounted by the advice of other learned men, and efpecially by the order of a great perfonage, for whom I fhall always retain the greateft deference. The following fheets however ought to be confidered as written at firft merely for my own amufement.

During the courfe of our voyage, I obferved the latitude at all opportunities, and have fo defcribed feveral fifh and birds, that if they fhould occur to others they may be known by them though they had never feen them before. Some which I have only feen at a diftance, I have (till further examination) only mentioned under the name which the failors generally give them in the latitude, where they either ftay for a feafon or throughout the whole year. I have remarked fwallows and other birds when they approached our fhip, that by a variety of obfervations of that kind, we may become better acquainted with the history of their migrations.

DURING my stay in *China* and other foreign places, I have been exceedingly attentive to the exterior aspect of the inhabitants, their dress, customs, religion, manner of subsistence, trade, &c. but especially to the condition of the country, the soil, the quadrupeds, amphibia, fish, birds, insects; likewise the trees, herbs, plants, seeds, &c. of which I have brought a good many with me. Most new plants and other natural bodies I have described in Latin [d], that foreigners might likewise avail themselves of these descriptions: but some few run in my mother'tongue, on account of those who understand no other. I have minuted the particular spot in which I found every plant, such as plain, mountain, valley, whether in shade, &c. because an ignorance of such circumstances frequently frustrates the labour and expence used in the cultivation of foreign plants.

[d] In the *German* translation these descriptions are not in Latin, for which reason I have translated them into *English*.

I HAVE

I HAVE ſhewn, that moſt foreign nations, and eſpecially the *Chineſe*, live for the greateſt part on fruits, roots, and plants, and that they cultivate ſuch plants in their marſhes, as will not ſucceed in other places: we might alſo find ſufficient proviſion among our own ſpontaneous plants. The *Chineſe* inſtruct their children in a religion both irrational and pagan, yet the principal objects of their education are morality and œconomy.

IN ſome places I have taken notice of things not uncommon in *Sweden*; which are however worthy of remark, becauſe they are found in ſuch diſtant climates, where every thing elſe is different: from hence we might at leaſt draw ſome uſeful concluſions.

WE are uſed to aſk what a thing is good for? And often raſhly think, that alone uſeful, which ſerves for medicine, cloaths, and food: as if the eye had no claim to its gratifications, and as if what is agreeable was not connected with what is uſeful. The dreſſes and

and utenfils of diftant countries are admired and carefully collected; why fhould not then the works of the Creator deferve at leaft an equal degree of attention?

THE obfervations which I have made in feveral places, efpecially fuch as were much frequented, are fhort and inartificial : and it will appear from my ftile, in how languid a manner the pen performs its office amidft the fcorching heat of the *Chinefe* fhores, where, to avoid the fufpicion of the people, I frequently wrote with my hand in my pocket, on a pocket book. Let every reader confider my fituation, and apply the cafe to himfelf. The hurry of the prefs has excluded fome additions [e] which I intended to have made.

I ONLY wifh that my obfervations may procure half as much approbation from the world, as they have coft me trouble and attention. I ventured on fhore at the ifland of *Java*, where the woods are filled with tigers and crocodiles ; and hazarded my life in *China*; (where

[e] Thefe additions were inferted by Mr. *Ofbeck* himfelf in the *German* tranflation, which is here followed.

the heat of the fun on barren hills, robbers on the roads, and petulant children in back ſtreets, are continually annoying a foreigner); and landed on the iſland of *Aſcenſion*, where the fun hatches the eggs of the tortoiſes, and in a ſhort time ruins the conſtitution of the moſt healthy. On the whole, however, I have no reaſon to be ſorry for my voyage, from the kind reception with which the directors of the *Eaſt India* company have honoured me on my return: the ſame year they gave me leave to go on a ſecond voyage, which ſome intervening obſtacles obliged me to lay aſide.

I HAVE added the letters of the late chaplain of the Gothic Lion, Mr. *Toreen*, to my journal. This perſon died ſoon after his return from *Suratte*; but deſerves always to be remembered by his friends, on account of his learning and integrity. Other *Swedes* (deſirous of extending knowledge) are ready alſo to publiſh accounts of their travels, would but the affluent give encouragement to thoſe who endeavour to be uſeful to the public on their voyages, by promoting diſcoveries in natural

hiſtory

hiſtory or œconomy. But for this purpoſe expenſive books are required, and money is very neceſſary for the voyage; on proper occaſions, I have expended not only my ſalary, but the voluntary contributions of my protectors, whoſe munificence will always make the deepeſt impreſſion on my mind.

Stockholme,
25th of *April*, 1757.

PETER OSBECK'S

VOYAGE to CHINA.

GOTHENBURGH.

North latitude, 57° 42′; and 6° weſt longitude from Upſal.

The year 1750.

November the 18th.

FROM Gothenburgh (where the Swediſh Eaſt India company's ſhips are fitted out, and to which place they have always returned, ever ſince the year 1731, when they obtained the firſt charter for carrying on this trade)

trade) I went to *Vargoe Hoala*, in very bad weather, the place where the East India ships usually anchor, when *Riff* and *Fcol*, and the other creeks in the Gothenburgh rocks, are filled with ice; by which means they avoid the inconvenience of sawing the ice in order to clear their passage. The above place, which derives its name from the Isle of *Vargoe*, or the *Isle of Wolves*, is a Swedish mile[a] and a half from Gothenburgh. I made this journey by land as far as *Hinsholm*, and there went on-board the *Prince Charles*, which was the first three-deck ship employed by Sweden in the East-India-trade. It was lately built at Stockholm, and its bulk was 390 tons; it was manned with 132 men, almost ready to set sail, and bound for *Canton* in *China*.

Wood is much wanted in this country; and for this reason the pilots, and all the other islanders, are obliged to buy this commodity in town, where of late its price is greatly risen; or to burn turf, which is dug in parallelopipeds, as it was formerly in *Holland*. In

---

[a] Eleven Swedish miles make one degree; consequently two miles are $12\frac{6}{10}$, or still nearer $12\frac{7}{11}$ English miles. F.

this province turf was not common fo early as 1670, fo that the citizens of *Falkenbergh* and *Laholm* petitioned for the free importation of it, but were refufed. In 1672, the town of *Laholm* obtained, that the turf dug in that diftrict fhould pay no duty. At prefent the turf is managed in Holland in a different manner from what it was before: which method the peafants of *Fiaré* learnt only 30 years fince from the inhabitants of *Salkenbergh* and *Wardbergh*; it is thus done. As foon as the farmer has fown the fummer corn, he goes to the turfmoor: the firft comer takes the beft place: feveral parifhes divide a moor amongft themfelves. They at firft take off the green fods, as far as the roots of heath and grafs reach: they then pour water upon the turf mould, and dig it out by little and little, till they reach a fandy foil. In the middle of the moor they may dig a fathom deep, but not fo deep on the fides. The hole is made floping on two fides, fo that they may drive into it with a horfe and cart. The mud is then carried out of the hole upon the field, there fpread with the fpade to the thicknefs of three or four inches, and cut crofs-ways, fo that it may be broken into quadrangular pieces. But thofe who defire to have their turf ftill harder, fqueeze the mud, whilft foft, into round pieces refembling loaves, and let them dry in the fields, laying them clofe by one another. The turf which is grown a little harder is laid in heaps, yet fo that the wind may pafs through, and is fheltered from rain. In fummer, the turf is carried home, put under a roof, and ufed in brewing, baking, boiling, and for warming rooms. The turf foil is either reddifh, brown, or black, all which is equally good according to the account of the peafants; but they add, firft, that the turf muft never be mixed with fand, which increafes its bad fmell; fecondly, it muft not be mixed with clay, which hinders it from burning; and thirdly, it muft be clear of all wood and great roots, becaufe the ground about them is always very loofe. They commonly find the beft moors in large fields, becaufe the roots moulder better there than in woods, and the water is more eafily carried off. Often the beft turf foil is found upon moors where heath grows. This plant is always to be met with in good turf-moors, where the wind blows freely, and where other plants are

mouldered

mouldered away [b]; as we find in Holland, and other countries, which are in want of woods, and where turf has been in use for a long time. Yet I know that the soil in such mosses or moors, where heath is not yet rooted, is used also for turf, especially where there is no choice. It has been observed, that turf-earth is a sort of soil produced from mouldered plants; and seems to consist chiefly of a mouldered, red mofs, *Sphagnum palustre*, Linn. which in Westrogothia is called *hwcetare Mofs* (and from this probably the mosses, *Mossar*, take their name; which else are called *Myror*, perhaps from *Myror*, ants, or pismires, for they frequently are met with in this mofs); I myself found this mofs in a woody moor, every where at a fathom's depth, and always fresh.

[h] *Erica*, heath, never grows in turf moors before they are quite dry; for it cannot bear wet, and often perishes when the place where it grows is under water, as Dr. Linnæus has observed in his *Iter Scanicum*. But the *Erica myricæ folio hirsuta*, Bauh. pin. 485. grows in marshy mosses and moors; and I have found this variety of heath (which is uncommon in Germany) in Mecklenburgh, amongst the *ledum palustre*, or marsh cistus, and the *vaccinium uliginosum*, great bilberry bush. But in what manner the common smooth heath changes into this rough sort is unknown to me, and is worthy of farther enquiry. D. S.

December 6th, 61° 14′ N. L.

THE *Fœroe* isles, which we saw this morning, looked as gloomy as the weather of this season. You scarce see any thing else than high mountains covered with snow, a cloudy sky, and a roaring sea. These islands belong to Denmark, which provides them with corn; and the islanders, who are said to be very industrious, re-pay it with stockings, waistcoats, gloves, quilts, and train-oil, &c.; for breeding of sheep and fishing are their principal trades. It is said, that they catch a great many *whales*; that they eat dry cod-fish instead of bread; and that they put their sheep-tallow under ground, in order to use it afterwards as butter or oil.

December 9th, 60° 10′ N. L.

WE thought to have passed in the night-time, *Rochelle*, a small island about the size of a ship.

December 19th, 56° 42' N. L.

Our seamen gave the name of *Northcaper* to a sort of whale which is discovered by its throwing up the water; it is *Delphinus orca*, or the *Grampus*. The Danish missionary *Hans Egede* speaks thus of it, in his treatise called *Gamle Greenlands nye perlustration* (or a New Review of old Greenland): " The species of " whales called the Northcaper derives it's " name from the North Cape, in Norway, " where they are numerous; yet they are " likewise found about Iceland, Greenland, " and other countries; for they look for the " places where herrings and other small fish " are in plenty, and often a ton of herrings " have been found in the stomach of such a " whale. The Northcaper is very like the " *Balæna physalus*, or fin-fish, which being a " very nimble fish goes into the open sea, as " if it were afraid of becoming a prey to its " enemies if it approached the coasts. This " kind has a more solid fat, and its whalebone " is not so long and good as that of the for- " mer, and therefore is seldom pursued." For a further account, see Klein. Hist. Piscium, Miss. II. p. 12. *Balæna Borealis, Northcaper*.

The year 1751.

January 1st, 36° 35′ N. L.

In the forenoon we saw *Cape Vincent*, a promontory in Spain. The shores appeared high and white, and the ever-green trees made the country look very fine.

January 4th.

The *Granate mountain* shewed itself to the right at a great distance, on account of its prodigious height.

The *Rock St. Pedro*, which was to the right, was quite fresh in our memories, on account of the ship called *Sweden*, which the crown of Sweden had designed for a present to the Turkish Emperor, but was lost here in November 1738, when Captain Wagenfeld, was conducting her to Constantinople. Of the artillery which was recovered out of the water, six brafs cannon and a mortar are still to be seen at Cadiz, all inscribed with the name and arms of that most glorious-King Charles

Charles the Twelfth and are kept there for the Swedish service.

WHITE *gulls* and *herring gulls (Larus canus et fuscus)* were here in such flights, as if they would dispute with the fishermen about their right of fishing.

THE greater and lesser *Porcos* are two rocks on the starboard, at the entrance of the port of Cadiz: we happily passed by them. When the water is low, they are very conspicuous; but when it is high, they are known by the breakers only.

ST. *Sebastian's* is a castle upon a little island near Cadiz, which, with two other castles, serve to defend this town.

THE *Gulf of Cadiz*, or the Road, is well known under the name of the Spanish-bay, where the ships of many nations yearly come, and where we likewise cast anchor after a six weeks voyage, and having suffered a great storm. After saluting, we were welcomed by several of our countrymen. We saw *Cadiz* and *Puerto real*, on the bay; *Puerto de Sancta Maria*

Maria directly oppofite Cadiz, and *Rota* further on towards the fea.

THE *Quarantine-boat* (or practic-boat, as the Swedes call it) was a floop covered with green, which was rowed by twelve men, and in it were two or three gentlemen of the college of health in Cadiz. After the floop had joined our veffel, they afked whence the fhip came? what was her name, and that of her captain? how many men fhe had? &c. The anfwers they received were written down upon paper. We likewife fhewed them our fhip's journal, and told them that they would find in it the name and manner of the death of a man that was killed by a fall. They took the journal with them on fhore, in order to fhew it to the college; but firft ordered us to let none go out of the fhip before they had obtained leave: for this reafon we put a goofe upon our foretop-maft, which is a fign of a fhip's keeping the quarantine.

January the 13th, and the following days.

I SAW on-board a Swedifh fhip fome orfelle, or oricelle *(Lichen roccella)*, a fpecies of mofs which

which grows upon the Canary Iflands, efpecially on Teneriff; and I was told that it fold in Leghorn at two dollars copper coin ᶜ per pound, and that it was ufed to dye red with.

THE climate here is not very agreeable, for the heat obliges the inhabitants to keep within doors on the fineft fummer days, to fleep during the day, and to go out at night. Without doors the heat is very difagreeable; and from May to the middle of October they muft fuffer a great deal from gnats.

SEA plants are very fcarce along the fhores here, whereas the Swedifh fhore has all forts of fuci, confervæ, &c. in plenty.

CADIZ *miol'ya* is a fuburb without the city walls, where all travellers land that come to town by water. In this part are two columns of white marble, erected by the governor of the city during the reign of Philip the Fifth, as expreffed in the infcription. Befides this, there is a watch-houfe for the foldiers, and a little cuftom-houfe.

ᶜ About 11 d. Englifh.

There are two gates in this approach, one for those that enter, and the other for those that go out. Both of them have draw-bridges, guarded with some soldiers; and about those are a number of lynx-eyed *visitors* (or custom-house officers) dressed in a sort of wide jackets, called *Casa guillas* in Spanish, which are used in this country as riding-coats. Under these coats they are said to have always a brace of loaded pistols, for their defence. The usual dress of their countrymen are these brown coats and flapping hats. They can make signs to one another through the gates if any thing happens; and they are obliged to look very strictly with regard to all unlawful importation or exportation, particularly that of money, which must pay somewhat *per cent*. Those that go out are visited with a strictness beyond description; as I once wanted to get out of the gate in great haste, with my pockets full of stones, it occasioned a suspicion in one of the visitors, who, in an earnest manner, put his hands into my pockets, and looking at me with a threatning countenance, searched every thing very carefully; but finding nothing but stones, he only smiled at my folly. To im-

port

port tobacco and fnuff is capital, or at leaft the perfon who imports it is condemned to the gallies for life: but they except that which the Spaniards bring from their American colonies. A fnuff-box therefore, if full of fnuff, may occafion great trouble to the bearer.

CADIZ, or *Cadix*, or, as the Englifh fometimes call it, *Cales*, is the principal fea-port in Spain; it contains a great number of inhabitants, is fituated on the fea-fhore of the province of Andalufia, at the extremity of an ifland, in 36 deg. 33 min. north latitude and 23 deg. 45 min. weft longitude from Upfal. The city is furrounded with fine gardens and fortifications, and is faid to have three hundred brafs cannon [d].

[d] The origin and antiquities of this town are defcribed by *Juan Baptifta Suarez de Salazar*, in his *Antiguedades de la civdad de Cadiz*, 1610, quarto, 317 pages; and afterwards in the *Emporio de el orbe, Cadiz illuftrada, invefigacion de fus antiguas grandezas, difcurfida en concurfo de el general imperio de Efpaua por el R. P. F. Geronimo de la conception, religiefo defcalzo de el order de nueftra Senora de el Carmine, y gaditano de origen, que la dedica a la muy noble y muy leal civdad de Cadiz*, Amfterd. fol. 1680, 663 pages: the price of it here at Cadiz is four pefos duros, that is, about feventeen fhillings and fix pence fterling.

THE

The walls, and moſt of the houſes in this town, are made of a ſort of ſtone which they call *Selleria,* and which is

Tophus *particulis teſtaceis, argilla & arena coadunatus,* or a mixture of ſhells, clay, and ſand. It is ſaid that the before mentioned rocks *Porcos* conſiſt of this ſtone. It is broken on the ſea-ſhore and carried from the *miol'ya* (when the tide is low) in high carts to the town; and thoſe pieces which are too heavy to be put into the cart are faſtened with ropes below it. The ſtone is ſoft in cutting, and therefore very proper to build with, as it hardens by time. The inner terras of the wall, to which a ſtaircaſe leads on the right hand ſide of the gates, is covered with Dutch clinkers [c], and as broad and even as the fineſt road. From thence you ſurvey with pleaſure (over the outward part of the wall, which is about four feet higher and very narrow) the ſhips riding at anchor, going out and coming in: among the firſt, is the ſilver-fleet. Towards the city you behold a ſtreet where ſalads,

---

[c] Clinkers are a ſpecies of Dutch bricks.

roots,

roots, and all forts of fruits, are expofed for
fale, winter and fummer.

The Spaniards make ropes and cables, for
fhips and other ufes, of a certain grafs which
they call *Sparto*. This is the *Stipa tenaciſſima*,
Linn. or *Spartum herba Plinii*, Cluf. Hift. 2.
p. 220. which is faid to grow in wet places [f].
The ropes they make of it are fo durable,
that they need not be tarred; but the Spaniards dry and fpin it without preparation,
contrary to what we are ufed to do with our
hemp. This might, perhaps, furnifh hints to
us to look out for fome of our own wild
graffes in order to employ them in the fame
manner, and we might make a beginning with
the *Elymus arenarius*. The Spanifh mats which
are brought to Sweden are made of the fame
Sparto.

Olive trees *(Olea Europæa)* and white
poplars *(Populus alba)* are planted on both
fides the ramparts, and are watered by fubterraneous pipes. Thus the city has the ad-

---

[f] Linnæus in his Species Plantarum, and Loefling in his
Journey through Spain fay it grows on the fandy hills of
Spain.

vantage

vantage of a garden's being within her walls; and therefore every one, if he choofes, can at once enjoy the pleafure of living in town and country. The road which goes further on will foon be adorned in the fame manner. The ramparts were, in all other places, of an equal breadth, and covered with fand, which makes it very eafy walking round the town.

On the ramparts, and even in other places, wooden croffes were erected.

The beggars were every where crying, *Una limoneta por el amor de Dios y por las benditas almas à efte pobre,* or fome fuch other petition for God's or for the Saints' fakes.

The foldiers upon the ramparts diverted themfelves with fifhing, when the tide was in. My defire of contemplating their art a little nearer was fruftrated; as I experienced now, and at other times, that foreigners are not permitted to ftand ftill upon the ramparts, to look about them.

The country fide has ftill higher walls; and its ditches, ramparts, and batteries, are more
curious

curious than I can defcribe, and are daily improving.

The market near the above mentioned fea gate, as well as a ftreet on the right hand of it along the high walk, are always well provided with victuals in bags, &c. and every perfon cries what he has to fell; thus, one cries *Caſtanas calientas y cocidas*, boiled warm chefnuts; another has a mug of water upon his back and a glafs in his hand, and cries *Agua del Puerto*, water from Port St. Mary.

Fish, in particular falted fea-fifh, were fold in vaft quantities in this market; and I heard them cry more than thirty different forts.

The houfes, as well private as public, are built of the above mentioned ftone (*Tophus*), and fometimes of limeftone. They are generally two or three ftories high, and have balconies which have no windows, except in the houfes of people of quality, and are provided, inftead of them, with two fhutters, which are opened when you want to let in the day-light, or to look at the great crowd of people paffing by. On thefe balconies they put their ftone water-

water-jugs, in which the water ufed in the houfe keeps beft.

FLOWER-pots, with rue, rofemary [g], &c. are likewife ranged in the fame place. The houfes of the people of condition are built round a fquare: at the fecond ftory on the infide, a gallery goes quite round, except on one fide, where they ufually have a little garden, out of which the *Paffiflora cærulea* creeps over the fecond-ftory windows; where, upon particular ftands, are feen cypreffes (*Cupreffus fempervirens*), *Capficum frutefcens*, lemon and orange trees, &c. which are likewife to be found below in the little gardens.

THE rooms are very high, white wafhed, and without tapeftry or painting, but generally ornamented with portraits and gilt furniture.

THEY keep the fpecies of parrot called *Pfittacus garrulus*, canary birds (*Fringilla Canaria*), red-legged partridges (*Tetrao rufus*),

---

[g] We bought fuch pots with flowers, to put upon the deck, for three pieces of eight each.

Loxia

Loxia violacea, and cardinal birds (*Loxia cardinalis*), which latter were faid to eat the above mentioned *Capficum frutefcens.*

Stoves and chimnies are as much unknown in this country as froft and fnow.

Floors and roofs are made of bricks and tiles. The former are covered with mats made of *Sparto* [h]. The rafters, laths, and tiles or flates of the roof are by no means concealed, and are rather difadvantageous to the beauty of the houfe, was this mode not in fome meafure juftified by the ufe refulting from it, and did it not increafe the height of the rooms.

The roofs are flat, and it is very agreeable walking upon them. They are moft commonly adorned with flower-pots on the fides, which make them look like gardens; in the pots are queen's ftock-july-flowers (*Cheiranthus incanus*); but where thefe are wanting, their places are fupplied by mapleleaved blite (*Chenopodium hybridum*), chickweed (*Alfine media*), common fow-thiftle *(Sonchus oleraceus)*; and befides this *Parietaria Lu-*

[h] See page 15.

fitanica.

sitanica. Where the water gathers on the roofs, *Bryum murale* and navel-wort (*Cotyledon umbilicus*) are found; and on dry walls *Lichen parietinus.*

Towers without spires are put upon several roofs: they have four sides, a height of some yards, and command a fine view of the town and the ships.

In the houses of consuls, the colours are hoisted upon such towers at the arrival of ships.

The doors are high, commonly folding ones, and in the inner apartments often without locks.

The gates are shut in the houses of people of rank, with a latch on the inside without any handle; but on the outside is a little bell: when this is pulled, the porter opens the gate from the balcony by a string, which pulls up the latch, and thus opens one half of the gates, which shuts of itself, by means of weights, as soon as the porter lets go the string. But if any one comes in the night-
time,

time, the porter muft go down to open the gates, left fome difagreeable guefts fhould flip in.

In the lowermoft floor are the ftables.

They ufe little caution againft fire, for the coachmen go into the ftables with torches; yet this accident feldom happens in Cadiz, as all the houfes are built with ftone.

Oil is ufed in lamps, inftead of candles; and likewife in dreffing meat oil is employed inftead of butter.

Their yards are paved, fome with flags of *Tophus*, and fome with flags of *Talcum*.

Some have wells in their yards; but the water is not fit to drink, and muft therefore be ufed for other purpofes in houfe-keeping.

The ftreets are paved with round pebbles, and have a channel in the middle filled with fhells of fifh, peels of fruit, or the like; which, putrifying by the heat, occafion a difagreeable fmell in many places.

The inhabitants are tawny, from the heat of the fun; moſt of them have long but narrow heads, great ears and eyes, black eyebrows and hair. They are lively, and have an eafy carriage.

A great mixture of other European nations is to be met with here; and befides thefe, they have negroes who ferve in the kitchens.

Their language is very expreffive, for they accompany their words with motions of the head, fhoulders, and arms [i]. The officers, as well as common foldiers, are reckoned very civil to foreigners: but the feamen are continually curfing and fwearing; and when they meet each other in their boats, it is their common falutation.

The drefs of the men is very commodious, for if they do not drefs fumptuoufly, they cover their heads with a linen cap, and above that they put a flapped hat, round which they faften a ribband with a little buckle, and tie

---

[i] Thefe geftures rather imply the contrary.

it to the head with another below the chin, so that the wind may not blow it off. They use no cravats. The rest of their dress is a waistcoat, the sleeves of which are open before, and the cuffs small, like those worn by the Prussian soldiers.

Over these they put on a long wide jacket, which is commonly of a black or brown colour: they wear linen stockings, and under them linen socks, and shoes with low quarters and heels, though the dirty streets seem to require higher. They carry two handkerchiefs about them, a coloured one to wipe off the sweat, and a white one. I sometimes saw young people walking with muffs, though it was then as warm here as it is in Sweden in summer-time. Gold-laced cloaths are as scarce with the quality as with the poor. People of rank carry sticks (which are said to be particular badges of honour) when they are not dressed. Some who have survived heavy diseases, or have escaped great misfortunes, wear, agreeable to their vows, no other than grey cloaths.

The ladies wear their own hair, either in long and broad tresses, or short with a toupee and an aigrette, or tied up at top as the Swedish country girls do. Hoops are not ufual here. They wear a fort of hood, which fits very clofe; this they put over their heads when they are in the ftreets, but throw it back when they are in their houfes: two ftraps, of a hand's breadth, hang down from it to the feet. If they go to church, a rofary, or paternofter, and a fan, are neceffary to their drefs.

The Swedifh Conful, Mr. Jacob Bellman, is honoured and beloved by every one, on account of his obliging behaviour. At the gate of his houfe, oppofite to the entrance, the Swedifh arms are put up: in his rooms were the portraits of the late King of Sweden, Frederic, of the prefent King and Queen, and of the Hereditary Prince Guftavus.

Churches, chapels, convents, and hofpitals, are all very fine. The church of white marble, which is not yet finifhed, and to the building of which the town pays a certain fum yearly, is the fineft and largeft of them all. The fubterraneous vaults below this church are almoft as large as the entire ftructure of the other churches, and fome corpfes have already

ready been depofited in them; they are faid to be quite finifhed; but the walls of the church are not raifed to the height intended; and yet candles are continually burning in it for its patron St. *Francis Xavier*, who fuffered martyrdom from the heathens for preaching the gofpel in Japan, and is faid to have wrought as many miracles as there are wax tapers burning round his image; to which the inhabitants pull off their hats whenever they pafs by.

WAX tapers are burning in the churches day and night. At the entrance is *Agua bendita*, or holy water, in a difh or veffel, into which they dip their fingers, and crofs themfelves when they go in and out. The church pavement is every where covered with matts; upon which men and women, of all ranks, kneel down for want of feats.

THE bells are always ringing, but not fo as with us; for they make a noife almoft all day, firft in one fteeple, then in another, then in all together, for prayers, or mafs, on account of lightning, or the dead: the latter is always in the evening, for their maffes for the dead are kept about that time.

ROSARIO,

ROSARIO, or a rosary, is neceffary to both ſexes, to regulate the number of their prayers; it confifts of a fine filver or brafs chain, with glafs or coral beads, or pearls, &c. and a crofs, from which hang two or three medals, with the images of faints, which are much valued.

CROSSING is performed with the thumb, before and after church fervice, or prayers, three times: viz. upon the forehead, mouth, and breaft, fo that nothing may befall their eyes, mouth, or heart; which is the more neceffary, as the crofs, according to their catechifm, is the principal mark of a Chriftian.

THEY marry very young; and a boy of fourteen years may marry a girl of twelve.

THEIR burials differ from ours in many things: before the corpfe a crofs with lanthorns is carried; as foon as it is depofited in the grave, fome quick-lime is thrown in along with it. In the evening a mafs is read for the dead, and the organ is played, though none but the living are the better for it. Their burying-grounds are out of the town; but they

fuffer

suffer no proteftant to lie in their church-yards.

The proceffions might almoft be confidered as funerals by ftrangers: they confift of a number of people of high and low rank, who follow a crofs through the town, accompanied by many lanthorns, and finging the *Te Deum* and *Litany*. Thefe proceffions are fixed to certain days; as the 2d of February, the 25th of March, the 15th of Auguft, the 8th of September, and the 8th of December ; and befides thefe, they have others on certain faints days, and when meat is to be gathered for the prifoners; and then they take kettles, difhes, pots, &c. with them. If they meet with fuch a proceffion, the people ftand ftill, take off their hats, and fall on their knees, though the ftreets be ever fo dirty. They have the liberty of making themfelves merry three days before Lent; and then they throw carraway comfits at the people who pafs by, with other things much more difagreeable.

The fchools have mafters and ufhers, who teach children the firft principles of religion, and the form of the mafs, which they inftruct them to mumble all together.

THEY

They seldom teach any other than their own language ; and it is said, that, besides the Jesuits, there are but few who understand Latin, and those make use of a particular pronunciation ; thus, for *mihi* they say *micki*. The Hebrew language and the Jews are equally in disgrace with the Spaniards, and therefore are both excluded from the colleges.

The Spanish poetry is greatly esteemed, particularly the works of *Quevedo* are praised beyond measure ; comedies in verse are frequently printed and acted, and the reading of them is the principal amusement of many people. The state of the sciences in Spain is best represented by the learned Spanish Benedictine friar *Geronimo Fejoo*, in his *Cartas Eruditas*, or Learned Letters, 1750, Tom. III. carta xxxi. p. 384.[k]

Here are several booksellers shops, in which may be procured Spanish books on religion, printed on a wretched paper, bound in soft pasteboard, with leathern straps instead of

---

[k] In the original is a long quotation from Fejoo's book, which the translator does not think interesting to an English reader.

clasps ;

clasps; as also some few French well-bound books, on natural history, physic, history, &c. Old books are exposed for sale, in the market and in other places, upon tables.

NONE but ecclesiasticks are permited to read the Bible, and the Inquisition is very strict in this article. For this reason it is only sold in Latin; and as the Spaniards seldom trouble themselves about any but their own language, this order is very seldom disobeyed.

THEIR catechism, or, as it is called, *Doctrina Christiana*, is very short. The first question is, What is the sign of a Christian? answer, Crossing; of which we have given an account above. In this catechism, seven sacraments are mentioned, baptism, confirmation, penance, communion, extreme unction, orders, and matrimony; and it is observed, that the five first are absolutely necessary.

WORKS of mercy are fourteen, among which one is the giving alms to strangers. It likewise mentions seven *Peccados Capitales,* or capital sins, and as many virtues:

1. Pride.
2. Luxury.
3. Avarice.

3. Avarice.
4. Anger.
5. Intemperance.
6. Envy.
7. Laziness.

Virtues are,
1. Humility.
2. Chastity.
3. Charity.
4. Patience.
5. Temperance.
6. Benevolence.
7. Industry.

In order to learn the Spanish language, there is no better Dictionary than that of *Sobrino*, which was published in the year 1744, in two volumes in quarto. The Grammar and Dialogues of Sobrino are also of great use [1].

---

[1] In this place, Mr. Osbeck inserts, for the use of his countrymen, the Spanish alphabet, with the pronunciation of the letters; but as the great commercial connections of this country make all European languages more common among the English, and many grammars and teachers of the Spanish langnage are to be procured, it is entirely unnecessary to insert an alphabet which the author had made with a view to be beneficial to his countrymen only.   F.

No proteſtant book is permitted to be brought into the city before the inquiſitors have peruſed it.

To avoid this inconvenience, I did not venture to take any books on-ſhore, though I often wanted them, in particular ſuch as treated of natural hiſtory.

THEIR diſhes are ſometimes very peculiar, on account of the many ſpecies of fiſh, fruit, and roots, which are unknown to us.

I HAVE ſeen no rye bread, and much leſs any of inferior quality; it is chiefly made in the Spaniſh or French manner. The latter, which is here made of Engliſh wheat, is well known to us. Great drought often occaſions a bad crop, which was the caſe the year before I arrived.

THEIR ſugar-bread, which is equal in taſte to the French biſcuit, is called *Viſocho* in Spaniſh, and is dipt into wine at table. They have likewiſe a ſort of ſugar-bread in Spain, which is like ginger-bread; it is gilt at top, and made of water melons, called *Calabaſſa*.
Nobody

Nobody is permitted to eat flesh in Lent, except the sick, who may obtain a dispensation for a certain fee. Cow beef is reckoned best in this country, because the cows are seldom milked; but in their stead goats, sheep, and asses. We bought two oxen for our ship; their flesh was exceedingly dry, occasioned both by the larvas of the gad-fly which nestle in their skins about this time, and by the want of good pastures; for our fine Swedish grass is much wanted here, and in its stead the pastures are covered with thistles, and other prickly plants, which I shall mention in another place.

SOVAJA is a sort of corn which is sown in the inclosures of the town, not for the use of men, but only for the cattle. They sold it to us in bundles, whilst it was green, and had no ears, which do not appear till March.

BEES are here in great estimation, or else the Spanish proverb could not take place:

Abeja y oveja,
Y piedra que traveja,
Y pendola trans oreja,
Y parte en la Igreja,
Desea a su hijo, la vieja.

THE beft wifhes of a mother to her fon are, bees, fheep, mill-ftones, a pen behind the ear, and a place in the church.

POT-HERBS *(Plantæ oleraceæ)* are fown both within and out of the town; as purflane, fpinage, and onions. The gardens are inclofed with walls, on which the *Agave Americana* is planted inftead of a hedge; but where this is not to be had, the prickly glafswort *(Salfola Kali* Linn.) or a hedge of twigs twifted together becomes the fence. *Origanum Creticum,* Spanifh *Oregano,* known by the name of Spanifh hops, is ufed to make anchovies and other meats more palatable[m]; and for that reafon, it was bought up very much in the apothecaries fhops, where there is plenty of it to be had.

ROSEMARY, which we reckon among the ornaments of our green-houfes, is carried for fale by whole cart-loads.

SWEET or China oranges, and other fruit, are daily eaten after meals, and likewife at

[m] I was told that this fort of fpice fold well in China.

other times; and that they may not occasion sickness, they use bread with them. It is no small advantage (at least to a Swede it appears so) to be able to take one's amusement all the winter-long in the gardens, and to pluck there the most delicious fruits; but, to balance these blessings of a genial climate, there is not one good draught of water in all the town, as it must all be brought from *Port Mary* in boats, or carried by asses, and is afterwards preserved in great stone jugs. This water-trade pays its merchants very well, for, if I remember right, each boat that fetched water at the abovementioned place gained about forty Swedish dollars silver coin (that is nearly 50 shillings): the passage is easily made in 24 hours, in case they go with the tide, and return with it.

WINE of Xeres [n] is the best and most common sort, which is made in a little town near Port St. Mary, called *Xerez de la Fronteras*, and derives its name from it. As our East India ships sail from their own port with but a small store of wine, they generally take in at Cadiz a proper quantity of Sherry for the

[n] Our Sherris or Sherry.

whole voyage and return; becaufe this wine is ftrong, and preferves its goodnefs in all climates. A quarter of a calk, containing from ten to eleven gallons, cofts forty Swedifh dollars filver, or nearly fifty fhillings fterling. *Tinto* or *Rota* wine is reckoned lefs wholefome than the white, and is therefore cheaper. Raifins are alfo bought here, and fold in China with great profit.

SPANISH brandy is very ftrong, and may be ufed as fpirit of wine. We gave it every morning to the men, mixed with two-thirds of water, and it was ufed in the punch which we had twice a week at dinner. Befides this, the captain ufually cheared the failors in a ftorm with punch or brandy.

THE people drink chocolate here in the morning, and fometimes in the afternoon inftead of tea. The following is the manner of making chocolate: the chocolate nuts (*Theobroma cacao* Linn.) are dried and rubbed into a foft pafte on a flat ftone, and fome cinnamon is added during the rubbing. This pafte is made into proper forms, fo that the chocolatecakes refemble the fhape of bricks. Such a piece of chocolate weighs one pound. If chocolate is to be made for drinking, you take such a piece to ten dishes of water; it is broken, and whilst it is boiling it is stirred with a ladle, the thickest end of which comes to the bottom of the chocolate-pot which it fills. At each filling of a dish, they stir it over again. It is probable that the manner of preparing it is the reason why it has a better taste here than in Sweden, though they do not mix the vanilla (*Epidendrum vanilla* Linn.), a very precious American fruit, with it. I never saw tea or coffee drank here.

The tradesmen are Frenchmen, Englishmen, or Italians, who work pretty well, but demand exhorbitant prices. Cloth and stuff are generally imported by the French, English, and Italian merchants.

The Exchange was kept in a broad street called *Calla nueva*, or New-street, close to the market. During the time that the merchants are assembled in it, the opening of the street towards the market is shut up by a bar, as is usual at our custom-houses.

THE Spanish pine-tree, *(Pinus pinea)* the olive-tree, and, as it is said, the cork-tree *(Quercus Suber* Linn.), are all sold for fuel by weight.

THE Spanish weights are accurately described in the Memoirs of the Swedish Academy of Sciences, 1746, p. 279. and afterwards both the measures and weights in the same Memoirs, 1755, p. 180.

THE quantity of specie which circulates here is rather astonishing to a Swede.

IT is said that some people carry a good deal of this out of the kingdom; and even the Spaniards themselves send great sums to the East Indies, and other places. If any one carries a sum of money out of town, and is discovered, he not only loses his money, but is sent to prison, and also suffers other punishments.

THE people of this country do not make use of horses for carriages or any other purpose; when an inhabitant of Cadiz goes out of town,

he

he puts on a wide jacket, or *Caffaquilla*, and wears neither coat nor boots, though both would be very neceffary. He makes ufe of wooden ftirrups, which have fome likenefs to a fmoothing-iron without a cover; he puts his feet into them, and they not only ferve as a fupport to him, but likewife as a cafe for his fhoes, to keep off the dirt.

MULES (*Equus afinus mulus* Linn.), called *Mulo* and *Mula* by the Spaniards, draw their carriages, but they move very flowly. Their coaches have no feat for the coachman, fo he is forced to ride on one of the mules. She-mules do not propagate their fpecies, at leaft fuch inftances are very fcarce. They are the offspring of a mare and an he-afs, or of a mare and a mule. The common people believe that the fterility of the fhe-mule is in confequence of a curfe laid upon it by the Virgin Mary at the birth of our Saviour, becaufe it had eaten the hay which the ox had collected together. Their common food is cut-ftraw with corn.

THE afs (*Equus afinus*) is lefs than the leaft horfe, and is very common in Spain, both in towns and in the country. The he-afs is called

called *Vurro*, and the she-ass *Vurra*, which is read as *Burro* and *Burra*. *Burrico* is the diminutive of this word, and denotes a little ass, whence the Swedish name *Borica* is derived. They are lean, and ash-coloured, but grow blackish after being shorn. They are fed like horses with cut-straw, but they likewise content themselves with what they find in the streets or road. When they come to market, their disagreeable braying even drowns the noise of the crowd. They are used to all sorts of work, except drawing a cart, which is never done but on the sea-shore, from whence they carry stones to town: sand, straw, street-dirt, in short every thing that is to be removed from one place to another, is loaded upon the backs of asses in panniers, made of mats, and open at top. But if they carry water or milk, they have saddles made of oaken planks, on which the casks are laid on both sides. When you have asses, you want no bridles to them; for as soon as the ass-driver cries out *Are* or *Araci*, all those which have strayed out of the road turn in again. Many hundreds of these animals were at the country-gate of Cadiz, whither they brought sand to make the ground even on the outside of the ditches, not to mention all those which are to be met with

with in every part of the town. Their hoofs are never shoed, though asses are used like saddle-horses at the post-stations; but this kind of posting is very disagreeable to those who are not used to it, from the slowness of their motion.

PEOPLE of all ages smoak tobacco, though it is (as well as snuff) very dear. It is seldom smoaked in pipes, but either in leaves rolled together, called *Cigarro* by the Spaniards, or the tobacco which comes in packs is wrapt up in paper, and this serves instead of pipes. The best Spanish snuff comes from Seville, and they generally put it into snuff-boxes of olive-wood, which are very pretty.

IT is very agreeable walking before the gate towards the country, because you are not pestered there with custom-house officers, and only meet with a few civil centinels, who shew the way to strangers if they happen to miss it. The high-road is very magnificent, and has stone benches on both sides. The throwing of bombs into the air, and some other diversions of the same kind, attract a good many people hither, who repose themselves on these benches. In other places the

high-road

high-road is not so grand. Travelling is much more inconvenient and expensive here than in Sweden, on account of the delays and bad accommodation. Travellers always carry fire-arms and pistols with them, and seem as if they were marching to a campaign; for they have reason to be afraid of robbers, which, though less frequent farther in the kingdom, are often met with in Andalusia; whence the Spanish proverb,

De el Andaluz guarda tu capuz;
Al Andaluz haze la cruz:
Al Sevillano con una y otra mano:
Al Corduves con manos y piés.

Take care of thy head before an Andalusian, and sign thyself with a cross; before a Sevilian cross thyself with both hands; and before a Cordubian with hands and feet.

I FOUND neither animals of prey nor snakes; but I met a person having a long lizard, exceeding a foot in length, of green, yellow, and other colours, on a string. It was very spiteful, and when it was let down upon the ground, it opened its mouth at all who passed by it, especially if a stick was held near it, it. The man who carried it said he could sell it to the apothecaries.

EUPHORBIA *Paralias*, a kind of *spurge*, was to be met with in the sandy grounds near the sea-shore, where the waves of the sea often reached. It was at that time without fructification.

SPARTIUM *monospermum*, which the Spaniards call *Retamas*, grows like willow bushes along the sea-shore as far as the flying sands reach. This plant was particularly plentiful in the peninsula on which Cadiz stands, which is covered with a fine white sand, and where, besides this, scarce any other plant grows, except the *Ononis repens*, or creeping restharrow. The *Retamas* sometimes grows to the thickness of a man's arm; its bark is ash-coloured, the numerous branches are all green; its leaves shine like silk; the fresh leaves are lanceolated, but the old ones are more obtuse; a little split at top, and reflected: the flowers are innumerable, small, white, and have red *Calices*. The use of this plant is very great in stopping the progress of the flying sand. The leaves and young branches of it are very

delicious

delicious food for goats, but I have not observed that they touch the bark. It turns the moſt barren place into a fine odoriferous garden by its flowers, which laſt a long while. The twigs are uſed for tying bundles, inſtead of ruſhes; and all kinds of herbs which are brought to market are faſtened together with them. The whole ſhrub ſerves to ſhelter hogs and goats againſt the ſcorching heat of the ſun.

SWINE are kept in whole herds by a man who feeds them with acorns, which are commonly ſold at Cadiz and at other places. The ſwine are very large, thin haired, and black as jet. It is probable they came originally from Africa, as I am told that this ſort of hogs is very ſcarce higher up in the country. It would be worth while for an œconomiſt to get a breed of theſe ſwine; but they muſt alſo be fed as they are here, and have ſome exerciſe every day, which keeps them from growing too fat °, and makes them taſte well. The exportation of a boar of this kind is forbidden, but a ſow almoſt ready to farrow

° In England no man tries to prevent his hogs from growing too fat.

would

would be still better for the propagation of this kind of hogs. We bought a good many of these swine for our ship; and every Saturday we killed one of them, and had broth called *Puspas* boiled from part of it.

In the same island were some little gardens, and in the midst of them here and there a palm-tree (*Phœnix dactylifera*) which gave them a fine appearance.

January the 23d, and the following days.

PUERTO *de Sancta Maria*, which our sailors called *Port St. Mary*, is a little unfortified seaport, about three quarters of a Swedish mile from Cadiz. I went this day to that place; It is situated in a plain, not far from the mouth of a river. If you go up this river, the town is on your left hand, and on the right a small island, whose situation is low, and which is covered with shrubs, among which the *Nerium oleander*, called *Yerva mala*, or the noxious plant, by the Spaniards, grew in the sand near the water.

On our arrival we were met by the custom-house officers, who came to us, with loaded fire-arms, in a boat. We afterwards went in smaller boats into more shallow water, where we found a good many fellows who offered to carry the people on shore for some small matter, and they did it very cleverly. For the same purpose asses and horses were kept in readiness. Though the city is less than Cadiz, yet its streets are finer; all the private and public houses are of stone, the same as in Cadiz, but less. Some of them were not yet rebuilt since the plundering of this place by the English. In a monastery of this town I saw several repositories full of relicks, but I suppose my readers will pardon my omitting to enumerate them. The houses were ornamented with pots, in which were rosemary, carnations, and other odoriferous plants, in full blossom; but the *Sempervivum arboreum* had no flowers as yet. Where these ornaments were wanting, Flora herself had supplied the bare walls with *Bryum murale* and *Lichen parietinus*; and besides these, in some places with *Cotyledon umbilicus*, or navelwort, whose leaves grew between every little cleft, the *Mercurialis annua*, or French mercury, and *Parietaria Lusitanica*. The old ruined walls were quite yellow with the *Sisymbrium Irio,* and with the *Senecio communis* or common groundsel. This town has good fresh water, in such plenty, that, besides its own inhabitants, it supplies Cadiz and the ships in that port. This water is reckoned the best in this country, wherefore in Cadiz they cry *Agua del Puerto.* I am told that it is brought a quarter of a Swedish mile by subterraneous canals to this place. There are several houses in this town from whence the water may be fetched; one in particular was built for that purpose on the river side, during the reign of King Philip V. The ship-boats come thither and fetch fresh water, without loss of time, because they open the water-canal for a very small matter. The other house is an English inn, where all the strangers generally lodge.

The leaves of the samphire (*Crithmum maritimum*), pickled in vinegar [p], are eaten here and in Cadiz with roasted meat. This juicy plant grows on the coasts of England, and perhaps on those of Spain, but not in this

---

[p] The manner of pickling this, and all the like salt and juicy plants, as is usual in England, is described by Mr. Professor *Kalm,* in his Voyage to North America, Vol. II. p. 97. of the Swedish edition. *Dr. Schreber.*

place;

place: it is not found in Sweden; but we have other juicy plants, such as (*Salicornia Europæa*) marsh samphire, or jointed glass-wort.

THE country hereabouts was already beautified with many flowers. Dwarf-mallow (*Malva rotundifolia*), with large red flowers, grew both about the houses and out of town, and was greedily eaten by hogs and oxen; but they always passed by the sunspurge (*Euphorbia heliofcopia*), and would rather eat the *Carduus Syriacus*, the white spotted leaves of which, though they ornament the fields, I think, afford but a poor food.

THE cow-herds go with long sticks, like the Polish bear-keepers. All the Spanish shores are mountainous, except in this place. The soil also varies much. On the sea-shore you find during low water a blue clay, and near it a fine white sand, which covers the country here and there at a little distance from the sea. It often looks like large hills of snow, where pine woods or other plants hinder it from flying. Higher up from the sea, you find a mould mixed with sand and pebbles, sometimes of a red, and sometimes of another colour.

In

In the vallies is sometimes a sky blue or other clay, the same as in their wheat-fields.

The plants on the sea-shore were very few; *Spartium monospermum* and *Juncus acutus* were but just sprung up from the ground. A little farther from the water grew *Schœnus mucronatus involucri foliis scapo longioribus*. Still further off began the woods of the *Pinus pinea*, which hindered the sand from spreading any further. In these woods I found the restharrow (*Ononis*); there grew likewise queen's stock july-flowers (*Cheiranthus incanus*), broad-leaved mouse-ear chickweed (*Cerastium viscosum*), *Lotus cytisoides*, and *Crepis barbata*. The latter was in blossom; the stock-july-flower just began to flower at my departure; but the restharrow had no appearance of flowering at that season.

Some insects are found in this sand; in particular, *Scarabæus sacer, lævis, thorace inermi.*

Gardens or plantations take up a great part of the fields; and they contain lemon, orange, almond, and olive trees, which turn to a considerable profit to the owners.

THE lemon tree, the Seville and sweet orange trees, are much akin to one another, and are generally planted promiscuously [q]. The sweet smell of their flowers would almost revive a person when half dead. The fruit ripens so slowly, that the whole year is spent before it comes to perfection. It is said by some nursery-men, that they can produce fruits of which one quarter is Seville, the second sweet orange, the third quarter sweet, and the fourth sour lemons.

SOVAJA was sown in some places amongst the trees; sometimes parts of the plantations were sown with salads, radishes, onions, &c.

THE *Phœnix dactylifera* [r] is seldom to be met with here: there were some near the monastery, almost as high as the house itself, the dates of which were fallen down, and were of the colour and size of white plumbs. The

---

[q] In the Linnæan System they are all included in one Genus, viz. *Citrus*.

[r] This is the Date-palm. There are two such in the Governor's garden at Gibraltar forty-five feet high, and supposed to be some hundred years old.

leaves are twisted together by the friers, who make presents of them to ornament the houses on Palm-sunday; and on that day they are likewise strewed about the streets.

The vineyards looked very poorly, and are like our [*] burnt land (*Swedieland*), for there are neither leaves nor flowers to be seen. The vines were planted in rows, and little drains were made between each row. Medic or snail trefoil (*Medicago polymorpha*) and *Rumex spinosus* were now in flower.

The almond-tree (*Amygdalus communis*), in Spanish *Almendro*, is an ornament to the vineyards with its white and reddish-coloured blossoms.

The olive-tree (*Olea Europæa*) was planted in large fields, having a red-coloured soil mix-

---

[*] In Sweden, Finland, Livonia, and the greatest part of Russia, where woods are plentiful, the countrymen cut down large tracts, burn them, and then they sow the land for three years and more together, because the ashes of the wood manure the land for all that time; after which they chuse another place, and proceed in the same manner; so that in twenty or more years they may return to the first place, which is then again entirely covered with wood; and this is called in the north *Swedieland*. F.

ed with little stones. The Spaniards call the tree *Olivo*, but its fruit, or the olives, *Aceytuna*. On them grew the *Lichen cristatus*, and below the trees bloomed a species of stock-julyflowers (*Cheiranthus trilobus*), and *Valeriana cornucopiæ*. In one of these olive-tree plantatations I found *Arum arisarum*, the roots of which go very deep. The olive-trees shewed no blossoms as yet, and had but a poor inclosure.

I saw here some small flocks of Spanish sheep: they were all white, with some black spots near the eyes, ears, and mouth. See Dr. Linnæus's Voyage to Westrogothia, page 58.

Artichokes (*Cynara solymus*), in Spanish *Acanziles*, or *Alcachofa*, or *Cardillos*, were planted on little hills, as we do hops; the rest of the garden stuff, as beans, turneps, &c. is managed as in Sweden.

The tender plants are covered with skreens, which are erected almost horizontally at two yards from the ground: to water the plants, water is drawn up out of the well by means of a great wheel, turned either by men or by an afs. The circumference of this wheel touches the water, and there are feveral earthen pots faftened to it by double ftrings, which fetch up the water.

Garden beans (*Vicia faba*) were already in full bloffom in the open air, which we never can have before Midfummer-day in Sweden. This is a clear proof of the difference of the climate.

The earthen walls, with which the gardens and plantations are furrounded, are often three yards high, and are befides covered with prickly plants: among which

The *Agave Americana* [t] is the moft common, moft beautiful, and moft ufeful. This is called *Pita* in Spain, but it is by no means the *Aloe vera*, or *femperviva*, except you will call every thing *fempervivum* which is evergreen; which would be as ridiculous as to give the fame denomination to the fir and the juniper, becaufe they both continue green all the winter. The leaves of this plant, which I was told was about fix years old, were three feet long. The laft year's *fcapi*, which were already mouldering, were about two men's lengths;

[t] Vulg. American Aloe.

lengths; and the fresh ones, which were already a yard in length, began to shew their long *antheræ*. The *corollæ* were for the most part eaten away, but the *stamina* and *pistillum* remained unhurt.

THE American aloe is useful in many respects; for, besides the use that is made of it in quick hedges, the leaves are soaked and managed like hemp, and may be spun for purses and other things. With the points of the leaves, which are as sharp and as stiff as an awl, they bore peoples ears, and clear tobacco pipes; but they must not be used for tooth-picks, for the wounds their prickles cause are not easily healed. It is said, that if its leaves, when roasted by the fire, be laid upon wounds, the pain will cease. The Americans use the juice of the root to cure the venereal disease. Some further account is to be met with, in the book called " The Memoirs of Sophia Eliza-" beth Brenner," printed at Stockholm, in folio. In it she speaks of the qualities of this plant: Upon the first American aloe's flowering in Sweden, it began to blossom in September 1708, and continued till the next winter in *Noors Sates gard*. " The *Agave*, says she, is " a plant which supplies all the wants of the
" Indian,

"Indian, according to the best authorities [u] ;
"if he wants to make a hedge round his fields,
"he plants the *Agave* round them, because its
"leaves are stiff, and armed with innumerable
"prickles. If he builds any thing, he makes
"his planks of *Agave*, which he can use in‑
"stead of timber; and he thatches his cot‑
"tage with its leaves. The latter are of still
"greater use to him; as from the same mate‑
"rial he makes his paper, linen, cloaths,
"shoes, thread, dishes, plates, and other
"utensils. The points of the leaves are as
"good as nails, spears, or pins. If he chooses,
"he can make wine, honey, sugar, and vine‑
"gar, from its juice. If he puts the thick
"leaves of it under‑ground for some time,
"they taste better than melons, or lemons
"with sugar.".

CACTUS *opuntia*, whose stem is thicker than a man's arm, is likewise used to cover the walls; and besides this, several other plants, such as holly (*Ilex aquifolium*), called *Hou* in French.

[u] NARDUS ANTONIUS RECCHUS de re medica Nov. Hisp. Lib. VIII. Cap. xii. Romæ, 1651.

AMONGST the thorny plants are several others ornamented with fine flowers; viz.

Lycium Europæum.
Atriplex portulacoides, sea purslane.
Chenopodium ambrosioides.
Asparagus officinalis, asparagus.
——————— *falcatus.*
——————— *acutifolius.*
——————— *aphyllus.*
Galium aparine, cleavers, or goose-grass.
Aristolochia rotunda.
Fumaria officinalis, fumitory, called *Conojito* in Spanish.

Arundo donax, a species of reed called *Cana* in Spain, held up its head above all the rest; its flowers were already withered. It is used for walking-sticks and for fishing-rods.

On the steep sides of these walls, towards the road, grew *Bryum acaulon ericæ tenuifoliæ folio.* Dillen. Muscor. 388. t. 49. f. 55. γ. *Anethum fœniculum,* or fenel, *Phlomis purpurea, Teucrium iva, Targionia hypophylla,* and the *Palmetto,* or *Chamærops humilis,* which last throve best here, and hung downwards; but these were not in blossom; nor was the *Daphne gnidium,* a shrub which is very like to our

E 4   *Ledum*

Ledum paluſtre, or marſh ciſtus, and grew near the road; where I found in bloſſom likewiſe

Geranium cicutarium, hemlock leaved cranebill.
Clypeola jonthlaſpi.
Vinca major, great periwinkle, in one ſingle place.
Hyacinthus ſerotinus.
——— *monſtroſus.*
Veronica agreſtis, germander ſpeedwell.
Myoſotis ſcorpioides arvenſis, mouſe-ear ſcorpion graſs.
Thlaſpi burſa paſtoris, ſhepherd purſe.
Centaurea pullata.
——— *ſphærocephala.*
Silene conoïdea.
Reſeda glauca.
Anagallis latifolia.
Arum maculatum, wake Robin, or cuckow pint.
Matricaria chamomilla, corn feverfew.
Biſcutella didyma.

In the gardens were the following plants growing ſpontaneouſly, in full bloſſom:

Papaver rhoeas, red poppy.
Stachys hirta.
Vicia

Vicia lutea, yellow vetch.

One *Physalis.*

Solanum nigrum vulgare, garden or common nightshade.

Alsine media, common chickweed.

Borrago officinalis, borage, in Spanish *Boraja.*

Malva rotundifolia, flore majore rubescente.

Sonchus oleraceus, sowthistle, in Spanish *Serajas.*

Urtica urens, annual nettle, ⎫ in Spanish *or-*
—— *dioica,* common nettle, ⎭ *tega.*

Ricinus communis, in Spanish, *Higuera del inferno,* or infernal fig-tree; this was scarce.

Sisymbrium irio, smooth broad-leaved hedge-mustard.

Senecio vulgaris, common groundsel, which likewise grew on the roofs and gutters.

Punica granatum, the pomegranate-tree; it was then without blossoms.

In poor and waste fields, the *Palmetto* (*Chamærops humilis*), which is called *Palmito* by the Spaniards, is as common as the juniper-shrub with us: the *Palmetto* has a narrow, and as it were compressed stem, with thorns on the edges. The stem is about a quarter of a yard long, and ends with a leaf of the same length,

length, which at first is folded together like a fan, but higher up it opens and expands. When the stem grows longer, it lies down on the ground. At that time this little palm-tree had neither blossoms nor fruit. Its leaves are every where used for brooms. The roots, which spread very much, are sold in the towns, and eaten raw, after they have been peeled.

Upon the same fields grew the afore-mentioned thistle; and also

Illecebrum paronychia.
Crocus Bulbocodium.
Salvia verbenaca, wild clary.
Tragopogon Dalecampii.
Cynoglossum cheirifolium.
Iris Xiphium.
Calendula officinalis, garden marygold.
Stachys arvensis.
Marrubium vulgare (without flowers), white-hoarhound.

Between and below the *Palmetto* trees, the following plants were in blossom:

Lamium amplexicaule, great henbit.
Geranium molle, dove's-foot crane's-bill.

Andropogon bicorne?
Linum ufitatiffimum, flax.
Sherardia arvenfis, little field-madder.

ON the road, between the gardens, I faw in flower,

Anemone palmata.
Afphodelus fiftulofus.

Afphodelus ramofus, called in Spanish *Gamon*; this fine plant, which grows up to the height of five feet, was to be met with both within and without the gardens.

Doronicum bellidiaftrum.
Beta vulgaris, beet.
Echinops Ritro.
Anchufa officinalis.
Silene pendula.
Stellaria arenaria.
Lycopfis veficaria.
Hypochæris radicata, long-rooted hawkweed.
Ranunculus bulbofus, bulbous-rooted crowfoot.
Lichen phyfodes.
Panicum crus galli.

Euphorbia

Euphorbia peplus.
——— *falcata.*
——— *exigua.*
——— *helioscopia.*
——— *esula.*
——— *myrsinites.*
} different species of spurges.

Lagurus ovatus.
Rumex acetosa, sorrel.

Silene floribus lateralibus solitariis, calycibus lanatis, foliis ciliatis. The stalk is thin, one foot long, almost quite rough, and without branches: the leaves are lanceolated, and below on the margin covered with a white wool; their other parts are quite smooth, out of the lower leaves shoot up some imperfect *petioli:* but the flowers come singly from the corners of the upper leaves alternately, and not two by two, on very short peduncles. The club-like *calyx* has ten points, covered with a long white wool.

January 28th, and the following days.

I went again to the fields which lye before the city of *Puerto de Santa Maria;* and found, besides the above-mentioned plants, the water-crowfoot *(Ranunculus aquatilis),* whose white flowers

flowers entirely covered the ditches and ponds. In them I found also the *Conferva bullosa*. I came into a little wood of Spanish firs, where the *Byssus candelaris* cloathed the trees. The wood was surrounded, like the gardens, with hedges of *Agave*, or American aloe. It is no wonder that these woods are inclosed, for the thin and hard boards they afford for chests to pack lemons in are often dearer than the fruit itself. In the fir-wood I found a good many scarce plants, and among the rest the *Sisymbrium sylvestre*, on which I discovered a hairy caterpillar, which afterwards became a smooth, pale-green coloured, oblong-pointed, angulated, warty, black aurelia, having on the back a convex elevation. In its third change it became the *Papilio hyale* Linn. or *Papilio Carolinianus luteus apicibus nigris*. Petiv. Muf. p. 12, T. VII. fig. 10.

Orchis *fuscescens* Linn. *bulbis fasciculatis, nectarii labio ovato indiviso subcrenato*, was very worthy of observation, as appears from the following description: the root consists of two or more tuberous simple bulbs, excepting four or six fibres towards the beginning of the stalk; the stalk was about the length of a span, round and red; four leaves are near the root,

root, the lower ones are larger, and oblong-oval (*ovata lanceolata*); the upper ones are less speckled alternate, and cover the remainder of the stalk with the sheath in which they end at bottom: the *stipula* which is below every flower is lanceolated, and like the lesser leaves of the stalk of a red colour: the flowers at most are seven, flesh-coloured, and consist each of five petals, that is three outward and two inward, which are almost equal to one another, lanceolated, and rolled up (*convoluta*); the lower lip of the *nectarium* is oval, entire, and somewhat crenated; the two *stamina* had round green *antheræ*.

The *Antirrhinum arvense*, or snap-dragon, was very small, but discoverable by its yellow flowers.

Allium *subhirsutum*; the root consists of two, three, or more white bulbs, from which run out little fibres; their scales are hard, brown, imbricated, and very irregular; the stalk is round, and uncovered at top; the leaves grow commonly ensiform or sword-shaped towards the root, and carinated below; they end in a point, are hairy on the margin,

and

and longer than the stalk; the *spatha* is torn, and generally withered: the flowers which form the *umbella* are white, and consist of six oval, oblong, concave, erected petals: the six filaments are pointed at the top, as long as the *corolla*, and come from the *thalamus*: the *antheræ* are oblong, short, and upright: the *germen* is round, blunt, and triangular; the *stylus* is as long as the filaments; the *stigma* is erected: the *capsula* is globular and trilocular; the seeds are generally oval and angular. It thrives most under bushes of the

PASSERINA *hirsuta*; the stem of which has many branches similar to those of the juniper shrub, has no leaves, is round and diffuse; the branches are full of leaves, and bent every way: the leaves grow alternately, are sessile, carnose, small, ovato-lanceolated, depressed in the middle, with a concave margin, woolly and white at the top, and dark-green below: the flowers have no *pedunculi*; they are small, of a yellow colour, and come in great numbers from the same buds with the leaves: instead of the *calyx*, which is wanting, are four or more leaves under the flowers: the *corolla* consists of an *infundibuli*-form petal, whose

inside

inside is woolly; the tube is cylindrical; the *limbus* is quadrified and shorter than the tube; the *laciniæ* are oval and reflected; the filaments are fastened to the tube, and four of them are a little lower than the other two; the *antheræ* are almost oval, they lie across the filaments, and are composed of two valves. This shrub grows in the fir-woods like our juniper shrub, and in other places out of town: it is called *Torvicho* here, but in other places *Tomillo*. On this shrub lives the *Meloc majalis* Linn. *segmentorum abdominis marginibus dorsalibus rubris*.

Saltamatos are a species of locusts, so called by the people here, which are to be met with in the above-mentioned fir-wood. They were of so remarkable a size, that, when flying, they looked like little birds, which they imitated farther in not settling on the ground, but always on high trees, and often at such a height that they were scarce visible.

Besides the *Coccinella septem punctata*, I gathered many scarce insects, most of which were destroyed during my absence from the inn, all the apartments being open to every body.

body. Those that remained, and which I took on-board with me, were,

Scarabæus (*facer* Linn.) *lævis, thorace inermi, capite antico fexdentato. Habitat in arenofis maritimis.*

Scarabæus (*typhæus* Linn.) *thorace tricorni, intermedio minore. In campis.*

Scarabæus (*bilobus* Linn.) *thorace mutica, capite cornuto, elytris ftriatis.*

Carabus totus niger, ftrigis feptem in fingulo elytro muricatis.

Tenebrio (*muricatus* Linn.) *elytris muricatis.*

Papilio (*rumina* Linn.) *tetrapus, alis ex coccineo, luteo, argenteo et nigro variegatis, primoribus rotundis.*

Papilio medius gaditanus ex nigro et fulphureo varius. Catesby.

Onifcus (*afilus* Linn.) *abdomine foliis duobus obtecto, cauda femiovali. Habitat in pifcibus marinis.*

February the 8th, and the following days.

As my greatest amufement was in the country about Port Mary, I went there again to-day, and had fcarce gone in at my old landlord's, lord's, when I found something new; before the window was a plant which they called *St. Joseph's flower*, and which is said to grow hereabouts in low ground; the *scapus* was triangular, and the flowers quite white; it was *Allium triquetrum*. I went without any company on the road towards Puerto Real, but was forced to return again on account of the rainy weather. The following plants I found in blossom:

In low places.

Geranium gruinum.
Bellis annua, common daisy.

On the road.

Anemone palmata.
Antirrhinum bipunctatum, below the palmetto.
Cistus Fumana.
—— *Tuberaria.*
—— *salicifolius.*

On dry hills every-where.

Satureja capitata (sine flore).
Lavendula stœchas.

Orni-

Ornithogalum umbellatum, star of Bethlehem.
Ornithopus compressus.
Antirrhinum orontium, least snap-dragon.
Teucrium fruticans.
Leucojum autumnale.
Coronilla juncea.
Hippocrepis comosa, tufted horse-shoe-vetch.
Anthyllis tetraphylla.
Ruta graveolens, rue.
Cistus hirtus, ⎫ two species of *Cistus,* of
—— *salvifolius,* ⎭ which the latter is called *Ro* in Spanish, and is a small shrub which made but a poor appearance at that time: for the branches were of the same colour as the ground they lay on, and so were the leaves; but in March it surpassed all its neighbours, by its large odoriferous white flowers.

It began to rain harder and harder, which made me hasten back; but I turned into another road, which led to the town of *St. Lucas.* I here found about the gardens the *Spartium spinosum,* with its fine golden yellow flowers. At last I was obliged to turn off to the left of the road, and came on a common, which, excepting some little hillocks, was all under water: upon it I found a plant till then quite unknown,

known, namely the *Verbafcum Ofbeckii* Linn. of which I made the following defcription: the plant fpreads on all fides; the ftalk lies on the ground, is undivided, triangular, and nervofe; the leaves are oval, and cut into irregular fegments; the upper leaves are lefs, almoft feffile, the lower ones have *petioli:* the peduncles are woolly, moft of them bifid, and come from the bottom of the leaves; the *calyx* is deeply quinquefid, woolly, with lanceolated fegments; the *corolla* is rotated, the tube fhort; the *limbus* quinquefid; the five filaments are very fhort, and reft on a *fquama*, covering the *germen*; the *antheræ* are oblong, erected, and longer than the filaments; the *germen* is almoft round; the *ftylus* is longer than the filaments; the *ftigma* is entire and pointed: the fruit was not yet vifible: the whole plant had a fmell of mufk, and might probably find a place in the apothecary's fhop.

At three o'clock in the afternoon, I arrived at my inn quite wet; but an hour after I accompanied fome of my countrymen who went out of town to buy lemons. I foon obferved a particular tree in a garden, which had nothing but a few crooked pods, with neither leaves nor flowers, and confequently

nothing

nothing by which it could be known. The Spanish name of it is *Aromas*; and our industrious Mr. Loefling, who travelled into America, at the expence of his Spanish Majesty, in order to make observations on natural history, for some years together, wrote to me, in his letter from Madrid, that it was the *Mimosa Farnesiana*, a species of sensitive plant. One of the company said, he had seen this fruit eaten in the East in times of scarcity.

We walked from hence into a lemon plantation, where the *Tanacetum balsamita*, vulgo *Costmary*, which is here called *Terva de Santa Maria*, and the wall-flower, or *Cheiranthus cheiri*, were planted, and the latter in pots. Among the wild plants, the *Anchusa officinalis*, or officinal buglofs, and the *Spergula pentandra*, or spurrey, were in plenty.

Not far from the town, we passed a well surrounded by a very high wall, round which there was a trough, for the cattle to drink. The well was covered with a sort of rush (*Juncus acutus*) called *Paron* in Spanish. At night we returned to our inn, where we paid a piastre a piastre [w] a day for an open room and an ordinary. To this if you add some other unavoidable expences, the income of three thousand copper dollars [x] for the whole voyage to China will not admit of many more amusements on shore.

February the 10th.

THIS morning I left the town with an intention to go on board our ship; but a sudden east-wind made us pass her, and brought us to Cadiz, where, to our great surprize, we landed at nine o'clock the next morning. The way by land is much longer; but you pass through two little insignificant towns, *Puerto Real* and *Chiclana*.

I WAS glad to come from the boisterous sea into an agreeable garden; the summer-houses of which were covered with our common ivy (*Hedera helix*), called *Yedra* in Spanish.

[w] Rather more than four shillings sterling.
[x] A Copper dollar is about five pence, or five pence half-penny sterling.

APIS *violacea* fought its nourishment on the bean-flowers in the forenoon, but in the afternoon it rested on the vine-tendrils, or on the dry bushes, which were laid over the covered walks to keep off the heat of the sun. These summer-houses were covered with the blue passion-flower (*Passiflora cærulea*) which had neither flowers nor fruit at that time. Besides these beans, there were Indian cresses *(Tropæolum,)* vulgo *Nasturtium*, wild roses, *Ricinus communis*, and borrage (*Borrago officinalis*); which are likewise common in our gardens.

SPANISH locusts, called *Grillo* in Spain, are by the people of fashion kept in cages called *Grilleria*; whereas our locusts are not in the least esteemed, and sing their song without being taken notice of.

February the 15th and 16th.

I AGAIN went to the *Puerto de Sancta Maria*, where I re-visited the above-mentioned inclosed fir-wood, in which I found the fine *Orchis*, already withered; but as I could find no other plants besides those I have already mentioned,

tioned, I went into the open wood, which begins at the shifting sands, and goes a good way into the country. It was not surrounded by a hedge, and I saw nobody in it except an honest wood-man. In a low place I found a most beautiful flower, which would be an ornament even to a green-house: this was *Ophrys insectifera adrachnites (labio trifido)*: the root is a bunch of oblong bulbs, whereof those in the middle are longer than those on the outside: the stalk is of the length of a span, green, and uncovered above the middle; the leaves are green, those near the root are ovato-lanceolated, and four or more in number; the *bractea* are green, and are as long as the flowers; the flowers are about three in number; the three outward petals are oblong, and the two inner ones small, like teeth; the under-lip is softly lanated at top, dark-red, with very fine spots, and cut into three parts; the middlemost *lacinia* is the least, which makes the whole lip look quadrangular-heart-shaped; the *antheræ* are yellow, egg-shaped, and oblong.

At last I returned to the ship; and the next Sunday, seventeen of the crew received the Lord's-supper before the sermon.

March

March the 1st and 2d.

Rain and other circumstances had prevented me from going ashore: I therefore went with the Spanish water-boats to Port St. Mary, and from thence immediately proceeded on the road to Port Real, to which town I had got towards the evening; but I returned, as I longed to be at my former inn again. I found the following plants in blossom:

On a dry hill.

Anagallis monelli.

Mercurialis tomentosa; of this I found no more than two plants, one male, the other female; as they were but a few yards from one another, the fructification might easily be effected by means of the wind.

The *Conyza saxatilis* did not as yet shew its flowers.

The meadows which had no inclosure were ornamented with

Adonis annua, pheasant's-eye, which is one of our finest garden-flowers.

Lupinus

Lupinus albus,
———— *varius,*
———— *hirsutus,*
———— *luteus,*
} Species of lupins.

Cerinthe major.

On the roads.

Echium Creticum.

Cistus tuberaria, calycibus hispidis, unguibus petalorum et calycibus punctatis.

Cynoglossum cheirifolium, corollâ inflexâ cæruleâ.

Anchusa angustifolia.

In low places.

Chenopodium fruticosum (now *Salsola fruticosa*), shrub-stone crop, or glass-wort.
Cynara humilis.
Anthemis valentina.
Arenaria rubra, purple spurrey.
Chrysanthemum coronarium.
———— ————*segetum,* corn marygold.

Near a ditch.

Veronica anagallis aquatica, water-speedwell, or brook-lime.

Near the river.

Salicornia fruticosa, salt-wort.

On hills.

Scorpiurus sulcata, caterpillars, (the plant so called.)
Hyoseris radiata.
——— *hedypnois*.
——— *rhagadioloides*.
Rubus fruticosus, common blackberry.

In a clay ground, on high grass fields.

Scrophularia sambucifolia; and near it, *Ammi Hispanicum*.

In the olive plantations, and other dry places.

Cheiranthus trilobus.

In holes, and the like places.

Carex cæspitosa.

Between the high-grass on a barren mountain grew nothing but the

Ophrys insectifera myodes, labio quadrifido, fly-orchis, the root consists of two almost round bulbs;

bulbs; the ſtalk is double-edged (*anceps*), flat and twiſted; four leaves are at the root; they are ovato-lanceolated; the fifth is lanceolated, and ends below in a ſheath; the *bractea* of every flower is as long as the *pericarpium*; the three outward petals are oblong, with reflected margins, and the two inner ones equally broad; the upper lip is bigger than uſual in the other ſpecies, the lower or under-lip is quadrilaciniated, very much reflected on the margin, ſoftly lanated towards the point, and of a cheſnut-brown colour, acroſs which runs a ſhining ſtripe; the two middlemoſt *laciniæ* are the longeſt; the filaments are thread-ſhaped; the *antheræ* are oval, and yellow.

In the evening I had the honour of ſpeaking to two Spaniſh prieſts, one of whom offered to accompany me to the town of St. Lucar, but I was hindered from going by the night and other circumſtances. The next day I went on-board, and this was the laſt time that I ſaw this agreeable place.

March

SPAIN. 1751.

March the 6th.

ON my arrival at Cadiz, I saw the *Hedyfarum coronarium*, or French honey-fuckle, in plenty. The Spaniards call it *Soya*, and the French *Saint foin* [y]; it was brought to town in great bundles, as food for the cattle: the *Tillæa procumbens*, or the small annual house-leek, on every wall.

March the 16th.

I WENT up the Gulph of Cadiz, in the boat belonging to Captain Eckeberg, to a place where fresh water could be got as easily as at *Puerto de Sancta Maria*, although the way to the ship called *The Peace* was somewhat longer, which ship the above-mentioned Captain brought hither to sell on the Swedish East-India Company's account, as she was now reckoned too small for that trade. We passed the Spanish silver-fleet and the little castle *Pontal*, where

---

[y] What we call *St. Foin* in *England* is the *Hedyfarum Onobrychis*; the *Hedyfarum Coronarium* is planted for ornament in our gardens.

the Swedes may bury their dead for a certain sum: when we went out of our boat near the watering-place, I was delighted to find some natural productions which I had never seen before. Here were great dry heaths on all sides, which I should have been very glad to have gone through; but the remainder of the day only allowed of a partial examination. We went towards the town of *Isla*, and found the following scarce plants:

Spartium spinosum.
Genista Anglica, needle-furze, or petty whin, called *Espino* in Spain.
Pistacia lentiscus.
Smilax aspera.
Ulex Europæus, furze.
Orobanche major, broom-rape.
——— *ramosa,* branched D°, which had the following characters: the stalk is about a span long, entire, smooth, and succulent; the *bracteæ* are lanceolated, there is one of them under every flower; the *calyx* is quadrifid; its four *laciniæ* are linear and hairy at the margin; the *corolla* is monopetalous and gaping (*ringens*); the tube is almost cylindrical, and as long as the *calyx*; the *faux* is open (*dehiscens*); the upper-lip is bifid, and emarginated before;

the lower-lip is trifid, with equal *laciniæ* ; two *nectaria* are in the under-lip, and sometimes on the sides; the filaments are four, which are commonly pretty long, and almost all equal in size; the *antheræ* are white, didymous, erected, joined into a semi-cylinder, and end below the *stigma* in a short bristle (*seta*); the *germen* is oblong; the *stylus* is pointed; the *stigma* is elevated, great, bifid, and pointed downwards; the *capsula* is oblong, unilocular, and bivalve; the seeds are small and numerous.

Ophrys bracteis cymbiformibus, the root . . . . ; the stalk is of the length of a span (*scapus spithamæus*); the leaves are three or more in number, their shape is ovato-lanceolated, they stand alternately; the *bracteæ* are carinated, and like the leaves on the stalk not variegated; the innermost petals are small, oval, connivent, and not quite green: the upper-lip is the least, and coloured at the bottom; the lower-lip is succulent, oval, blunt, or emarginated with inflected sides, and coloured, except one part which is green, in the two opposite points; the filaments are thread-shaped, one of them is fixed to the lower-lip, and the others to the outward petal; the *antheræ* are globular,

globular, and yellow; the *germen* is furrowed. I only found a single plant, which was perhaps unnatural.

Scrapias lingua, bastard hellebore: the root consists of two hanging oval, black, bulbs; the stalk, and the flowers, are twisted to the left; the former is covered with about seven linear lanceolated leaves, which are red spotted, like the stalk itself; the *bracteæ* are of equal size with the petals, and like them lanceolated, pointed (*acuminatæ*), pale-red on the upper-side, but not dark-red at the bottom as the petals; the two innermost petals are broader at the bottom, waved (*undulata*), narrow towards the point, sharp-pointed, and with entire margins: the lips are long and red; the upper has narrow reflected points; the lower is dark-red, large, and lanceolated, has incisions on both sides towards the bottom, and its surface covered with some dark hair; the filaments are very short and yellow; the *antheræ* are green: it grows on the plains among the above-mentioned *Asphodelus*, page 59.

Serapidis linguæ varietas minor, is to be met with along with the former.

HERE

HERE I found likewife the *Ciftus falvifolius*, and in the garden was the *Myofotis apula*. I obferved the following things in this plant: the *calyx* has a thick wool upon its fegments; the *corolla* is quinquefid; the tube is long and linear; the *limbus* is quinquefid, with oval *laciniæ*; the filaments are faftened at the bottom of the *corolla*, and are hardly vifible on account of their fhortnefs; the *antheræ* are very fmall and oblong; the ftalk is of a fpan's length; the leaves grow alternately on the ftalk, are equally broad, have a prominent line below, and are rough.

AT laft we reached the town of *Ifla*, which is a little unfortified place, lefs than any I have hitherto mentioned. It is about a quarter of a Swedifh mile off the fea-fhore, in a plain country; it has on one fide a barren field, and on the other a river: the houfes are not very large, but ftrong; the ftreets are broad and fine. The (*Spartium junceum*) Spanifh broom fhewed its admirable flowers over a garden-wall which was higher than a man's head; this plant is difcoverable at a great diftance by its fine fmell. We lodged with an Englifhman who lived in this town; he accompanied us over a bridge, between the town and peninfula of *Cadiz*, to fhew us a fail-cloth manufactory which is carried on by gypfies and other prifoners, both men, women, and children. Thefe people are locked up in their prifons on holidays, from whence they infeft paffengers through the rails, in the fame manner as in *Cadiz*. In the yard of this building were the foldiers, who had mounted guard there. We were obliged to return without effecting any thing, and I only faw the *Arenaria rubra*, and fome common plants around the Englifhman's houfe, which was the laft on this fide.

AFTER dinner I was obliged to return to my congregation, on account of the next Sunday. I returned through a meadow, where I faw the following plants in bloffom:

Cratægus oxyacantha, hawthorn.
Ricinus communis.
Convolvulus althæoides.
Aftragalus bæticus.
Heraclium fphondylium, cow-parfnep.
Malva mauritiana.
Hypochæris maculata, fpotted hawkweed.
Plantago coronopus, buckfhorn plantain.

In

In holes I found:

Ranunculus muricatus.
Crepis fœtida, ſtinking hawkweed.

In the fields:

Fritillaria meleagris, fritilary.
Poterium sanguiſorba, burnet.
Anthoxanthum odoratum, vernal-graſs.
Teucrium fruticans.
Reſeda glauca.
—— *lutea? (tetragyna procumbens).*
Briza media, quaking-graſs.
Centaurea ſphærocephala.
Aſparagus officinalis, aſparagus, which is cut here in the fields, and ſold when young for the ſame purpoſe as in our country.

Near the ſhore the following plants were in bloſſom:

Hyoſcyamus albus.
Corrigiola littoralis.
Statice armeria, thrift.

At night the water ſhone in ſeveral places, which was owing to ſome pieces of rotten ray or other fiſh.

March the 18th.

To-day I got the *Meloe variegata* from a gentleman who had been near *Isla*. He said, that when he saw this insect, the Spaniards about him advised him not to take it into his hand, on account of its bite being poisonous. They feigned to take great precaution in catching this pretended noxious animal; probably in hopes of receiving a reward from strangers.

EUPHORBIA *serrata?* I likewise received from the same place: its *umbella universalis* was trifid, triphyllous, with a cordato, lanceolated, reflected leaf.

AND also the *Scilla Peruviana*.

March the 20th.

ON weighing the anchor, some crabs were pulled up; they were *Cancer brachyurus, hirsutissimus, subovatus*; and likewise

CHITON *læve*, which Petiver calls *Oscabrion*: the *shell* is carinated, and consists of eight transversal pieces, which are furrowed transversly;

tranfverfly; the *margin* of the fhell is foft, the reft is hard. The animal is flat, foft, and covers the inner part of the fhell; which, when touched, it contracts, fo that one point touches the other.

CANCER *brachyurus, ovatus, fpinofus, poſticè lævis.*

IN the room of our furgeon, whom we left fick in Spain, we took an Englifhman called *Thomas Druit* with us. A Spanifh paffenger alfo, *Jofeph Garcias Domingo Rivero*, a merchant's fon from *St. Ander*, about twenty years of age, came on-board in order to go to *Manilla*.

ANIMALS of all forts, *viz.* oxen, hogs, chicken, pigeons, &c. were in fo great plenty in our fhip, that we ftill had fome of them left on our return from *China*.

AFTER a ftay of ten weeks in Spain, we failed at fix o'clock at night from Cadiz, with a good wind, though the eaftern trade-wind is feldom found below the thirtieth degree of latitude.

The weather was very changeable during our ſtay in Spain: ſometimes it was dry almoſt a whole week, ſometimes foggy, often for three or four days together rainy, then we had thunder, and it was almoſt always ſtormy.

March the 23d, 33° 15′ N. L.

WE little expected to meet with our *Hoopoe* (*Upupa epops* Linn.) ſo far from Sweden. This bird approached our ſhip to-day, and went along with us a good way. I have before ſeen it in Spain; and in order to ſhew what alteration the ſeaſon or the climate might cauſe, I drew up the following deſcription: the *beak* is angulated, compreſſed, arcuated, long, ſharp: both the *jaws* (*mandibulæ*) are equally long, and triangular: the *noſtrils* are oblong: the *head* is adorned with a creſt of yellowiſh brown feathers with black tops, of the length of the beak; though the middlemoſt feathers (of which there are twenty-four) are ſomewhat the longeſt: the *neck*, the breaſt, the belly, and the foremoſt part of the back, are of a yellowiſh brown: the *vent feathers* are white, and the back black, with white ſtripes; but the

coverts

coverts of the tail are quite white. The sixteen *quill feathers* are black, with broad white crofs ftripes; the nine foremoft of which have one, the tenth two, and the reft three or four white lines a-crofs, excepting the three lefler coverts of the wing. The eight *feathers of the tail* are black, and have at top and below a white ftripe: the thighs, and the beak as far as the noftrils, are covered with little yellow-brownifh feathers: the *feet* and *toes* are dark grey; of the three fore-toes the middlemoft is the longeft, the reft are of the fame length with the back-toe. This bird was of the fize of a pigeon. I was told that the Spaniards called it *Coccis* on account of the note which is peculiar to this bird.

March the 26th.

AT half an hour after fix in the morning, we faw the Ifle of *Teneriffe*, (in N. N. W.) which belongs to the Spaniards, with the other Canary ifles, *Canaria, Palma, Gomora, Lancerota, Ferro, Port Sancto, Forta Ventura,* and *Madeira. Teneriffe* feems very barren towards the fea fide, on account of the high mountains without trees; but it is faid to be very agreeable

able further up the country, and to produce a quantity of wheat, lemons, oranges, but particularly grapes. The city of *Sancta Cruz* lies on the sea-shore; we passed pretty near to it, and counted in its harbour about fourteen ships at anchor, one of which hoisted the Swedish, one the English, and one the French flag, after we had hoisted ours. This town is well known; we fetch many sweet wines from thence, such as Canary, sack, and malvasy, or malmsey; and carry them the staves with which they make their pipes. In the last war, Spain had the treasure of the silver fleet in this harbour: from whence also our East India merchants fetched the money necessary for the Chinese trade. The city is surrounded by walls, ramparts, and other fortifications. The bishop of the *Great Canary* is said to have chosen this place for his summer residence. The *Pico Teneriffe*, which is situated at twenty-eight degrees, and twelve minutes, northern latitude, and thirty-four degrees, and fifteen minutes western longitude from *Upsal*, was, at twelve o'clock, two or three leagues off to the N. W. this mountain is reckoned among the highest in the world. It lay on the other side of the isle, but was nevertheless very conspicuous above the other mountains.

mountains, and seemed in shape like a haystack. It is affirmed that its summit continues burning, and for that reason nobody dares ascend so high. *Teneriffe* being on our right, *Canary* was consequently on the left, but out of sight. The passage here is reckoned more safe than on the other side of *Teneriffe* [z].

The 28th of March, 22° 12′ North Lat.

PAST eight o'clock in the evening the wind abated, and such a continual lightning ensued, that it seemed as if the whole ship was on fire. Afterwards it likewise thundered a little, and about nine o'clock fell a violent hail-storm; the largest of the stones were of the size of beans. The figure of the hail-stones was not alike, yet they all had two or three white rings in the middle, like fishes-eyes. This was a remarkable Maunday-thursday, especially so near the tropic of Cancer, which we passed the midnight next following.

---

[z] For a full account of *Pico Teneriff.* see Bishop Sprat's History of the Royal Society.

The 30th of March, 19° 34′ N. L.

BESANTYES is a word as familiar to our people who go to the East Indies, as it has been strange and unknown hitherto to naturalists. A multitude of *Besantyes* sailed by our ship at this time, with their bow-like, expanded skins; but sometimes they turned over and dipped their sails into the water. I was not able to get one of these little animals, although I wished it very much. At a great distance they look like green fish-bladders, with little sails, from whence they derive their name.

THE flying-fishes (*Exocœtus volitans*), which generally live about the tropics, and especially in the Western ocean, now began to appear near the ship. They have many enemies both in water and air: in the former they are pursued by the *Scomber Thynnus*, or tunny, by the *Scomber Pelamis*, or bonnet-fish, and by other fishes; in the latter, the *Phaëton æthereus*, or tropic-bird, the *Pelecanus Piscator*, or booby, and the *Pelicanus Aquilus*, or man of war, are their enemies. All these look upon

upon the flying-fishes as created for their use. Providence has given them longer pectoral fins than any other fish, with which they fly as light and as swift as a bird; but are forced to dip into the water, at the distance of a common gun's shot. They sometimes fall upon the ship's deck when flying; they are then quite unable to help themselves off again, and die quickly. On the evening we saw a swallow in our ship; but it was so wet, that it seemed as if it was but just out of the water.

The 31st of March, 17° 40' N. L.

The swallow which we saw yesterday, was so tired to-day, that we could catch it with our hands. It was the *Hirundo rustica*, or house-swallow. It is somewhat extraordinary, that it should be met with at so great a distance from Sweden, and in so different a climate. I do not pretend to assert, that it came yesterday from the bottom of the sea, as it was taken so near the Canary islands [b].

[b] Our author, with the northern naturalists, takes it for granted, that swallows retreat under-water when they disappear in autumn; there is good evidence that many of them migrate from Europe to Africa; and it has been fre-

The 1st of April, 15° 20′ N. L.

WE now saw a sea-turtle sleeping on the surface of the water, but it was wakened by the passing of the ship: we likewise saw a kind of birds which our ship's-crew called *boobies*[c].

The 3d of April, 10° 22′ N. L.

OUR passenger told me, that the *Sepia loligo* Linn. a species of cuttle-fish, or ink-fish, was eaten by the Spaniards, and that they called it *Cangrejo*. They have their enemies in common with the flying-fish. As soon as the *Sepia* wants to fly, it expands its arms (*tentacula*) like a brush, and also its rhomboidal tail-fin. It has peculiar characteristicks:

THE black *bill* looks like that of a vultur; the *jaws* are pointed, short, and bent; the

---

quently asserted, that a few have, at times, been found in a torpid state, hid in old buildings: but how a bird so much lighter than water, can contrive to keep itself half a year at the bottom of the sea, seems inexplicable.

[c] Our sailors call the *Pelecanus sula* Linn. a booby.

bill is furrounded by a circular *mouth* which has ragged incifions (*os lacerum*); round the mouth ten arms are fixed, whereof eight are trigonal, pellucid, thread-fhaped, ending in a point, at the outward end warty and dentated; the two others are round, thread-fhaped, longer, fmooth at the bottom, but warty at top. The *fhell* is foft, cylindrical, thicker before, fmooth, and red fpotted: the *eyes* are large and black: the *head* and *tentacula* are tranfparent, marked with little black dots: the *back* is of a golden colour, inclining to brownifh; and tranfparent towards the tail, with black dots: the *belly* is pale red: the *tail* is fharp pointed, and covered with a foft rhomboidal *fin*. The animal is faid to contain an ink-like juice in a bladder; it is eaten by the Chinefe.

The bonnet, from the Spanifh *Bonito* (fine), is a fpecies of fifh which is always very plentiful within the tropics, and lives upon flying-fifhes and ink-fifhes. The bonnet is a fpecies of mackarel, but much larger than our fort. It is eaten, although its flefh is very dry. It is caught in the following manner: you take a fifh made of lead or tin, put on a large fifhing-hook and faften the tops of two feathers to it, oppofite to each other, that it may look ftill more like a flying-fifh; you add another top of a feather or two for the tail-fin; at the end of this artificial flying-fifh you faften a ftring: you then move it up and down over the water on either fide of the fhip, till the bonnet bites. The bonnet is likewife ftricken by harpoons, which is another way of taking it. The name of this fifh is to be met with in many accounts of voyages; however, I fhall give the following defcription for thofe who have no opportunity of viewing the fifh itfelf:

Scomber pulcher [d], *pinnæ dorfalis anterioris officulis quindecim, pinnalis fubtus inter Caudam & Anum feptem.*

In Swedifh *Bonnet*; in Spanifh *Bonito*.

THE *dorfal*-fin has fourteen or fifteen radii, the *pectoral* fins each twenty-eight, the *ventral* fins each feven, and the *anal* fin fourteen: the *tail* is large, bifurcated, and has twenty-fix rays: the *head* is compreffed: the *body* is rather elevated than flat on the fides: the *belly* is not fo round as the back: the *mouth* is large, or rather very wide: the lower *jaw* is the longeft: the *forehead* runs into a point: the *eyes* are of a middling fize, they are placed in

[d] *Scomber Pelamis* Linn. Syft. Nat. p. 492.

the sides of the head, are roundish, oblique, and shine like silver. The *opercula branchiarum*, or coverings of the gills, are two round plates. The *membrana branchiostega* has six radii, and is covered; the upper radii are very long, the lower very short. The *teeth* are all in one row in the jaw; they are pointed and numerous. The *tongue* is wedge-shaped, with the skin a little convex on the sides. The *linea lateralis* is bent, near the head it approaches the back, and is thicker thereabouts. The *scales* are very small, and lie quite singly. The colour of the belly as far as the *linea lateralis* is silver-coloured; on each side run four blackish lines lengthways. The back is blueish and very little elevated. The appendages on the sides of the tail are very thin: the first dorsal fin from the head to the second has fifteen hard radii or rays distant from each other, ten of the hinder rays usually fold into a furrow of the back after the death of the fish. The second dorsal fins consist of ten or fourteen soft rays covered on the sides with little gristly scales, hardly to be distinguished. The pectoral fins are of an elliptical lanceolated figure, and have twenty-eight rays, divided at top, of which the lowest are the shortest. The ventral fins are long, with seven ramose rays, which are almost grown together at the bottom; the inner ones are the shortest. The anal fin is somewhat nearer to the tail than the dorsal fins, and is about the same size and form, consisting of fourteen rays which are distinguished with difficulty. The ventral and anal fins are surrounded like the following little softer fins, with a gristly skin. Below the two dorsal fins are eight, and below the anal fin to the tail seven other little fins with different rays. The tail is furcated, very much extended, and consists of twenty-six rays. The pectoral and the ventral fins are directly opposite to the beginning of the dorsal fin, and their length is equal to that of the first ray of the first dorsal fin. The *swimming bladder* sticks to the backbone and is long. The heart is tetraedrous. The belly is an oblong oval. As this fish is dying, it trembles and quivers much. Its length is scarce two feet. I have been enabled to examine many of them, and always found that the first dorsal fin is the surest specific distinction.

The 4th of April, 8° 19′ N. L.

LAST night about one o'clock we passed in the 9th deg. 20 min. N. L. and

3° 15' West longitude from *Teneriffe*. The Sun being west in *Aries* 25° 25' 42". For this reason no observations were made to-day. A dolphin was wounded by an harpoon, but broke it and got off.

The 5th of April, N. L. 6° 28'.

The heat was very great to-day as well as yesterday. Our water, which began to stink before we were quite clear from *Cadiz*, now grew sweet again. This change may be explained from natural causes; for on straining the water through a coarse cloth many gnats and *onisci* were found in it in a perfect state.

April the 6th, N. L. 4° 40'.

We now lost the north-east trade-wind, which helps the ships forwards all the year thus far from the thirtieth degree of N. L. because it continually blows from north-east, or at least with little variation. In the morning it began to rain; afterwards it grew calm, as is always usual about the Line.

The tunny is a fish very like the abovementioned bonnet, but may be easily distinguished from it by the longer pectoral fins, and the white belly. The difference is more plainly seen in the following description:

Scomber albicans [e] *pinnæ prioris dorsi osficulis quatuordecim, pinnulis subtus inter caudam et anum octo* P. D. *prior osficulis quatuordecim: posterior duodecim.* P. *pectoralis triginta duo.* P. *ventralis sex.* P. *ani tredecim. Cauda triginta osficulis.*

The *first dorsal* fin has hard rays, and the hindmost of them fold into a furrow of the back: the *second* dorsal fin is flexible, triangular, as in the bonnet; its eight first rays are longest; they are single, and of the length of the first fin; the remaining rays were gradually shorter and divided into many branches; it is connected with the eight flexible small fins, whose rays are divided: the *pectoral* fins are about six inches long, and treble the length of those of the bonnet; they have thirty-two rays: the *ventral* fins have six rays:

[e] *Scomber Thynnus,* Linn. Syst. Nat. 493.

the

the *anal* fin confifts of thirteen rays, the hindmoft being the fhorteft; it is flabelliform and connected with the eight little fins: the colour of the fecond dorfal fin, of the anal fin, and of the eight little ones, is yellow at top and at bottom: the *tail*, which has thirty rays, is longer than that of the bonnet, but not fo much expanded. The length of the fifh is not quite two feet: the *body* is compreffed, has flat fides, is white below to the *linea lateralis* and above it, with little fcales: the *head* is lefs fharpened: the *mouth* is wide; the lower *jaw* longer than the upper: the forehead fomewhat pointed: the *teeth* and *tongue* are fimilar to thofe of the bonnet, however the former are more diftant from each other: the *opercula branchiarum* confift of two large round plates: the *eyes* are large, round, and filver coloured. It trembles as it dies. The veffel that is the conduit to the gall is formed like a worm, and is blueifh. The *belly* is oblong.

The tunny is caught in the fame places, and much in the fame manner, as the bonnet; they are equal in fize, and are both eaten.

A large fort of fish, called the *Springer* in Swedish, shewed its back fins above the water near the ship.

April the 7th, 3° 47′ N. L.

We caught the *dog-fish* to-day, which is reckoned the moſt voracious animal of prey. Authors have already deſcribed ſeveral kinds of them, though not very clearly. The reaſon thereof is probably that ſome ſorts are no-where to be found but in great ſeas, where they can be but ſeldom examined by inquiſitive people; whence all ſorts are called by the ſame name, becauſe they all look alike at a diſtance. Very ſeldom does an opportunity offer of comparing ſeveral ſorts together, that ſpecific marks might be aſcertained, which otherwiſe is difficult, as their fins do not conſtitute the only difference. The dog-fiſh moſt commonly met with about the line is

The *Squalus conductus, Squalus Canicula,* (Linn. Syſt. Nat. p. 399. n. 8.) or the greater dog-fiſh.

Its *length* is five feet: the *body* is of a blueish grey above, and white below: the *head* is flat, with a fhort, half-round forehead: the lower *jaw* has four rows of ferrated teeth: the *mouth* is lunular, large, about an inch from the point of the head: the *tongue* is thick, round before, and dentated: the eyes were covered on both fides with a fkin after its death, excepting one crofs ftripe, which was to be feen in the middle. The *ventral* fins are near the *anus*, they are broad, fhort, blunt, and in fome meafure connected: the *anal* fin is fhort, and in the midway between the *anus* and the tail. At the tail there is a triangular cavity. The *pectoral*, *ventral*, and *anal* fins are white, with black points; the others are of the fame colour with the body, but they have white points. It is viviparous, and is caught on very large hooks, which have a joint not far from the hooks, faftened to ftrong ropes: on this hook you put a large piece of bacon, or half a chick, or fomething which the fifh fwallows greedily. It is very tenacious of life; and will move about, though its head or tail be cut off; from the wound the blood gufhes as out of a fpout; nay even if the bowels be taken out of its belly, it lives more than

than an hour, as we faw when we caught it. In its belly were bonnets, fepiæ, and whole chicken with feathers, which we had thrown over-board when dead. When a dog-fifh is caught, it flounces about the deck; and people muft take great care, for with its teeth it is faid to bite off a leg with great eafe, at leaft it would not be fafe to try the experiment. When the feamen want to get into a boat where thefe fifh frequent, they muft take care not to put their feet into the water, for I once faw a dog-fifh attempting to fwallow a large wooden quadrant, but it was not able to do it, as it was too broad, and therefore only left the marks of its teeth on it. It is owing to its great greedinefs that the feamen are able to catch it: they cut off its fins, and then throw it again into the fea; befides many other cruel tricks, which I fhall pafs over. If a failor dies in a place where dog-fifhes haunt, and is thrown overboard, he is fure to be buried in the bellies of fome of them. Large dog-fifhes are never eaten, and fmall ones but feldom, and in cafes of neceffity only. They are cut into flices, which are fqueezed in water till no train-oil remains in them: after being thus wafhed, it is boiled or roafted, and eaten with butter: the part towards the tail is the beft;

the

the fore-part is seldom eaten. The skin and fins are made use of in polishing, and are called *shagreen* [f]; they are found in plenty in the Chinese apothecaries shops, and in other places. In the head, above the eyes, in two cavities, is a thick white matter, which, the skin being taken off, is taken out, dried, reduced to powder, and used as an *Emmenagogue*.

THIS dog-fish had two companions:

Echeneis Remora, Linn.

THE *membrana branchiostega* has nine parallel bent rays, which are black, as well as the *opercula branchiarum*. The length of the fish is about one span: the *dorsal* fin has twenty-two rays; the *pectoral* fins twenty-six each: the *ventral* fin, which is joined together by a skin, has five rays: the *anal* fin is opposite to the dorsal, and has twenty-one rays: the *tail* is sickle-shaped, and has about sixteen rays. The whole *body* is covered with a black skin; but young ones have a greyish-white skin, shaded with black. The *head* is flat: the

---

[f] True shagreen is part of the skin of a wild ass, and is brought from *Turky*.

teeth are in two rows in the gums, and on the tongue: the upper *jaw* is the shortest: the *eyes* are small; their *iris* is white. From the foremost point of the head, to the point of the pectoral and ventral fins, runs a *skin*, or elevated flat *shield*, which is oblong, hangs on the back, is as broad if not broader than the fish itself, but its smooth margin is never fastened. This fish fastens itself on the belly or breast of the dog-fish with this skin, which consists of eighteen rough, double-crest-like, transversal lines, cut in-two length-ways by a middle line. The fish which *Artedi* described was much larger than I ever found any. It often sticks so fast to the dog-fish, that it is pulled upon deck along with it.

April the 8th, 2° 49′ N, L.

PILOTS are a sort of small fish which are similar in shape to those mackarels which have a transversal line across the body. Sailors give them the name of pilots, because they closely follow the dog-fish, swimming in great shoals round it on all sides. It is thought that they point out some prey to the dog-fish; and indeed that fish is very unwieldy. They are

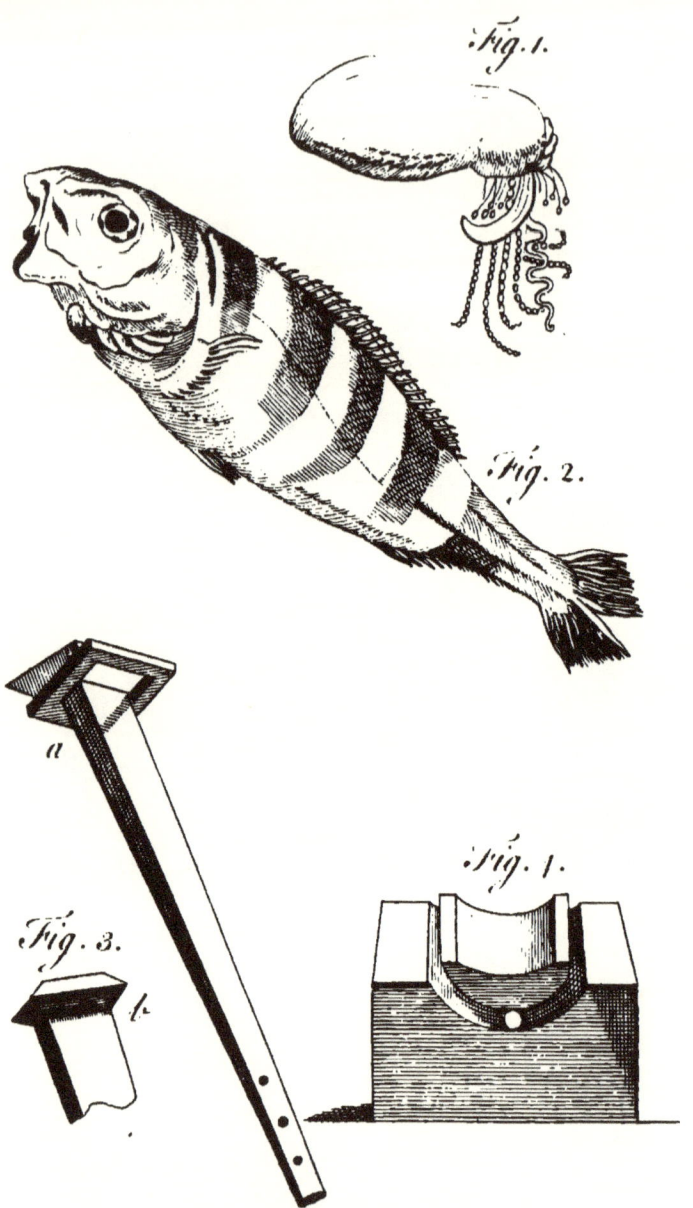

Fig. 1. HOLOTHURIA Physalis.
2. GASTEROSTEUS Ductor.
3. a chinese pair of Tongs.
4. a chinese Roller or calender.

not only not touched, but also preserved by it against all their enemies. Psalm cvi. ver. ii. *" Who can utter the mighty acts of the Lord?* *" Who can shew forth all his praise?"* This scarce and remarkable fish I had an opportunity of describing: it is *Scomber cæruleo-albus cingulis transversis nigris sex, dorso monopterygio.* See the Memoirs of the Swedish Academy of Sciences, for the year 1755, vol. xvi. p. 71, of the Swedish edition. Or

Gasterosteus Ductor, Linn. Syst. Nat. a species of stickle-back. *Pilote piscis*, by Ray Pisc. 156. Vid. tab. 12.

The *membrana branchiostega* has six rays: the *operculum branchiarum* consists of two entire gristles: the elevations on the sides of the tail are sharp and soft: the *dorsal* fin begins on the middle of the back and ends near the tail: it has thirty rays, whereof the three first are hard, short, and scarcely perceptible; the next following are longer; but the rest keep decreasing, and are divided: the *pectoral* fins are small, and have nineteen rays: the *anal* fin has sixteen rays: the tail is furcated, and has twenty-six rays, with black tops: the head is narrow: the forehead is blunt: the jaws are about equal in length, yet the lower

seems

seems longer when the fish opens its mouth: the *mouth* is oblong and small: the *teeth* are very small, and very numerous in the jaws; in the palate are none: the *eyes* are small and round: the *pupilla* is black; the *iris* is shining like gold and silver: the *back* is blue, the *belly* is a silver colour: the *head*, the belly, and even the tail, are ornamented with seven blueish black lines: the scales are extremely small, and stick very fast.

The 10th of April, 1° 50′ N. L.

THE *Southern-cross*, called the *Croziers* by the *English* sailors, is a constellation consisting of four stars, of which two are of the second, and two of the third magnitude. It is situated at the hindmost part of the constellation called *Centaur*, which appears on the south side of the line, as soon as the polar star disappears. This cross we now began to discover.

The 11th of April, 8′ N. L.

IN the afternoon we passed the Line. On this occasion the old custom was observed; namely,

namely, all the men were called upon the deck, and some pails full of water were thrown upon those who had not crossed the Line before, and those who have very often partake of the bathing. It appears from *Holms's* Description of New Sweden, that this ceremony was usual in 1642, on his voyage to *America*. The first cause that gave rise to it is unknown. It is true, in the neighbourhood of the Line, it is usual to wash the ships every morning and evening with sea-water, that the intolerable heat may be less noxious; which, particularly if the sailors drink brandy, is sufficient to make them mad. But we cannot from hence derive the ceremony of drenching them in water, as it is a practice more likely to occasion diseases than to prevent them.

AFTERWARDS all those who had been here for the first time collected a sum of money among themselves, to serve as a treat at a *Gothenburgh* tavern, in case they should return; and it amounted to three hundred and sixty-four copper dollars, and fifteen ocres. Another collection was made for the orphan-house at *Gothenburgh*; every one contributed to it, and it amounted to eight hundred and thirteen copper dollars, and twenty-four ocres.

The 14th of April, 5° 16' Southern Latitude.

THE wind called *the south-east trade-wind* was of great use to us at this time. This wind has this name because it blows from the south-east, or nearly, all the year long. It forwards the ships on the side of *America* very much, till they get a west wind at about twenty-two degrees of southern latitude, which carries them on still farther.

April the 26th.

ABOUT half an hour after nine we passed the tropic of *Capricorn*. We saw flying-fishes (*Exocœtus volitans*).

May the 2d, 31° 19' S. L.

MALMUCKS was the name given to a sort of brown gulls, with short wings and white bellies, which flew about the ship; and we saw them afterwards in other places, but were never able to catch one of them.

THE

The south-east wind, which generally turns west about the tropic, did not turn before last night.

May the 5th, 33° 16′ S. L.

SEVERAL sorts of birds flew about our ship, and in particular the *Albatros*, or *Diomedea exulans*: their size is that of a goose; they are white every where, excepting the quills and tail, which are black at the end, but white at bottom. We found them also in other places, viz. in thirty-six degrees, and likewise in thirty-five degrees and eighteen minutes of southern latitude.

CAPE *Pigeons* are a species of birds so called by mariners; they only resemble pigeons in size: their country is the *Cape of Good Hope*. A great many of these birds flew to and fro, and kept us company as far as the southern tropic. This bird is the

PROCELLARIA *Capensis* Linn. or the middling spotted Petrel of Edwards's Birds, 90. t. 90. part 2. The following is its description:

The

The *size* is that of a common dove: it has very fine black and white down on its *body:* the *bill* is black, narrow, conical, and short: the *upper jaw* is pointed, bent, and gibbous in the middle near the nostrils. About the *nostrils* are elevated *lines* running lengthways, but not parallel: the *lower jaw* is streight, flat, somewhat elevated on the point, not very sharp-pointed, compressed, and has parallel incisions towards the point; below covered with a skin of a dirty black colour: the *skin* within the bill is whitish: the *teeth* are foliated, and stand crofs-ways: the *tongue* is whitish, smooth, lacerated near the basis, broad, truncated at its extremity, and fits the bill exactly: the *epiglottis* is furcated: the body below is quite white. The *head* and all about the eyes is covered: the *upper* part of the *neck* is black, as is likewise the fore part of the back; because the feathers are grey, with black tips: the hindmost part of the back is black, spotted with white, and the feathers are white with black extremities: the *under* part of the neck is commonly white, but sometimes a little blackish, when the feathers have black tips. This is perhaps a difference of sex. The *wings* are long; below white,

white, with white fides; on the upper fide black with two large white fpots : the *quills* are white with black points; the three *firſt* are the longeſt; twelve or more *leſſer* ones are joined by them, and next to thefe again ten longer *fecondary* ones: the outfide of the quills is black; as the next decreafe in fize, fo their black margin decreafes, and the reſt of the fhort ones have only black tips: the *greater coverts* of the wings are white with black tips, and the *leſſer* ones are quite black: the *lower* coverts are quite white, except thofe at the extremity, which are black. The fourteen outward feathers of the *tail* are fhort, and white with black tips; the others are of the fame number, and are covered at the top and below: the *thighs* are covered to the knees, partly with the vent feathers, and partly with their own down: the *toes* are palmated, and, like the legs, of a dirty black colour: the *web* of the toes is very flightly notched: the *outward* toe is the longeſt, and has five articulations; the middlemoſt has four articulations, of which thofe two which are neareſt the bafe of the toe are white on one fide: the outward toe of the three fore toes has but two joints, and is whitifh on the inner fide: the fourth or *back toe* is the fhorteſt, for

it

it has but one joint or nail; the last articulations of the toes are hooked (*hamosi.*)

This bird makes a noise like a parrot, and throws up train oil when touched. It is caught without any trouble, with some tarred string, or a piece of lard on the fishing-rod. They are seldom eaten, and only in great necessity. We once boiled and tasted some of them, but they were extremely oily.

The two congeries of stars, of which the one which is near the *Polus eclipticæ* is called *Nubecula major*, and the other *Nubecula minor*, are well known to our *East India* navigators [f]. They observe how the one, which appears at night lower on the horizon, gradually mounts up higher than the other; and from this they can tell the hour of the night on the south side of the Line, as our common people can by the turning of the *Great Bear*.

May the 6th, 34° S. L.

We were obliged to dress in our winter cloaths, for the cold was no less intense than

---

[f] Our sailors call them the *Magellanic clouds*.

in *Sweden* in winter time. This change occasioned many diseases, and no less than twenty-two men were laid up at once, most of them having an ague; some had the head-ach, and others different complaints.

The storm-finch, (*Procellaria æquinoctialis*) has got this name from seamen for shewing the bad omen which its appearance forebodes. A couple of these little birds accompanied us, and always flew quite close to the surface of the water, if the sea was ever so rough. We saw them likewise the following days.

May the 16th, 36° 22' S. L.

The trumpeter, *Zetermark*, a comely and decent young man, died about noon of an ague, and was buried in the sea, about four o'clock in the afternoon.

May the 18th, 36° 8' S. L.

Although the abovementioned storm-finches were but very small, yet they were bold enough to feast along with the large sea-birds, when we threw the guts of pigs overboard.

board. They were generally firſt and laſt on ſuch an occaſion.

May the 21ſt, 35° 15′ S. L.

We caught a ſort of dog-fiſh to-day, which I have often heard of: it was by far larger than any of this kind we had ſeen till then: its colour was grey, like ſteel, and white below.

This *Squalus catulus*, Linn. or leſs dog-fiſh, had the following characters:

The *body* without the tail is eight feet long: the *colour* of the back is grey, like lead, and that of the belly white, without ſpots: the *mouth* is thin, oblong, and near it are two ſmall noſtrils: below the head it has ſeveral ſmall *apertures*: the *teeth* ſtand alternately, and their edges are ſlightly indented: the upper jaw is the longeſt: the teeth in the firſt row are ſtreight, like thoſe of the above deſcribed dog-fiſh (*Squalus canicula*), but they are more ſharp pointed, and larger below: the teeth of the ſecond and third rows are bent: the eyes are black, ſhining, and quite covered with a white ſkin, as ſoon as the fiſh is dead:

dead: both *dorsal* fins are short, and of the colour of pewter: the length of the *pectoral* fins exceeds a foot: they have parallel margins, but a joint on the insertion; they are white below, and above of the same colour with the back: the *ventral* fins are joined near the anus; they are white, short, and cylindrical at their insertion: the *anal* fin is of the same colour with the dorsal fin, and is very short: the *tail* is two feet long, and lead coloured. This whole animal shines, and is covered with a fine skin. The heart and the eyes were in motion a long while after it seemed to be dead. One of its bowels was like a long string of pearls, the joints of which were of the size of acorns, and contained thick blood. On one of the pectoral fins many *chrysalides mucronatæ, thorace imbricato*, were fixed. But the pilot-fishes which accompanied the *Squalus canicula* did not attend on this species.

May the 22d, 35° 14′ S. L.

It is in this latitude, that a seaman must be more cautious than any where else, for the least cloud often changes the finest weather into

such

such a storm, that the bare masts are sufficient without any sails.

The continent of *Africa* began now to appear to us, between N. N. E. and E. N. E. About five o'clock in the afternoon we buried one of our men, who died of an ague. We now thought that *Cape Falso*, as being the nearest land, was eight or nine miles off, N. by E. We found that (by heaving the lead) we had ground at ninety fathoms depth; and here we fished for cod, but in vain.

May the 23d, 35° 46' S. L.

About one o'clock in the afternoon, we again found ground at ninety fathoms depth. The effects of the deceased were sold by auction.

May the 25th, 36° 56' S. L.

One of our men, who had been sick for some weeks together, died of an ague, and was buried the next day before the sermon.

May the 27th, 37° 19' S. L.

Six dolphins [h] followed our ship, and generally were on the surface of the water. I never saw a finer fish than this for the variety of its colours. The dolphin is the same in a large size, as the gold-fish is in a small.

May the 29th, 37° 33' S. L.

THIS morning, about two o'clock, I saw an eclipse of the moon, which began on the south-east side, and continued till three quarters past three o'clock, when only the northwest border was eclipsed. The moon after-

---

[h] The reader must here take care not to confound this dolphin (which is the *Coryphæna hippuris*, Linn. and the *Dorado* of the *Portuguese*) with the dolphin of the ancients, (*Delphinus delphis*, Linn.) which is a cetaceous fish. If by *gold-fish*, Mr. *Osbeck* means, as we do, to express the *Cyprinus auratus*, Linn. one cannot but wonder that so good a naturalist should use so little precision in his account as to say, ". The dolphin is the same in a large size, as &c." merely from the resemblance of colour: for the *Dorado* and gold-fish are so little alike as to be not only of different *genera*, but also of different *ordines:* for the former is a thoracic fish, the latter an abdominal.

wards continued to increafe on both eaft and weft fide, fo that fhe was full about five o'clock. Yet before the end of the eclipfe, a fog, as the certain fore-runner of an imminent ftorm, began to increafe more and more; and the ftorm accordingly happened when the fky was quite covered.

At a great diftance from the fhip we faw fome animals which were faid to be *fea-lions*; but I could not diftinguifh whether they were fifh or *belluæ marinæ*. According to the figure of the fea-lion in Anfon's Voyage, it feems to be a fpecies of feal. Thofe which that admiral caught and ufed as provifion near the ifle of *Juan Fernandez* were twelve or twenty feet long, and eight or ten thick.

June the 7th, 37° 30' S. L.

About eight o'clock at night we heard, at feveral times, a deep and harfh noife. We fuppofed this was the voice of fome large fifh, and perhaps of that which we faw the next day. Some faid that they faw its way, and that it fhone a little in the dark. This light might probably arife from the violent motion
which

which its swift passage gives to the water; for in the night something shone about our ship: yet this might also be occasioned by many sorts of little worms, dead fishes, and other putrified bodies.

June the 12th, 36° 54' S. L.

THE sea raged excessively, and was driven by the wind, as the snow is on the land. The colour of the waves, and their height indeed, resembled hills of snow. At three o'clock in the afternoon a great body of water burst into the cabbins through the windows, and spoiled all the sugar, cloths, books, &c. which it met with. This accident put us into great confusion. Such was the reception we met with at the rocks of *St. Paul and Amsterdam*, from whence, the next night, a storm attended with hail so effectually helped us away, that the reefed mizzen and fore-sails only, were sufficient, whereas at other times we were obliged to add twenty more sails.

June the 14th, 35° 16' S. L.

WE saw some sea-grafs swimming by the ship; it was perhaps a *fucus*, for our navigators call this whole genus sea-grafs; which is one of the furest signs that rocks, iflands, or lands, are near.

June the 15th, 34° 1' S. L.

ANAS *nigra* Linn. or a *Scoter*, almost of the fize of a goofe, was feen to-day, and afterwards in thirty degrees of fouthern latitude. They look brown at a diftance; the head and feet black; and the bill white: the wings are greyifh at top, but blacker below.

June the 21ft, 30° 49' S. L.

WE affembled as ufual to attend our morning fervice; but a fudden ftorm made us leave off, when we had fcarce begun.

June the 22d, 29° 34' S. L.

A GRAMPUS, or great fifh of fome fathoms length, which fwam about the fhip backwards and forwards, once fwiftly paffed before her, though the fhip failed very faft; but at laft was forced to give the precedence to us; where-

whereupon it (and perhaps some others in its company) spouted the water up to such a height, that it was both heard and seen at a great distance.

July the 3d, 23° S. L..

THE sea being smooth, our sailors were employed in cleansing the ship.

SOME of the *Lepas anatifera* Linn. had fastened themselves during our voyage to the ship, and particularly to the rudder, but were now all destroyed. As soon as the water passes over them, they stretch out their *tentacula* like hooks to get their food by, which is either the *conferva rivularis* which grows about them, or some other things which the water carries to them. The reason which made the ancients call this lepas *Concha anatifera*, appears from *Grew's* Museum, p. 148. where he says, that some assert it as a certainty, that in the *Orcades* were some worms, which grew in hollow trees, and got, in time, a head, feet, wings and feathers, as perfectly as a seabird; and that they became as large as geese[i].

[i] Dr. *Grew* did not believe this absurd tale of the *Bernacle*; but old *Gerrarde* asserts, that he has seen with his own eyes the several stages of this metamorphosis.

The

The animalcules inhabiting it had the following shape:

They are of the *Triton* kind, and have ten pair of comb-like arms, which are bent towards each other like skrews, are black or grey, connected together at bottom, and are an inch long; each pair is inserted below, and entire. Besides these ten pair of arms, there is a single arm in the middle, like a worm, which is hairy at the top, and is perhaps the instrument they make use of to bring that kind of food to their mouth which they catch by their *tentacula*. Besides, there are a pair of arms on each side, which are like the abovementioned ten, but stand a little more off, are shorter, and as clear as water. The mouth consists of seven valves, which are serrated on the inside: on the sides of the mouth are some scales, that are like the former; they all stick to an oblong bladder: the shell sticks to the ship by means of a wrinkled leather-like tube, made of a spongy substance, which is tough and blueish, and has ten or more wrinkles: its shell is of the *lepas* kind, bivalve [k], oval, compressed, water coloured,

---

[k] Linnæus in the last (twelfth) edition of his *Systema Naturæ*, ascribes to the *Lepas anatifera* five, smooth, compressed valves. F.

and with yellow futures; each valve is divided in two by a crofs future, of which that is the leaft which forms the fummit: the fide which opens has yellow linear edges: but the back defcribes almoft a circle: the ridge of the back is brown, and has on both fides black and yellow futures: the bottom is faffron coloured.

ADELPHOZION I call a fpecies of worms which were joined together in the water by hundreds, and we at firft took them to be fnakes; but when we caught them by a hook they parted: each of them was an inch long; fcarce as broad as a finger; had compreffed fides, and at firft fight looked like a little fifh without fins: the whole body was foft, pellucid, but a little more folid at the ends: there were no bones in them, and only a fine finew or fide line; and a red brown edge quite in the middle fomewhat diftant from the fnout. As I wanted time and opportunity to confider them more attentively, I preferved fome in fpirits, and others in fea water; but they loft their former figure in both. I afterwards faw a drawing of many worms connected together, at Mr. Affiftant *Braad's*, who met with them in his voyage to *Suratte,* in the fhip called

The

The Gothic Lion, which perhaps only differed from these in age; but they had, for the most part, a rhomboidal figure.

July the 6th, 19° 5′ S. L.

WE were come so far, that we expected to see *New Holland* soon; but were disappointed, and fell into a very good trade-wind.

July the 9th, 14° 15′ S. L.

Two tropic birds (*Phaëton æthereus*), so called by seamen because they live within the tropics, were observed soaring in the air at a considerable height, as larks do. They seemed to be large and white, with a long narrow tail, consisting of a few feathers, with smooth, black edges, and a red bill. The description of this bird may be met with further on.

July the 11th, 9° 37′ S. L.

ONE of the greatest inconveniencies that attend a voyage to the East Indies is, that worms spoil both meat and drink. In our ship-

ship-bread some worms had lived ever since the beginning of May, and they now were of the following figure: the larva was white, somewhat hairy, and had a bristly tail: the fore part was flat; the hind part cylindrical: the three pair of feet were yellowish, and fixed near the head: the body has twelve articulations, the head included. The whole head, with the next articulation, and the tail, are dark brown: the jaws are prominent: the *antennæ* short and setaceous. I have also found smooth ones, less than the former, of a light brown colour, and middling ones likewise smooth. The head and tail of the latter was brown: but the former was not punctated; and the articulation nearest to the head was not brown as in the former. Perhaps these are only varieties arising from different ages.

July the 12th, 7° 53' S. L.

WE now got sight of *Asia*, and first of all of the isle of *Canibas*, the eastern point of which was about twelve o'clock N. E. by N. the western N. and the middle N. N. E. and it was reckoned two or three leagues from us. The eastern part of *Java* was to us E. N. E.

N. E. and the weftern N. N. W. We afterwards failed along the coaft of *Java*.

Some thoufands of porpeffes (*Delphinus phocæna*) were playing about our fhip, and made a great noife in leaping. They feemed a yard and half long, and of a ferrugineous colour: the *tail* is horizontal, and the *dorfal* fin lacerated behind.

The air was very cold here at firft, though the climate is one of the hotteft. This perhaps may be occafioned by a draught of air between the mountains.

The country is covered, both vallies and hills, with green trees, the reflection of which gives a green caft to the fea, even at a diftance from land. The fun fhone very hot, fo that a vapour rofe from the land like the fmoak which is feen in our country when woods are burnt down; yet the air along the coaft was very cold.

July the 13th.

Bubbi, from the *Englifh* word *booby*, is a fort of bird fo called by thofe of our nation

who

who fail to the East Indies, becaufe, though they frequently fettle on fhips, yet they never fly away if any one attempts to catch them; but only cry out, bite, and fpout out the train-oil, or fifhes, which they have fwallowed. Such a bird we caught to-day with our hands, which enabled me to know it better than merely by name. It was the male of the

PELECANUS *Pifcator* Linn. Its *bill* is pointed, elevated, narrow, blueifh on the outfide, has a ferrated margin, and is two palms long: the *throat* and all about its eyes are without feathers, and covered, as the bill, with a blueifh fkin: the *upper jaw* is elevated, and has on both fides a furrow running towards the *point*, which is bent, and has a prominence: near the head the bill has an elevated part: the *lower jaw* is narrow and ftreight; the tongue, which is faftened to it, is arrow-fhaped: the *cere* is light blue: the *noftrils* are wanting, unlefs the notch at the bafe of the bill can be taken for them: the *pupils* of the eyes are black: their *irides* are white, and furrounded with black: the *head*, the neck, back, the upper fide of the wing, and the inner margin thereof, together with the tail, are quite black: the *breaft*, the belly,

and

and the *uropygium* are white, waved with blackish grey: the *down* and the *lower coverts* of the wings, in particular the ten longest and innermost, are white: all the sixty-four *quill feathers* are very black, with whitish grey below: the first quill feather is the longest; the next to it decrease gradually: there are ten quill feathers on the first joint; on the second thirty; and on the third or innermost fourteen; and more secondary feathers. The *upper coverts* are tipped with grey: the *lower* are dirty white, with little black edges: the tail has fourteen feathers: the *thighs* are covered with grey feathers: the legs naked and whitish, like the four toes: the *first toe* has five, the *second* four, the *third* three, and the *fourth* two joints: no *back-toe* is to be met with: the *heart* is oval; the *liver* is long. The bird is the size of a raven.

The *female* is somewhat less: the *bill* is more serrated, and reddish towards the head: the *neck* and the *upper coverts* of the wing are white: the three first quill feathers are quite black, as in the male: the next following ones are grey, spotted; and the last white, mixed with black: the *back*, the *coverts of the wings*, and the thirteen *feathers of the tail* are white, spotted

spotted with a reddish yellow: the middlemost feather in the tail is the longest: the *toes* and *legs* are red: the rest the same with the male: Whether this is the female of the first described bird, I leave to others to examine. It may be compared with the *Anser Bassanus* of Albin, vol. i. p. 86. I found a black [k] *Hippobosca* upon it.

BOTH these birds were exceedingly lean, and not eatable on account of their oily taste. In flying they spread their tails like a fan, and bend their long necks towards the side they fly to. They settle upon ships, and sometimes stay on them (if not scared away) whilst they sail many miles. They are much plagued with lice, and for that reason are not agreeable to keep. These lice run very swiftly, and soon creep upon the men. They are small and white, and black on the middle: some are brown; and some have four long feet.

AT five o'clock in the afternoon, *Wincopers* point was N. by W. and the middle of the isle N. N. E. to us. *Flying-fishes* were to be met with here.

[k] *Hippoboscæ* abound on the *Hirundo apus*, or swift.

On a little isle, which we passed by in the dark, we observed strong breakers.

July the 14th.

To-day we had clear weather and but little wind. In the afternoon, at four o'clock, we found ground at ninety fathoms depth.

The Cape of *Java*, which we passed at nine o'clock before noon, was at first N. N. W. to us, and at ten it was N. by W. This high steep promontory is called *Java head* by the *English* sailors and ours, or the *Pico* of the *Prince Island*. It is on the right if you are sailing into *New Bay*, which is the first port in that road. This mountain is of a brown red colour. Near *Java head* is a neck of land every where covered with trees, and therefore is entirely like that side of *Java* which we passed by. Higher up the country the ground was rising, and the palm-trees were taller than I ever saw any where else. In a few places we observed, between these thickets, some spots of ground the surface of which appeared quite yellow from the blooming flowers: this gave a charma charming appearance to the country, but increased my chagrin as I was not to go on shore; and I was forced to languish like a hungry person who views his food only at a distance. These woods are said to be so full of tigers and other beasts of prey, that nobody ventures to live on the eastern shore of the island. At night it was extremely agreeable upon the decks, for we were refreshed by the sweet smell which exhaled from the trees and other vegetables. We were visited by many little white birds, like our gulls, which fluttered about us and whistled; and afterwards another larger sort of birds came to us, but soon after left us.

NIEU *Eyland*, or the *New Island*, whence the new bay, or the new road, derives its name, is the place where the *Swedish East India* company's ship *The Gothic Lion* (which had lost the trade-wind) was obliged to stay, and whence all our ships on their return fetch fresh water; and even on their voyage from *Europe*, if in want of it, or if detained by calms or by contrary winds. At eleven o'clock we had a coral bottom, twenty fathoms depth.

The second port in *Java* is *Welcome bay*, the third *Pepper-bay* and the fourth *Angeri*, which are all on the right coming from *Europe*. On the left or south side is *Prince Island*, which is said to be very populous, and belongs to the king of *Bantam*. From this island the ships of other nations take water for their return, as the *Swedish* ships formerly did: but they have since found *New-bay* more convenient for that purpose.

Sumatra, which we saw at a great distance behind *Prince Island*, is much larger than *Java*, and is computed to be two hundred *Swedish* miles long[1]. The country was on this side like *Princes Island*, and for the most part covered with thick woods, between which were some open places.

On the shore of *Java* we saw some small reddish rocks, and sea-turtles on the water. In the evening the sky was covered with some clouds shining like gold, upon which rain and thunder ensued. The inhabitants along the shore lighted several fires to frighten wild

[1] That is, about one thousand two hundred and fifty *English* miles. F.

beasts

beasts from their huts. About eleven o'clock all was silent, and we anchored in the fourth harbour, viz. *Angeri*.

July the 15th.

The thunder clouds lay low on the mountains, so that the high rocks were prominent above them. Thunder and lightning, together with rain, ensued.

We weighed anchor at eight o'clock in the morning, having had *Angeri* point N. N. E. and the island called *Quer im Wege* (that is *Across the way*) between N. and N. by E.

The isle of *Kraka toa* was to the left of us. About nine o'clock we cast anchor; we had fifteen fathoms depth, and a clayey ground, on which lay little shells. We had the fourth bay from *Java*, between S. and S. by E. The before mentioned island N. E. and *Angeri Point* N. E. by E.

Some moths came aboard our ship and were caught, viz. *Sphinx atropos* Linn. or the *Jasmine Sphinx*: its *upper wings* are black, with

whitish

whitish spots; but at the extremity of an orange colour: the under side of the upper, and both sides of the lower wings, have black lines: the *antennæ* are blackish, prismatic, and have a brown spot on the point: the *eyes* are large and black: the *back* of the *thorax* is marked with a blackish brown figure like a skull: the *body* is black below, with orange rings: it is marked at top with rings of black changing into blue: the *feet* are shaded black and brown; and their spines, which sting like nettles, have the same colour: this *Sphinx* has a strong spiral tongue. When caught, it made a noise something like a bird.

At half an hour after four in the afternoon we sailed, and about six o'clock we dropped the anchor at ten fathoms depth, in a blue sandy, clayey ground.

The island called *Across the way* was now N. N. W. and *Angeri* S. by E. We saw two fires on the coast of *Java*.

July the 16th.

For the greatest part, calm and fine weather.

About

ABOUT eleven o'clock we weighed anchor, but foon after dropt it again, at a moderate diftance from *Angeri*. Here at laft I got leave to go on fhore with the boat, which fetched fome refrefhments for our men, fuch as cocoa-nuts, &c. but only on condition of returning immediately as foon as the commanding officer fhould defire me. We had provided ourfelves with fire arms in cafe of a bad reception.

As foon as we reached the land (which we did with great difficulty, on account of the coral bottom, and becaufe the tide ran very much to the fhore), fome natives of the country met us: thefe at firft feemed undetermined whether to look upon us as enemies or as friends; for they were then at war with the *Dutch*. Each of them had a dagger on his fide, which looked like a kitchen knife hung in a belt, and its point was made poifonous by the *Toxicaria* of *Rumphius*. One of them carried a couple of javelins on his back, and a cane in his hand. They were almoft naked, being covered with nothing but a brown cotton cloth, fpotted with blue, tied round the body with a handkerchief; between which their dagger is put. With thefe poifoned daggers they

they cut the cocoa-nuts, and other things; but they likewise defend themselves againſt their enemies with them. Round their black hair they wear a check handkerchief tied, yet ſo that the crown of their head remains uncovered. When they came on-board they ſometimes cloathed themſelves in a looſe ſhirt, which was commonly blue or check. Some of them wore on their fingers braſs rings with ſeals of ſtones like blue ſaphires. Theſe Indians were of a middle ſize, but generally ſhort; their hair and eye-brows black, their teeth of a blackiſh red, their eyes and noſes little, their mouth large, and moſt of them had no beards. They were civil, grave, ſimple, and willing to oblige; but cried like children if any thing was taken from them! They want no chairs, becauſe they ſit upon their heels like monkeys. Their ſalute is *Tabu tuani*, or Good day to you, Sir. At laſt they offered us their cocoa-nuts, plantains, chicken, beer, buffaloes, tortoiſes, and bed-mats; which latter were either *double*, that is, ſuch as have larger meſhes on one ſide; or *ſingle*, which are always brought here and uſed as ſheets, on account of their coolneſs. In payment they received *Spaniſh* ſilver money, or wares, ſuch as old ſhirts, handkerchiefs,

kerchiefs, mirrors, glafs, knives, pins and needles, flints, &c.

The fea-fhore here confifts of a grey fand, in which are feveral corals, fuch as madrepores, millepores, &c. as alfo fhells, viz. *Cypræa alba* and *Cypræa punctata*, two fpecies of *Cowries*, were found here. The country was fcarce a yard higher than the furface of the water. A number of fmall crabs ran very nimbly on the land.

A little hut, confifting of four poles, open on the fides, but covered with cocoa leaves at the top, and ufed for fires at night, was found on the fhore. The people live fo contented here amongft apes and parrots, that the ftatelieft palaces in *Europe* do not contain fo happy inhabitants.

All the trees are different from thofe which are found with us, and ftand fo clofe together on the fea-fhore, that it is almoft impoffible for a ftranger to penetrate into the country.

The inhabitants of *Java* had a little path through the wood, but they forbad me going through it. They accompanied us to-day
along

along the fhore towards the fide of *Angeri*, on a brook which was about the diftance of a gun-fhot from our boat, where we filled a tun full of water, which was not very good. On the fide of the brook ftood a tree of about ten or twelve feet high, which had both flowers and fruits, and which the *Indians* called *Vientaro*: it is *Cerbera Manghas*; the *germen* is oval like the *ftigma*, which is bifid: the *outward fhell* of the fruit contained a milky juice, which raifed a fufpicion of its qualities; and befides, the people of the country more than once told us that it was poifonous. It may be compared with the *Arbor lactaria*, Malaicè Bintaro Rump. iii. p. 234. and *Jafminum Indicum*, Merian Surin. p. & t. 8. *Quauthlepatli f. Arbor ignea.* Hern. Hift. Mex. cap. xxxiii.

The other plants which I gathered here, were

Acanthus ilicifolius: the *perianthium* is double: the *outermoft* is lefs; and both of them have two oppofite leaves fomewhat larger than the reft: the four *ftamina* are fhorter than the *corolla*, and two of them longer than the other two: the *filaments* are broad, pointed, and ftriated in the middle: the *antheræ* are

are oblong, erect, hairy, and shorter than the filaments: the *germen* is almost oval, and situated below the *corolla :* the *stylus* is filiform, and is of the same length with the filaments: the *stigma* is undivided : the *pericarpium* is a bilocular oval capsula, turned upside down; in each partition were two flat, oval seeds: the *smell* is like that of an *Agaric.*

Catesbæa? *Javanica :* the *perianthium* is short and infundibulous-form : the *tube* of the *corolla* is very long, and nearly cylindrical : the *limbus* is short and quinquefid: the four filaments are filiform, remarkably long, and inserted in the tube of the *corolla :* the *antheræ* are small : the *germen* is round and small : the *stylus* is filiform, and longer than the *stamina :* the *flowers* are blue and axillar; each peduncle bears three flowers at the utmost: the *peduncles* of each flower in particular are short : the *plant* is a *frutex :* the *branches* hang downwards, and are quadrangular: the *leaves* are ovato-lanceolated, opposite, smooth, pointed, petiolated, inclining to one side and deciduous. It grows on the sea-shore.

Convolvulus pes capræ Linn. lay on the shore, with its long tendrils and fine flowers.

Ischæmum

Ischæmum muticum procumbens Linn. was the most common grass along the sea-shore.

Vitex trifolia: the *perianthium* is monopetalous, quinquedentated, cylindrical, and very short: the *corolla* is monopetalous and ringent: the middlemost *lacinia* of the upper line is longer and broader than the four others, which are equal: the four *filaments*, two of which were longer than the others, are inserted in the base of the limbus: the *stylus* is longer than the *stamina*: the *antheræ* are bifid; and so is the *stigma*, which is reflected: the *berry* is obovated: the branches are quadrangular, lanated, like the leaves and *petioli*: two, three, or four *leaves* sit together; but on the branches they are single: the *foliola* are lanceolated and serrated. The *tree*, or *shrub*, has branches hanging down, and a *smell* of wormwood. It grows on the sea-shore.

Asclepias gigantea: the *nectarium* looks like a lion's mouth.

Memecylon capitellatum: its *styli* are filiform, as long as the *nectarium*: the *stigmata* are lamellated and joined together: the *leaves* are elliptical, and lanated below.

Verbesina

Verbesina lavenia: the leaves have two little glands at their base, and one or two about the middle.

Sida cordifolia.

Urena sinuata: the *leaves* are ovated, cordated, serrated; and the lower ones have generally an angulated edge: the *flowers* are red and at the extremities. The *plant* is a little tree.

Michelia champaca: it has no *calyx:* its *corolla* is double: it has fourteen lanceolated *petals,* of which the outward six are greater: the *filaments* are numerous, short, inserted at the base, and surrounding the *pistillum:* the *antheræ* are longer than the filaments: the *stylus,* &c. like that of the *Nymphæa:* the *flowers* are yellow, and have a very fine smell. The *Javanese* offered them to us as an agreeable present.

The *Tetradapa of the Javanese*; *Erythrina corallodendron?* the *perianthium* is monophyllous, spathaceous, short, and oval: the *vexillum* of the *corolla* is great, including four oval, short petals: the *filaments* are ten in number, nine of which are grown together half-way in one;

one; they are all fubulated: the *antheræ* are erected and oblong: the *germen* is long, and lanated: the *ftylus* is fubulated: the *ftigma* is deflected and barbated: the *flowers* are verticillated, red and deciduous. The *fruit* which lay under this tree (if it may be called fo) was a narrow rhomboidal *pod* (*legumen*): it contained two kidney-fhaped *feeds*. The tree was as high as a man's head, and very ramofe: it had no leaves at that time, but fine fcarlet flowers. It may be compared with the *Gedala litorea*; Malaice *Gelala laut* et *Gelala itam*; *Badenfibus Dadab. Rumph. Tom.* iii. p. 231. *t*. 77. This author fays, the tree is in bloffom at the latter end of July, and the leaves fall off about that time. In the middle of Auguft the flowers drop. In September comes the fruit and the frefh leaves. The blood-coloured parrots called *Luris* like thefe flowers exceedingly; about the time that the trees are in bloffom, they flock about them, and fuck the juice out of the *Nectaria*; and at that time they are caught in fpringes fixed to the boughs of the trees. The above-mentioned author fhews the ufe of the leaves and bark in phyfic; on the latter of which grew *Byffus candelaris*, and on the root *Onoclea fenfibilis*
Linn.

Linn. vel *Filix indica polypodii facie*. Mentz. pugill. tab. penultima.

Crinum Afiaticum Linn. *Tulipa Javana*. Rumph. t. v. page 240. t. 105.

The *fpatha* has two leaves: the *flowers* form a knob at the top of the ftalk, and have an agreeable fmell: the *corolla* is monopetalous: the *tube* is cylindrical, and very long: the *limbus* is fexfid, with long, linear, reflected *laciniæ*: the *ftamina* and the *ftylus* are very long, and alfo reflected: the filaments are inferted in the mouth of the tube: the *ftylus* is longer than the filaments, but does not reach fo high, becaufe it ftands much lower: the *leaves* are fword-like and broad. It grows in the fandy fea-fhore. It was brought to *Sweden* perfectly alive.

Coccus nucifera (*Palma Indica major*, Rumph. t. i. p. 1.) called *Calapa* in the *Javan* language, is a very high, but not very thick palm-tree, with a rough bark, and a ftem which is undivided up to the crown. On the bark grows a white flour-like mofs. The cocoa-nuts, which hung at the top, looked like cabbages, and were fomewhat triangular: the exterior fhell of the nut is yellow when it begins to ripen,

ripen, and grows brown: it confifts of an outer cafe, like hemp, and is ufed as fuch, and therefore is commonly peeled off before the nut is fold; excepting a narrow ftripe, which is left to fhew how ripe the nut is; and accordingly is either green, or yellow, or brown. Yet thefe nuts may be had quite perfect if they are ordered, and in that ftate they contain the greateft plenty of frefh water. The fibrous fhell is ufed for matches and ropes, but the latter foon rot in frefh water. The next fhell below this is white before it is ripe, but it afterwards becomes brown and very hard: near the ftalk it is fomewhat angulated. The *Java* people make ufe of it to put their brown fugar and other things in. People going to the *Eaft Indies* make drinking veffels and punch ladles of it: and befides this fome very pretty little bafkets. Oppofite to the bafe, or to the part where the ftalk is faftened, are three little holes, but only one of them is eafily opened. The innermoft fhell, which fits clofe to the hard fhell, is white, and not much harder than a turnep before it is boiled: it may be eaten raw, and it has a tafte of fweet almonds; and for that reafon feamen mix it with cinnamon, and make a fort of almond milk with it. It may alfo be ufed

as a fallad, when prepared with vinegar, falt,
and oil. The nut is filled with a pale, fweet
water, which turns four if it is not drunk foon
after the nut is opened. Every nut contains
about a pint, or fomewhat more, of this water. We ufed it for fome weeks, whilft it was
frefh, inftead of tea. It is faid that this juice,
if it is ufed as water to wafh one's felf, gives a
fine complexion. When the nut grows old,
the water congeals into a fpungy white kernel,
from which, after the fhell is opened, fome
leaves fpring up, which keep very long without putting the nut into the ground or water-
ing it. A hundred nuts coft a *pefo duro*, or
Spanifh dollar. The trees ftood along the
fhore in low places, and were very plentiful.
Authors fay very circumftantially, that this
tree affords cloaths, meat and drink, houfes,
or huts, utenfils or houfehold implements, and
other inftruments, to the natives. To the laft
mentioned purpofe the ftem is of ufe; out of
the branches they make the arched entrances
to their huts, to which they faften flowers on
their wedding-days: the leaves are made ufe
of for thatching, fails, bafkets, brooms, and
may be wrought upon with bamboo nails:
the kernel and water of the nut afford them
their meat and beverage: the outward fhell

Vol. I.   L   affords

affords cloathing, painting-brushes, &c. If an incision is made into any bough, a clear juice runs from the wound in the night time, which makes syrup and vinegar if properly prepared. Without this juice of cocoa no arrack can be made: and the Chinese, for this reason, are obliged to buy this liquor here. The Indians breakfast on the kernel of the cocoa-nut, sagoe-bread and dried fish: but those of higher rank add some boiled rice. The shell is used like *Areca*, for chewing, but first they mix it with *Betel* and chalk: it is likewise put into water, and afterwards they make a milk of it, which they call *Santar*, in which they boil herbs, cabbage, rice and fishes: this milk turns sour in one night. If it is mixed with a certain quantity of water and boiled in a pot, it loses its white colour; and when all the water is gone off, a pure oil remains, which it is said is as clear and sweet as oil of olives; it is used as butter, and is a very nutritive food. Both men and women anoint themselves with cocoa oil, both against certain diseases, and because it is fashionable to have black hair. The ladies of *Java* and *Balaya* mix part of the root of turmerick (*Curcuma* Linn.) with it, which gives a lustre to their complexions. The *Portuguese* doctors prescribe

scribe cocoa oil with syrup of violets against coughs and asthmas, and order gouty people to rub the parts affected with it, &c. The roots are used against dysenteries and fevers. The strangury and the *gonorrhœa virulenta* are healed by means of the flowers taken out of the spatha and eaten with *Lontaris* or a reddish sugar. If fresh cocoa-nuts are roasted and grow cold again, or when they are exposed to dew, they are said to put a stop to agues and the like diseases: it might be of use to try this receipt in the *East India* voyages. In *Malabar* the kernels of the ripe nuts are dried by the sun, and exported into other countries by the name of *Copra*; and oil is pressed out of it, with which all sorts of weapons are rubbed to prevent their rusting.

The inhabitants of this part of *Java* had no wild birds to sell at present; however, for two knives, I got an *Ispida viridis supra ferruginea: (Merops viridis* Linn.) One might see by its aspect it was not formed for a songster, but only to clear the earth of grubs and other insects. It made some noise now and then as long as it lived; but it survived but a few days. After its decease I took down the following particulars: the *bill* is black, sharp, arched,

arched, and has a narrow ridge at the top: the *eyes* are black: the *irides* are red: the *jaws* are triangular: the *tongue* is every where equally broad, narrow, and lacerated towards the tip: the *nostrils* are round and naked: the *head* and *neck* are brownish: the *breast*, *belly*, and *tail* are white, and somewhat greenish: the *wings* are green on the upper side; the upper margin, the extremities, and the under side are ferrugineous: the *back*, the *throat*, and the *tail* are blue: it has twenty-one *quill feathers:* of the twelve feathers in the tail the two middlemost are the largest: the *legs* and *feet* are ash-coloured and naked: it has three *fore-toes* and one *back-toe*. This specimen is preserved in the *Museum Upsaliense*.

Several insects, particularly butterflies, flew about us on all sides; but it was their good fortune that we stayed no longer on shore. I only caught an *Apis rufa, thorace antice linea alba, abdomine fusco*; and some black ants. The latter were frequent in the trees.

The *flying-boats* or *proas* of the *Java* people were pulled on shore and carried into the woods, lest the great heat of the sun should spoil them: they are sharp and very narrow, with

an

an out-rigger of bamboo, going in the water on one-fide, which makes it more fecure[m].

JAVA tortoifes (*Teftudo Javanica*) were fold here two for a piaftre. They were both females. They are dreft for eating in the fame manner as the tortoifes in the *Afcenfion* Ifland, as will be found in the fequel; but the latter are much larger, and of a quite different kind, as will appear from this defcription: the *upper jaw* is ftriated inwardly; the *lower* is dentated: the *upper fhield* is of a reddifh brown, and ftriated: the five middlemoft *fcutella* are pentagonal: next to them are, on each fide, four oblong pentagons, crofs-ways; and on the margin are twenty-five leffer oblong quadrilateral ones: the *fhield* on the belly is yellowifh-white, and reticulated: on each fide are eight ribs: the *paws* and *feet* are entire, but fomewhat notched on the inner fide.

AFTER we had paid a vifit to the inhabitants of *Java* for about a quarter of an hour, and bought a hundred cocoa-nuts for one *pefo duro*, the above tortoifes, and other things, we returned on-board, where we arrived about

[m] See Lord Anfon's Voyage, book iii. chap. 5.

twelve o'clock, and found other *Java* men there, exposing cocoa-nuts, and the following things to sale:

Tobacco, which they chewed with *Areca.* The tobacco was cut from broad, thin, green leaves, into narrow stripes. It is said that it is very good for smoaking, and might be the *Nicotiana peniculata.*

Brown powder sugar in half cocoa-nut-shells, put together and tied with leaves.

Bottles of Gourds, (or of the *Cucurbita lagenaria* Linn.) filled with water, as it is made up for their own use, and for sale.

Shells, particularly *Cowries.*

Cucurbita pepo.

Citrus decumana Linn. the shaddock, is a great, roundish fruit, like sweet or *China* oranges, and eaten instead of such; yet it is much larger than a *China* orange, and rather sourer, and is therefore better to quench thirst. The peel is spungy, of the thickness of a finger, bitter as a *Seville* orange, to which this fine fruit is very near akin.

There

There was another round fruit like small *China* oranges, with a green warty peel, which was called *Pompelmuss* by the *Java* people: I have seen but few of them. They were reckoned more valuable than the *Citrus decumana*, and had a sweeter and more agreeable taste. *Limon tuberosus Martinicus*; Malaice *Lemon-Martin*, Rumph. ii. p. 101. t. 26?

Musa *paradisiaca* Linn. *Plaintain* tree, or *Pisang*, has yellow, soft fruit, which looks like fingers, being seated on the stalks in such a manner as to resemble two hands. If you will keep the fruit for some weeks together, you must buy it green, and then it gradually ripens, and is pretty good to eat as soon as the rind is turned yellow, which easily peels off. It is said that this is the forbidden fruit, which threw our first parents into misery.

Java monkies, *Simia Aygula* Linn. *caudata subbarbata eminentia pilosa verticis longitudinalis*. The seamen call them *Tjacko*, and this is perhaps the true name which the people of *Java* give to this animal. It is no bigger than a little cat, of a light grey, or greyish colour, and this is likewise the colour of the tuft

tuft at the top of the head: below the belly it is whitish: the *snout*, from which an elevated sinew runs down to the lip, is narrow: the *eyes* are brown; the *pupil* is black: the *eyebrows* are large: the *beard* is so small, that it scarce deserves that name: the *nails* are narrow and long, but the nail of the thumb is short. They flatter both men and those of their own species, and embrace one another. If they perceive an ape of a different kind, they greet him with a thousand grimaces. They play with dogs if they have no nearer friends about them; at first they are uneasy at being separated from their own species. When a number of them sleep, they put their heads together. They make a continual noise during the night time; and in day time, if they are tied to one place, they continually move backwards and forwards. If any body looks cross at them, they are angry, and begin a smacking. They resemble all others of that genus in dirtyness, lasciviousness, drollery, in shewing a liking to all glittering things, and an appetite for greens and fruits. They crack nuts and eat the kernel with great alacrity. It is said that the monkies in *China* gather rhubarb, and pound rice. Females are but seldom sold. These animals in general are

not

not eafily brought home from fuch diftant parts. Their conftant nocturnal mewing is intolerable. Sometimes they are attacked by the fcurvy, which makes them fo ftiff that at laft they can fcarce move out of one place, and this very often kills them. If you let them go about freely, they play a thoufand tricks, jump over every thing, fteal the peoples meat away, hunt after chicken, break the necks of birds; and even carry their mifchief further, which has been attefted by many men of veracity: fome years ago there was a great monkey in a fhip, and the boys being ordered to get upon the yard to take in the fail, the monkey mounted after them, and one of them not doing his bufinefs to its liking, it bit off his ear. Thefe and other inconveniences are the reafons why we bring no more of thefe diverting animals with us.

July the 17th.

FINE and calm weather.

A JAVANESE man, who conducted a Dutch yacht from *Batavia* to the weftern coaft, with a Dutch flag, came on board us, after we had fired

fired a cannon, and presented us with two large water-melons marked with Chinese characters.

About three in the afternoon we sailed from hence, with very little wind, and anchored again at five o'clock on a stony ground at twenty fathoms depth; the next night we had some lightning.

July the 18th.

The weather was fine, but wind and current were against us.

The *Java* men came to us, and had cocoa-nuts, large oranges, (*Citrus decumana*), great coffee-beans, chicken of different colours, pale-grey ducks, powder-sugar, tobacco, several mats to lie upon in the heat instead of sheets; some birds in cages, particularly little parrots of excellent green, blue, and red colours, especially the following:

Psittacus galgulus, viridis, uropygio et gulâ rubrâ, vertice cæruleo Linn. *Psittacus viridis, remigibus rectricibusque supra viridibus, subtus cæruleis, uropygio pectoreque coccineo, vertice cæruleo.* Edw. t. 6.

[It

Its *size* is that of a little sparrow; the *bill* is of the same shape with those of other species of the same genus; the round *nostrils* are high up on the bill, and are surrounded by an elevated skin; the *eyes* are surrounded by a bluish skin, with elevated points near the margin; the *head*, the *back*, the *belly*, the *uppersides of the wings*, and the coverts of the *tail* below, are green; but the under-side of each feather is purple at the bottom; the *crown* of the head is adorned with a blue spot; the *uropygium* and the *throat* are red; on the *neck* is a brownish spot; the lower part of the back has a yellow spot, and towards the uropygium it grows red; the nineteen *quill-feathers* are blue on the outward edges, the rest is green; the eleven tail-feathers are green on the upper and blue on the under side, and they are almost concealed under the coverts; the people of *Java* call these birds *Parkicki*, and our people call them *Paroquets:* these little birds are beautiful on account of their high colours, and this is the only thing that recommends them to all nations; if it is put into a cage, it whistles very seldom, and commonly grows quite sullen; it hangs itself with its feet so, that the back is turned towards the earth, and seldom changes this situation; it is fed with
boiled

boiled rice, in which manner, in the year 1752, one was brought alive to *Gothenburgh* in the ship the *Gothic Lion,* and I brought a stuffed one.

PSITTACUS *Javanicus* (*Psittacus Alexandri* Linn.) This Parrot is twice as big as the preceding one, and is here universally exposed to sale. The *core* is black; the *wings* have seven quill-feathers in the last joint; eleven secondary feathers are in the next; and in the lowest, which is very short, are a few small ones; the midlemost of the eleven *tail-feathers* is the longest; the *upper-jaw* is the longest and pale red; the *lower* is pale yellow; the *nostrils* stand very high up in the bill, and are round; the *membrane* of the head goes round about somewhat lower; the *head* is every where covered with very short feathers of a pale blue, and pale yellow; the *temples* are black on both sides; all the other parts of the bird are grass coloured, except the *throat* and *breast* which are pale red; the *wings* are light grey below, but five of the *coverts* are yellow; the *down* close to the body is grey; the *tail* is yellowish, the *thighs* are long and covered; the *legs* are short, and like the *feet,* of a greenish grey; the latter have two *fore-toes* and two
back-toes

back-toes of which the innermoſt are the ſhorteſt.

CORVUS *Javanenſis* (*Gracula religioſa* Linn.) The *Java* people call them *May-noa*; they may be compared with the *Lef-koa* of the Chineſe; it looks like a great blackbird with white membranes near the ears; the *bill*, the *legs*, and the *feet* are pale yellow; each of the outermoſt *quill-feathers* has a white ſpot; the whole bird is black beſides; each *ear* has two white membranes; the *eyes* are black; its little oblong *noſtrils* are in the middle of the bill; the *jaws* of the bill are of an equal ſize; the *irides* are moſtly covered and blue; the *legs* and *feet* are whitiſh and ſcaly; the latter have three *fore-toes* and one *back-toe*; of the ſixteen *quill-feathers* the ſeven outward ones have each a black ſpot in the middle; the ten *tail-feathers* are ſhort; the *head* is naked: this bird eats greadily, cries loud, ſmacks with its bill, and it is ſaid, it may be taught to ſpeak: we bought one here, but it died at *Canton*.

MOTACILLA *familiaris* (*Emberiza familiaris* Linn. Syſt. Nat. 311.) *capite & roſtro nigro, uropygio luteo:* the *head* is black and has a little a little tuft; the *bill* is fubulated, ftreight, narrow, black; the *neck*, the *breaft*, and the *head* are afh-coloured; the *coverts of the tail* are yellow. It was one of the prettieft birds I ever faw; for, when a perfon whiftled to it, it fang very fweetly; and if any one offered his hand when the cage was opened, it would jump upon it; if it faw a difh of water, it went and bathed itfelf, which it did almoft every day; at night it was reftlefs till we hung fomething over its cage; we fed it with rice till it was devoured by rats at *Canton*.

JAVA Turtle doves (*Columba turtur*.) The *head* is reddifh-grey; the *bill* is blackifh and narrow; the *upper-jaw* is the longeft, and ends in a fharp point like a nail, but a little bent; the *lower-jaw* is ftreight; the *noftrils* are long, equally broad, oblique, raifed up at the edges; the *irides* are red; the *throat*, the *breaft*, and the *belly* are of a reddifh grey; on the *neck* are white and ferrugineous fpots; the *quill-feathers* and the *tail* are undulated with a red and ferrugineous colour; the *legs* and *feet* are red; it has three *fore-toes* and one *back-toe*.

JAVA *Sparrows. Fringilla capite & gula nigra, temporibus albis (Loxia oryzivora* Linn.) The Cock-paddy

Cock-paddy or *Rice-bird.* Edw. t. 41. The *bill* is sometimes more, and sometimes less red; the *lower-jaw* is a little longer than the upper one; the *tongue* is sharp and lacerated; the *head* and *cheeks* are black, but grey in young birds; the *temples* are white; the *neck*, the *back*, and seven of the *quill-feathers* are blue, and blackish grey on the upper side; the quill-feathers are whitish below; the *belly* is reddish; the twelve feathers of the tail are black; the *vent-feathers* are white; the *legs* and *feet* are of a pale colour; the *back-toe* is as long as the middlemost *fore-toe*.

We now got a sight of the *Patiallinga*: they are small Dutch merchant ships, which cruize hereabouts, between the islands, to prevent smuggling on the coasts.

Every time we heaved the lead we got pieces of corals.

Being obliged by the contrary current to anchor at *Topenshuth*, overagainst which is *Brabandshuth*, the Dutch Commodore's ship, the *Middelburgh*, commanded by Commodore *Suavenbourg*, with four other men of war, cruizing about the coasts of *Java*, passed by us.
They

They brought advice, that the Queen of *Bantam* was killed, that the King was taken prisoner, and that five thousand Dragoons and one thousand five hundred Hussars were at that time ready to kill all the inhabitants of *Bantam* without distinction, who would not acknowledge the King whom they had appointed, and who should refuse to look upon the Dutch as their protectors. The prince of *Madura* supported the Dutch in this affair with all his power.

The island of *Great Java* is situated under the sixth degree of south latitude, between *Summatra, Banca, Borneo, Madura, Baly* or *Little Java*, and the country of *Eendraught* (Union). It appears from hence that it must be very hot, and the heat would be intolerable if the thick woods did not retain the moisture after the rains are over, and if all kinds of animals were not refreshed by the shade.

Batavia is the celebrated capital of the Dutch in this isle, who built it in the year 1610, in the place where the old town of *Jacatra* formerly stood; but as it lay on the other side of the isle we did not get sight of it. I am told there are fine houses in it, and that

it

it is inhabited by merchants of all nations, and even by *Chinese,* who contribute much to the riches of this place. The Dutch *Council of India* has its feat there ; and from thence directs their *East-India* trade.

THE *Dutch* intend to possess themselves of *Bantam,* a town and kingdom which has formerly been governed by a *Mahomedan* King, and carries on a great trade in pepper.

IT is said that the language is either that of the natives or the *Malaic. Leidecker* has wrote the first *Malaic* and *Dutch* dictionary in *Batavia,* which Cardinal *Barberini* got published in *Latin* at *Rome,* 1631, in quarto, by David *Hixio. Hadrianus Relandus,* in his *Differtationes miscellaneæ,* has likewise published a sylloge of the dictionary of *Leidecker.* Not to mention some other works which the *Dutch* have published in the *Malaic* language, such as the *New Testament,* &c. [n]

THE *Malaic* language is said to be more universal in *India,* than *Latin* in *Europe.*

BATS? of the size of ravens, flew every evening from *Summatra* to *Java,* to spend the

[n] Mr. *Bowrey* published a Malayo and English Dictionary, in Quarto, at Lond. 1701.

night there, and returned in the morning to *Summatra*. This is undoubtedly a fingular circumftance, deferving a clofer examination. In flight and fize they were like our ravens; a man of veracity affured me, that he had feen them in a garden at *Batavia*; do thefe animals find fome food at *Java* which they cannot meet with in *Summatra?* or are they molefted during the nights in *Summatra* with enemies which are not to be found in *Java?* what elfe can be the reafon why they fo often change their habitations?

July the 19th.

We paffed by the point of *Bantam* in the morning, in fair weather and with favourable wind; and in the afternoon about two of the clock, two ifles which are fo like one another that they are called the *Two Brothers*. The ground was a blue clay mixed with white fand; it was at ten or thirteen fathoms depth.

July the 21ft.

The water looked yellow, and was now in bloffom °, as our people told me.

° In the northern countries of *Europe*, it is faid, that *the water is in bloffom*, when it is tinged with a green or

We

We saw *Lucipara* before us. It was a very shady isle, like all the isles hereabouts which have thick forests: it is thought that this isle had its own inhabitants. Our ship required at least eighteen feet depth of water before, and nineteen and a half behind; for which reason we always sent our boat and sloop before us, as soon as we had but five fathoms depth: in some places we had scarce four fathoms depth: thus we sailed here according to the depth, and by the direction of our lead, and not according to the course, which was the cause that we did not approach *Summatra* nearer than at five fathoms depth; nor did we venture to keep further off than at seven fathoms depth.

The isle of *Summatra*, which was continually on our left, and to which we sailed so near, was low in this place, and covered with trees, which stood very close, whose stems were without branches, and all of a height; and for that reason, the forest looked like a cut

yellow hue, by a kind of *Byssus* or *Hair-weed*, with which it is then filled: and from thence even the sea is said to be in blossom, when its surface is tinged with a preternatural colour. F.

hedge, or as a clump of reeds in the water; but further on a row of higher and darker trees made their appearance. Perhaps the former trees were those called *Spanish* reeds: the landing is said to be very inconvenient, on account of the deep clay, which extends a good way into the wood: however, there are *Swedes* who have sometimes been on shore for pleasure, and to cut wood. *Juan de la Serna* says, in his *Diccionario Geographico*, that the above mentioned island is three hundred leagues long, and seventy broad; that it produced rice, several sorts of spice and fruit; that it is subject to a great deal of rain; and that the heat is much greater than in *Java:* that the petty Kings have a King superior to them all at *Akhen*; and that the inhabitants are black, ugly, proud, tyrannical, treacherous, and faithless *Mahomedans,* who despise all strangers.

The isle of *Banca* lay on our right. The mountain called *Monopin*, which is upon it, may be seen at a great distance.

We cast anchor in the evening.

July

July the 22d.

We failed with a fair wind, however, not above half a mile from *Banca*. The isle of *Nanka*, or *Polo Nanka*, where fresh water is to be got, was observed on our right. We approached very near to the North side of *Summatra*, which looked as before mentioned; we anchored towards the third promontory or cape.

Insects came to us from the land.

The 23d July.

Having seen in the morning a *Junke* (for that is the name of a *Chinese* yacht), we happily passed a little rock hidden under water, which has frightned many *East-India* sailors, and which they call the *Frederick Henry*. This place is dangerous, because the low water prevents the ships from approaching the shore; but if they go too far off, the above rock may make an end of the whole voyage, as happened to a *Dutch* ship, and is still quite fresh in our memories.

I HAVE often been told that squirrels sometimes sail across the sea; but to-day I experienced, that birds likewise are possessed of that art; for a *Booby* (*Pelecanus Piscator*) sailed by us on a root.

MONOPIN upon *Banca* we left out of sight in the afternoon, together with *Summatra*.

The 24th July.

WE now saw those called the *Seven Islands* on the right; but they were at a greater distance than the isles *Polo-Taya* on the left: the isle of *Lingen*, which is one of the former and lies exactly under the line, was overagainst us at 6 o'clock in the evening.

The 25th July, 1° Northern Latitude.

THE wind was fair, and we saw land.

The 26th July, 2° 39′ N. L.

WE thought that *Polo-Tingey*, where the *Swedish East-Indiaman* the *Ritter House*, was lost,

loſt, was on our left, among the iſles; but we afterwards found, when we had paſſed by ſome of them, that it was amongſt the iſles of *Anambo*. The firſt was a little high white rock; and the others were covered with ſoil and ſome ſmall plants. We therefore turned and took another courſe. We ſaw birds of ſeveral ſorts at a diſtance; we were accompanied by ſome dog-fiſhes, and likewiſe a ſpecies of eels, with yellow tranſverſal lines, if they were not ſnakes; they kept behind the ſhip, in that part of the water which the keel of the ſhip had cut through; and I ſhould ſuppoſe that they and ſeveral other little fiſhes followed us from the Streights of *Sunda*. We likewiſe ſaw them the next day.

The 27th of July, 4° 20' N. L.

THE weather was fair, and we ſailed exactly before the wind.

Two ſwallows came in the evening, and followed the ſhip.

The 29th July, 7° 16′ N. L.

The *Globulus* is a little white shell like a waistcoat-button. It is an univalve, very elevated at the top, flat below, and has depressed rays on both sides. The worm which lived in it lay in a circle towards the spire, was very narrow, and was in length a finger's breadth; had two setaceous horns, and a filiform tail.

The 30th July, 8° 59′ N. L.

Polo *Candor*, together with some other isles in the neighbourhood, appeared to the left. This isle is inhabited, and belongs to the king of *Cambogia*: it is fifteen leagues off *Cambogia*, and its latitude 8° 40′. In the year 1746 the ship *Calmar* was obliged to winter near *Polo Candor*. The chaplain, M. *Tarnström*, who made the first trial what a *Swedish* naturalist might expect from such voyages, died here, on the 4th of December, and his funeral was honoured by the firing of two guns. The abovementioned ship was forced to stay near this island from the 11th of October 1746, to the 15th of April 1747, on account of contrary

trary winds; for in the *Chinese* sea two continual winds blow every year; so that six months are taken up by each of them: from April to September you may sail to *China* with a south west wind; but the other months from *China* with a north east wind. It is very unfortunate to be here when these winds change, for then are usually exceeding great storms (called *Tayfun* [p] by the *Chinese*) which continue to rage twenty-six hours with such fury, that the people on-board the ships cannot get out of their places, but must stand as if they were lashed to the mast: and this our

---

[p] Although Mr. *De Guignes* in his *Memoire dans lequel on prouve que les Chinois sont une colonie Egyptienne*, Paris, 1759, 8vo. has endeavoured to prove the *Chinese* to be the offspring of an *Egyptian* colony: I must however confess, that his arguments were by no means satisfactory to me; though I very willingly allow that there is a great probability in his opinion. For a further investigation of this matter by the curious, and such as go to *China*, I will only remark, that the *Typhon* of the *Egyptians* was a physical divinity, the symbol of a fiery malignant easterly wind, for which reason this divinity was called *Theou phoou*, the *bad wind*, which bears a very great resemblance to this *Chinese* name *Tay fun*. Besides this, the pronoun of the first person ΝΓ in the *Egyptian* language is in the *Thebaic* or purest dialect, and which is pronounced *n'ye*, yet preserved in the *Chinese* language, both being equivalent to *J*. F.

East

East India sailors are able to assert from their own experience.

The 31st of July, 10° 30′ N. L.

Polo *Zapata* (which is called a *last* by the *Swedes* from its figure) appeared, being a little, naked, white, high rock, in the open sea.

Near this rock are a great number of birds; and by catching one of them, upon our return from *China*, we found that it was *Sterna stolida grisea, capite albo.* The boobies were plentiful here. I likewise caught a *Phalæna seticornis spirilinguis, alis planis, superioribus cocrulescentibus, maculis luteis:* the body, wings, and feet were white: the head green: the tongue ferrugineous.

The *Mill beetles* (*Blatta orientalis* Linn.⁋) annually come in ships from the *East Indies*. I was told that when the ship *Gothenburgh*, returning from *China*, foundered on a rock not far from the fortress *Elfsborg*, and the wet tea was carried to be dried in the ovens in the town, these insects came thither

⁋ The Cock Roach?

along

along with it; and have since continued there, and in other places. These infects, which conceal themselves in the day time, come out in the night, when they eat shoes and other cloaths, which are greasy: it is said that bugs are their most delicious morsels; so if any one chuses to exchange one pest for another, he might perhaps authenticate this notion. We found a female of this infect in a plantain tree (*Musa paradisiaca*) which came from *Java*.

The 3d of August.

THE sun was perpendicular to us to-day, and the latitude could not be observed for that reason; but as to our calculation, it was 14° 6' N. L.

I CAUGHT a *Libellula fusca, capite et lateribus viridibus*. The abdomen had eight articulations: the wings were all equal, and brown near the body; the outward edge had below a black right angled spot, but on the under side it was not quite black.

The

The 5th of August, 16° 48' N. L.

This day and the preceding night we had mostly calm and clear weather; afterwards the wind was changeable; towards evening it lightened; about twelve o'clock at night it rained very hard, with much lightning, during which the whole sky was covered with clouds. On the foretop something like a little star was perceived. The Counsellor of Chancery, Mr. *Klingenstierna*, says, in the learned speech which he delivered in 1755, on the newest electrical experiments, when he resigned the office of President of the Royal Academy of Sciences, that such flames are electric, being emitted from an electrical cloud, which serves as a conductor. Among the ancient naturalists these flames were mentioned under the names of *Helena, Castor* and *Pollux*.

The 8th of August, 22° 4' N. L.

Piedra *Blanca*, or the *White rock*, came within our sight, towards noon. The wind abating,

abating, the heat became intolerable. Towards the evening we anchored.

BALISTES *Monoceros* is a species of fish which looks like a flounder at a distance, and has almost the same taste, but is not so fat. The fish was half a foot long, and its body covered with a dark-grey rough skin. We caught several with a hook, and this afforded me an opportunity of describing them.

ON each side is a *spiracle*, and next to it, within the skin, two transversal bones: the first *dorsal fin* near the eyes, consists of a reversed brittle bone, which is armed with little hooks; it is the length of a finger's breadth, and a little longer than the other fins: the second *dorsal fin* has forty-seven rays: the *pectoral fins* are the least; each has thirteen rays: the *ventral fins* are wanting; in their stead is a long bone under the skin: the *anal fin* is opposite to the second dorsal fin, and has 51 rays: the *tail* has 12 ramose rays: the *mouth* is oblong and narrow: the lower *jaw* is somewhat longer than the upper; on each side of it stand three pointed, broad *teeth*, connected together below, of which the middlemost is split: the *lips* are moveable.

The

The 9th of August.

THE ship hardly moved from the place where it was the day before. We saw besides *Piedra Blanca* the isle of *Lantoa*, and some other isles on the *Chinese* coast, on our right.

The 10th of August.

IN the forenoon the sky was clear, but the wind against us.

BALISTES *scriptus*. Catesby, vol. ii. 27. A fish equal in size and appearance to the *Balistes monoceros*, but marked over the whole body as it were with blue letters of an Eastern language, was caught here, and put into *Spanish* brandy; but the fine colours vanished as soon as it was dead. In the afternoon we had a tolerable good wind, but at night again stood out to sea; because a cloudy sky and lightening are said to be the forerunners of a storm. We had cloudy weather, contrary winds, and showers of rain, the following days.

The 13th of August.

To-day it was refolved to look out for land, where we could, but all our endeavours were in vain.

The 14th of August.

RAIN, ftorms, and contrary winds, always drove us off from land: a fwallow, which had been feen fome days before, ftill accompanied the fhip.

The 15th of August.

DARK and inconftant weather: the flying fifh, which we faw on the 11th, now accompanied us.

The 16th of August.

CLOUDY and rain. We fteered W. by S. along the fhore, though we did not fee it: about noon we anchored and faw *Piedra Blanca* to the North Eaft; not from the deck, but

but from the foretop. *Porpeſſes* tumbled in great numbers about the ſhip.

The 17th of Auguſt.

In the morning we ſaw ſome land pretty near, and anchored afterwards, but were ſoon driven from ſhore with ſtrong wind and rain. Contrary winds and calms hindered our gaining the *Chineſe* coaſts till the 22d of this month: in the mean time we got the following ſpecimens of Natural Hiſtory.

The 20th of Auguſt.

Balistes *nigro-punctatus* and a *lump* of narrow, ſmooth, round, water-coloured worms, which hung together without any order, and ſeemed to be a torn *Meduſa*, at leaſt no mark of life appeared in it.

The 21ſt of Auguſt.

The heat to-day and yeſterday, was intolerable: the large dragon flies (*Libellula*) which

which had followed our ſhip for ſome days, were well pleaſed with this weather.

A GREAT dead ſnake floated on the water, and occaſioned a poiſonous ſtench, which commonly is aſcribed to the flowering of the water.

BALISTES *Chinenſis* is diſtinguiſhed from the aforementioned ſorts, by the following character; the *bone* which makes the firſt *dorſal fin*, is ſomewhat thicker, and behind it is a ſkin: the ſecond *dorſal fin* has thirty-four rays; the *pectoral fins* thirteen rays; the *ventral fin* conſiſts of a bone with eight bent rays; on that *bone* is a membranaceous fin, which gives a greater breadth to the fiſh; the eyes are very prominent, and have a red iris; on each ſide before the eye is a ſmall hole; the *anal fin* has thirty rays; the *tail* has twelve rays: this fiſh is leſs than the others of that kind.

The 22d of Auguſt.

IN the morning we weighed anchor and ſteered to the *Chineſe* coaſt, having been obliged to linger near it fourteen days, and having made a collection for the poor of 334 dollars in copper[r]. The pilot whom we got on board, and who brought us in, was to receive twenty *pesos duros* (four pounds seven shillings and sixpence), or 200 dollars in copper. We had *Lantoa* on our right and the Southern isles of *Limes* on the left: the sea formed high billows rolling in from the isles, which were quite green with plants, but had no woods. The most usual entry of *European* ships into *China* is by the *Ladrones*, which derive their name from the pirates who formerly lived upon them.

MACAO is a *Portugueze* town on an isle, which was now on our left, but so far off that we could not see it: our *Spanish* passenger left us here, and sailed for *Macao*, from whence he designed to go to the *Isle of Manilla*, where he intended to settle.

THE isle of *Linting* was on our left. We were obliged to anchor here, having no wind, and the tide against us: the fishermen sailed by

---

[r] A dollar in copper is about five-pence or five-pence halfpenny sterling; thus 334 dollars are about seven pounds sterling. F.

faſtening their net to the maſt. I here caught the *Papilio (Lintingenſis) tetrapus ſubtus pallide luteus nebuloſus, ſupra nigricans luteo impregnatus.* The *body* is whitiſh on the under, but blackiſh on the upper ſide: the *antennæ* are ſetaceous, blackiſh: the *wings* are all dentated; the primary ones of a pale yellow on the under ſide, with a few black ſpots; the *ſecondary wings* blackiſh on the upper ſide, and yellow below; towards the *baſe* they have a blue *Gemma*, or *Ocellus*, but towards the outward edge they are of a dirty yellow.

The 23d of Auguſt.

WHILST we tacked here, we met with a *Comprador*, or *Chineſe* who provides the ſhips with the neceſſaries of life, ſuch as fleſh, greens, and bread. He came from *Macao*, and had *Plaintains* or the larger ſort of *Piſang*, *Gujaves*, *Lantcyes*, and water-melons: his name was *Attay*, and his ſervants were *No-hay* and *At-yan*. The latter came every day with a large *Sampane*, and kept near the ſhip (or *Barcſkal*). I was told that this and other *Compradors* ſtayed all night in the *Wam-pu* cuſtom-houſe: in the factory at *Canton* there is likewiſe a *Comprador*, who

who in the fame manner gets ready every thing required for our fubfiftence, and who is obliged to accompany every perfon going on board, to the next cuftom-houfe, in order to fearch what he takes with him. If any body dies, the *Comprador* is to order the funeral: he that was to be the *Comprador* of our factory, was called *Luffy*.

The 24th of Auguft.

Bocca *Tyger*, in the *Chinefe* language *Phohaö*, the mouth of the *Tyger* or *Phomunn*; the *Tyger*, at its opening, is a narrow river, where we anchored about noon for want of wind. On the right hand fide of the entrance, was a low caftle, furrounded by trees; on both fides of it a path afcended the mountain to a fmall houfe; before which ftood a white hut, which is fuppofed to be a place dedicated to an idol: fomewhat further on the left were two caftles on two different hills, furrounded likewife by trees; the moft outward of them was furrounded by water, and had a little hut clofe to it: the inner one is higher, fo that it may command the other *.

* See Lord Anfon's Voyage round the World, book iii. chap. 9.

MANDARIN

MANDARIN, or *Commander*, is a denomination which our people borrow from the *Portugueze*, and which they give to all public officers in this country, even to lower officers of the cuftoms: if a *Chinefe* was to pronounce this word, he would fay *Mandeli*, for they cannot pronounce the letter *r*; whence it plainly appears that the word *Mandarin* does not belong to their language: fome of thefe gentlemen now came on board, to fee what fort of people we were; two *Mandarins* accompanied us up the river, to *Wam-pu*, where we met two others, each of which joined the fhip in his boat with his men, each having his appointed ftation. He who was on the right fide of the fhip, and was the neareft to it, belonged to the cuftoms, and ftayed with us whilft we were in *China*; but the other on the left was a military man, and was exchanged every month: their bufinefs is, to keep off the thieving *Chinefe* from the fhip, and to provide thofe, who muft, on account of bufinefs, go to *Canton* or other places, with *Tiapp*, or paffports, which muft be fhewn at the cuftom-houfe. Their people can almoft get a fufficient fubfiftence by wafhing of linen: it is remarkable, that no *Chinefe* can be a *Mandarin* in the place where he is born.

The fishermen brought several sorts of fish, as eels, at least a sort of them, called *Paling* in the *Chinese* language, soals, rays, and *Chinese* crabs.

CANCER *Chinensis*. These are as big again as the *Swedish* crabs; the *body* is almost transparent, as long as a hand is broad: the *rostrum* has eight incisions above, and four below; the *eyes* are excessively prominent, as if they stood on stalks; on the sides are two little leaves; the *sides* are lacerated and notched; the *body*, besides the tail and head, has six articulations; the *tail* has four oval leaves, except the middle one, which is sharp pointed, concave, and cylindrical; the five pair of *hind feet* are red, and covered with hair towards the inward margin; the five pair of *fore feet* are cheliferous; instead of the two *foremost* are two pair of bifid feathered ones.

AT night we advanced with wind and tide, and anchored near the *Lion's Tower*, which is the first of three remarkable towers in the way to *Canton*.

The

The 25th of August.

THE weather was clear: a rich *Chinese* threw a tortoise out of his boat, for the use of such poor people as would give themselves the trouble to go and fetch it.

AFTER a voyage of five months and four days from *Cadiz*, we at last arrived at *Huam-pu*, or, as it is commonly called, *Wam-pu*. This is the place where all *European* ships in the river of *Canton* or *Ta-ho* ride at anchor, and where they stay as long as they trade in this country. We reckoned this anchoring place about four *Swedish* miles from the mouth of the river, or *Bocca-tyger*. To *Canton* we had a mile and a half, and the town of *Wam-pu*, which is to the left when you arrive, was about half a mile off from hence. On both sides of the river we saw large low rice-fields. Here were already sixteen *European* ships, and one came in after us; so that, besides the *Chinese* boats, which anchor near the town, or in another place, this year there were 18 ships.

The *European* ships were the following:

Two *Swedish* ones.
Prince Charles.
The Gothic Lion, which came a little before us, from *Suratte.*

One *Danish.*
The Queen of Denmark.

Two *French:*
The Duke of Chartres.
The Duke of Monteran.

Four *Dutch:*
The Commodore's ship, *The Constancy.*
Friburgh.
Amsleveen.
Geldermousen.

Nine *English:*
The Essex.
Centurion.
St. George.
Cæsar.
True Briton,
Triton.
Hardwick.
Elizabeth.
Success Gally, a country ship.

AT night we heard a fort of mufic, partly made by infects, and partly by the noife of the *Gungung* in the *Sampanes* and *Bancfhals*.

ARRIVING at *Wam-pu*, you have a large field with rice on your right, for no other corn is ufual in this country : part of this field near the river is feparated from the reft by a ditch, leading to a bancfhal, or warehoufe for *Englifh*, *Swedifh*, and *Danifh* fhips; thefe fhips annually raife this place higher with their ballaft: but this time our people made a fine ftone quay where large boats could land. The *French* have their warehoufe on the *French* ifland, which lies on the left, fomewhat nearer to *Canton*. The *Dutch* are forbid to come here with feveral fhips at once, or to land any baggage, having once attempted to bring cannon on fhore in water-tubs; but, as they broke to pieces, their fcheme was difcovered. I am told that the *Dutch* have fince got a bancfhal, in 1761.

BANGSAL (in *French* bancafal, in *Englifh* bancfhal) is the place, or warehoufe, where we ftow all our unneceffary wood and tackle, pitch and tar; and keep our chicken, hogs, &c.

&c. during our stay in *China*. The ship which comes first has the best place. Each ship is obliged to give a sum for the place it takes up, besides paying the *comprador* for erecting (immediately after the arrival of a ship) a warehouse in form of a barn, made of bamboo and mats, in which there are two chambers for the mate or bancshal captain, who continually watches with some sailors at both ends of the building. As long as they do not suspect any thieves, they shout out from one bancshal to another, *all well*, and often beat the gungung, to shew their vigilance. A liberty was formerly given to the centinels of firing upon the *Chinese*, who ventured to get into those bancshals at night; but this is not now permitted.

When an eminent stranger pays visits, or when the colours of a ship are hoisted, the flags are displayed in the *bancshal*. Towards the departure of a ship, the necessary oxen, hogs, &c. are killed in this warehouse.

Gungung is the *Chinese* name of an instrument which has the greatest resemblance to a brass bason. In all *bancshals* and factories, a signal on this instrument is given every half hour, in the same manner as is done on-board

by

by a bell. They give one knock at half an hour paſt twelve, two at one o'clock, and ſo on till four o'clock, when they give eight thumps, to ſignify that eight half hours are paſt: at half an hour after four, they begin again in the ſame manner; ſo that at four, eight, and twelve o'clock, eight thumps are always given on this inſtrument.

The *Chineſe* drum on this inſtrument at their feſtivals, and ſet fire to little boats of gilt paper, and throw them into the ſea, as a part of their morning and evening amuſement on ſuch occaſions. On board the ſhips is a quarter-maſter, or cadet, who ſtands near the compaſs, and cries out, when the half-hour glaſs is run down, to him who is near the bell, how many pulls he muſt give.

The *Daniſh Iſland* (which bears that name becauſe that nation commonly bury their dead in that place) is oppoſite to the *Bancſhal*.

The *French* iſland is the next above the *Daniſh*: this is the burying-place of the *Engliſh*, *Swedes*, *French*, and *Dutch*. However, in both iſlands there are likewiſe ſome *Chineſe* graves.

graves. There are every where gardens, producing such fruits as in our country would be cultivated in hot-houses as rarities. But high places are never cultivated, because the sun entirely burns up whatsoever grows upon them.

The 26th of August.

IT began to rain, and rained for four days together. In the morning we saluted, and the *Danish* ship returned the salute.

THE *East India* company had recommended it to us, that nothing should be taken from hence to *Sweden* by the crew, except a few pounds of sugar, tea, and some gallons of arrack, as provisions for the voyage. This order I read the next day after the thanksgiving for our happy arrival; and it was afterwards twice repeated before our departure.

CYPRINUS *Cantonensis* was thought to be the common carp, but it was nearer allied to the *Grislagine:* Faun. Sue. 367. It is above a foot long: the *dorsal fin* has 10 rays, and stands in the middle of the back: the *pectoral fins*

fins have 21 rays: the *ventral fins* have nine rays, and are equally diſtant from the pectoral fins and from the anus: the *anal fin* has 11 rays: the *tail* is bifurcated, and conſiſts of 26 rays. This fiſh has no *beard* (*cirrhus*): the *iris* is yellowiſh: the *noſtrils* are at the top, in the flat part of the head, and are but little: the *membrana branchioſtega* is ſoft and prominent: the *ſcales* are rhomboidal, and are flabelliform.

The 30th of Auguſt.

FINE dry weather.

THE *French*, who ſaluted our ſhip, were honoured with ſome guns fired at their arrival and departure.

The 1ſt of September.

The lead which we unloaded to-day, and the day before, was weighed by a *Chineſe*, who proclaimed the weight of it aloud, and
three

three other *Chinese* wrote it down, in the présence of several *Mandarins* [r].

The 2d of September.

SAM *pan* is a *Chinese* boat without a keel, looking almost like a trough; they are made of different dimensions, but are mostly covered.

THERE are,

PASSENGER *Sampanes*, to carry people backward and forward between the town and the ships. These you may hire every day; and you may either take larger ones *Tow-cytin*, or less ones *Suutin*. They are quicker than you would expect, provided you take advantage of the ebb or flood.

THESE boats are as long as sloops, but broader, almost like a baking trough; and have at the end one or more decks of *Bamboo*

---

[r] Here our author has inserted an history of *China*, extracted from books in the hands of most *English* readers; we have therefore omitted it, as uninteresting.

sticks:

sticks: the cover, or roof, is made of *Bamboo* sticks, arched over in the shape of a grater; and may be raised or lowered at pleasure: the sides are made of boards, with little holes, with shutters instead of windows: the boards are fastened on both sides to posts, which have notches like steps on the insides, that the roof may be let down, and rest on them: on both ends of the deck are commonly two little doors, at least there is one at the hindmost end. A fine white smooth carpet spread up as far as the boards makes the floor, which in the middle consists of loose boards; but this carpet is only made use of to sleep on. As these boats greatly differ from ours in shape, they are likewise rowed in a different manner: for two rowers, posting themselves at the back end of the sampane, work it forwards very readily, by the motion of two oars; and can almost turn the vessel just as they please: the oars, which are covered with a little hollow quadrangular iron, are laid on iron swivels, which are fastened in the sides of the sampane: at the iron the oars are pieced, which makes them look a little bent: in common, a rower sits before with a short oar; but this he is forced to lay aside when he comes near the city, on account of the great throng of sampanes;

panes; and this inconvenience has confirmed the *Chinese* in their old way of rowing. Instead of pitch, they make use of a cement like our putty, which we call *Chinam,* but the *Chinese* call it *Kiang.* Some authors say that this cement is made of lime and a rezin exsuding from the tree *Tong Yea,* and *Bamboo ockam.*

THE sampane in which I went this time had, besides a couple of chairs, the following furniture: two oblong tables, or boards, on which some *Chinese* characters were drawn; a lanthorn for the night time; and a pot to boil rice in.

THEY have also a little cover for their houshold god, decorated with gilt paper and other ornaments: before him stood a pot, filled with ashes, into which the tapers were put before the idol. The candles were nothing else than *Bamboo* chips, to the upper end of which saw-dust of sandal-wood was stuck on with gum. These tapers are every where lighted before the idols in the pagodas, and before the doors in the streets; and, in so large a city, occasion a smoke very pernicious to the eyes. Before this idol stood some *Samso,* or *Chinese* brandy,

brandy, water, &c. We ought to try whether the *Chinese* would not like to use juniper-wood instead of sandal-wood; which latter comes from *Suratte*, and has almost the same smell with juniper.

FISHERMENS *sampanes* are the least of all, narrow like some of our fishing boats, and have a very little deck, of straw or bamboo; or are even without that poor convenience. Bad as these boats are, yet parents and their naked children are seen to get their livelihood in them both summer and winter, by fishing, and by picking up what has been thrown overboard by others. For this purpose they tie several hooks to a cord, and throw them out in different places, almost in the same manner as fishermen in our country lay their eel hooks. They have better or worse fortune as it happens. There is nothing so filthy but what these people will use as food: and the hogs which die and are thrown over-board, and, by beginning to putrify, float in a few days, are often the occasion of such quarrels as end in battles. The reason why the *Europeans* sink the hogs which die on board their ships is, that the inhabitants of this place may not feed upon them; for it is said that the *Chinese*, when they go on-board any ships, will give pepper to the hogs, which they think is poison to them, that they may get them again if they should die. It is certain that numbers of hogs die in the possession of the *Europeans*, whilst they stay in *China*.

DUCK *sampanes* are boats in which they feed four or five hundred ducks. They have on both sides a bridge which may be let down. In the day time the ducks feed in the river, upon herbs and fish; at night their master calls them into his boat; they immediately obey him, and come on-board as soon as he lets down his bridge.

SAMPANES *of burden* are the largest boats, by means of which all porcelain, silk, and other commodities, are conveyed from *Canton* to the *European* ships. But I do not mean that these boats serve for the above mentioned purpose only; for they are used besides as houses for whole families; which are born, marry, and die in them. They commonly have, besides hogs, some chicken, and dogs; and some flower pots, containing *Guinea* pepper, or some other plants, in these boats. All the above

above mentioned sampanes are not embellished by painting.

MANDARIN *sampanes*, are greater or less red-painted boats, ornamented with dragons, and such like figures, or with little flags.

THE *Chinese* also use *Galleys*, *Sao-Sjo-an*, with eighteen or twenty oars, and as many men. They lie near the city of *Canton*, and some of them near the *European* ships, probably for the security of the country.

JUNKS, called *Toan-sian* by the *Chinese*, or, as *Du Halde* calls them, *Thouen*, in the Portugueze language *Soma* or *Sommes*, are the greater vessels, about 200 feet long, and 20 broad. With these ships the *Chinese* sail along the coasts of *Batavia*, *Manilla*, *Ainam*, *Cochinchina*, *Cambogia*, *Chinchiu*. From the last mentioned place comes the white sugar candy, which at present costs six tale, three mace peckuls. Such a vessel holds 1000 chests of tea: it is high and round on each side: the rudder is very slender, and can be taken out with very little difficulty, and hung at the other end of the ship: it has no upper sails; but only one great sail, the fore-sail, the sprit-sail, and the mizzen-

mizzen-sail, all which are made of mats, tied together quite acrofs with bamboo-fticks. They ftrike their fails with difficulty, as they can only effect it by fending a failor up the yard to tread the fails down. In thefe veffels there is a continual noife, becaufe the perfon in command does not infift on filence; they are painted either black or white, and have always an eye painted on each fide. Their compafs is divided into 24 points. The timber of which thefe fhips are built, is called *Saaomock*: the anchors are made of hard wood, which is called *Tat-fiew*, or *Tie-mou*; but they are commonly plated with iron at the extremities, and are more handy than our anchors of iron, and of more fervice to little veffels.

I should have overlooked the *Dung-Sampanes*, if their fmell had not been fo difagreeable as we paffed by; arifing from the human excrements contained in thefe veffels.

In *Canton*, near the port, fome great tuns filled with it are put under ground, which after ftaying there fome time, are emptied into thefe veffels and carried to the plantations, where they have walled pits into which they put this dung, mix it with water, ftir it well, and afterwards

wards, use it every where in the country for manure.

THE rice fields, which are green on both sides of the river, as far as your eye can reach, the fine woods, which consist of many sorts of trees, the hills, and the vallies, make the view beautiful, particularly on the left side; but the wet condition of the rice fields, and a mistrust of the inhabitants, did not allow me to examine things more nearly.

THERE are three custom houses, where all those who go in the *Chinese* boats between the town and the ships are forced to stay. Our people generally call them *Tiapp-Houses*[u].

THESE *Tiapp-Houses* are built in part on a hard stony ground, and partly over the river, supported by posts. They have a bridge so contrived, that the boats may come to them at all times, as well during the ebb as the flood. And, that no one may plead ignorance, they paste their regulations on the walls; and besides that, close to the house, stands a flag, marked with large *Chinese* characters. The

[u] Called by the English Hoppo-Houses.

sloops of the Europeans pass free with their flags, to the factory, where the custom-house officers receive them.

If any one goes from a ship to *Canton*, and shews the *Tiapp* which the Mandarin gave him, in each of the two first custom-houses, an oblong red seal is put upon it; but in the last custom-house the *Tiapp* is left. Returning from *Canton*, you obtain a Tiapp from the Interpreter, and a Comprador goes with you to the next custom-house, where you are searched, and the *Tiapp* is sealed: in the other custom-houses they observe the same method as in the going to *Canton*.

To go with the tide to *Canton*, and likewise down with it, is by far the most expeditious and agreeable way. In coming from the ships, the first custom-house is on the right hand, not far from them, and is called—

The *Wampu Tiapp-house* by the *Europeans*; in the *Chinese* language it is called *Huamp-Siogun*. Near the entry stood a *Pomegranate Tree*, *Hibiscus mutabilis*, *Rosa Indica*, &c. *Huampu* is a little town behind the custom-house, having

ing a tower with nine stories, which the *Chinese* call *Pa-tiaw* [w].

THESE towers serve as ornaments to the cities, and, as the *Chinese* affirm, as a measure to the roads: but the inhabitants contradict what some histories have advanced, that these towers are used in times of war, as watch towers: on the different stories of these towers grew trees and plants, but I could not determine their kinds, being at too great a distance; somewhat further on, I saw the mouth of another river, through which the larger *Chinese* boats pass. There was a *Pagoda*, with several houses. On the shore grew in several places, *Saccharum pluviatile* and *Cyperus odoratus*.

THE *Chinese* here catch fish, by putting up mats along the shore, while the tide is in, which hinder the fry from returning with the ebb. As soon as the water was fallen, many people were seen wading up to the knees in the blue clayey ground mixed with sand, after the little fry, which jumped about in the mud like lizards; but when they saw no means of saving themselves, they crept a foot deep into

[w] Pagoda.

the oozy ground, not without the knowledge of the *Chinese*, who took care to observe them; and pulled them out with their hands; these fish, fryed in oil, are the principal food of the poor, besides rice; and are of two species, as will appear from the following descriptions.

1. *Fay-ye*, or (*Gobius pectinirostris* Linn.) The *membrana branchiostega* has four very small rays; the *dorsal fins* are ash-coloured, with blue transversal lines, and black spots at the bottom: the first *dorsal fin* is higher, reaches from opposite the breast, to the middle of the back, and has six rays; the *second* has twenty-six very short rays, and reaches from the middle of the back, to over-against the *anus*; the *pectoral fins* have eighteen rays; the single *ventral fin* is infundibuliform, sits close to the head, and has ten rays; the *anal fin* has twenty-six parallel rays: all the fins but the dorsal ones are brownish; the *head* is narrow, smooth, and of the same breadth with the middle of the body; the *mouth* is large and oblong; the *forehead* flat; the *tongue* lacerated and truncated; the *teeth* are little, pointed, strait, unequal in the *upper jaw*; they stand only in one row, in the *middle* are few, in the *lower jaw* they fill up the whole margin; the *lips* are short, and do not

not cover the teeth: I have not difcovered that
they have any noftrils; the *eyes* are elevated,
very prominent, oblong, and ftand near one
another on the head; the *pupilla* is blue; the
irides of a golden colour; the *back* grey, with
red and blue dirty fpots; the *belly* whitifh;
the whole *body* oblong, as long as a man's hand,
and as it were compreffed.

2. *Tan-noao* (*Gobius niger* Linn.) The
membrana branchioftega has four rays; the firft
dorfal fin is almoft quadrangular in the middle
of the back, and has eleven rays; the fecond
is longer, and lefs, oppofite the anus, has ten
rays, is tranfparent on both fides, with tranf-
verfal black lines; the fingle *ventral fin* forms
a funnel, and has twelve rays; the *anal fin*
has thirteen rays; the fpace between the
fecond *dorfal fin* and the tail, and that between
the anal fin and the tail, is equal to the
breadth of one's little finger; the *tail* ends in
a point, and has eighteen rays, of which the
outermoft are the fhorteft; the *body* is the
fame as that of the preceding fifh, except its
having more white and dirty black grey; the
head is large, and has very fmall white dots;
the *mouth* is much lefs, and almoft round: I

faw

saw here a net drawn by two *Chinese* up to their chins in water.

Duck Sampanes lay on the shore: hundreds of ducks came into the boat, as soon as the owner let down the bridge and called them.

The *Brandy Tower* was somewhat further off, on the left; the *Chinese* call it *Tie-koang*; When the sailors come over-against it, and can see light quite across the windows of the tower, from their sloop, they are entitled to a draught of brandy. This custom gives name to the tower, which is half way between *Wampu* and *Canton*.

The *Lazarus tree* is further up on the right; it was said, that people having the leprosy, and other nasty diseases, lived under this tree, which has very luxuriant branches. Some little inns, which stand several of them close together, somewhat higher up on posts, above the river, make the beginning of the suburbs: before them lie innumerable small and great sampanes quite crowded, as well as junks or large *Chinese* vessels; which occasion the passage to be very narrow and difficult, by the

boats

boats meeting each other in so contracted a space.

WE now stopped at the second custom-house, called *Toang-pack-toy* in the *Chinese* language; having just before passed a castle in the middle of the river, which was on our left; another castle is somewhat higher up; both were surrounded by trees: I was told, that the *Dutch* had built one of these forts.

THE third custom-house is the principal: it is near the factories, and the *Chinese* call it *Tay-quam-Song-gunn*; it is the last you meet with before you get to *Canton*: the custom-house papers (*Tiaps*) are taken in and kept here. If you were to go from *Canton* to *Bocca-tyger*, you need not stop at any other custom-house, except these three, though there are many others between these places; for next to *Huam-po* is the fourth, called *Oty*; the fifth is called *O-tyoang*; the sixth, *Baxia-tunn*; the seventh *Toann-tao*; and the eighth, *Pho-munn*, or the custom-house of *Bocca-tyger*, or the mouth of the *Tyger*.

THE tower of *Canton* was the third that we saw on this route,

THE Factory is the first place in the suburbs to which the *Europeans* come: this is a general denomination of the houses built towards the river, or over it upon piles, and which are let by the *Chinese* merchants to the *European* ships during their stay: this time is sometimes five months, and sometimes a year; which long delay, though it may arise from accidental causes, is often by design, lest several ships coming home at once should glut the market with *Chinese* goods: during this time the *Europeans* lend money to a great advantage in *China*; but a person who has not borrowed considerable sums himself runs great risque, when he lends his money in a place where the debtor is often sought for in vain. Commonly each ship takes a factory for itself; but sometimes two ships of a nation, may be together, and this time it happened so to two *Swedish* ships, and if I remember right, they paid 900 tel for it, which, at the rate of seven dollars per tel, make 6300 dollars in silver.

THE above-mentioned houses are but two stories high, but very long; and one end of them stretches towards the river, and the other to the factory-street: some are built of unburnt bricks, others of bricks and wood laid cross

cross-ways; but the partitions and upper floors, &c. are sometimes entirely of wood: therefore they are so poorly provided against fire, that on the seventh of *December* 1743, in three or four hours, more than 150 houses were reduced to ashes: the fire, for want of proper regulation, would have spread farther, if it had not been for Commodore *Anson* and his men: the inhabitants, who believe an inevitable destiny, were merely spectators, not attempting to extinguish it. The factories look like two houses built parallel and near to each other, between which there is a court-yard; the floor of the lower story is covered, like the court yard, with square or rather oblong stones; in these stones are here and there little holes, through which the water may run into the river; the stair-cases are either of stone or wood; the rooms are high, and the roofs are sloping and covered with tiles, like those in *Spain*.

Windows are made in the roofs, but they are square, and less than those in the walls: there are no ceilings up stairs below the roof: a room has seldom windows on more than one side; these are long, and narrow, with wooden bows, and have square panes of mother of pearl,

pearl, but the poorer sort make use of other shells; which are the breadth of a hand each way. Lead and glass are never to be met with in a *Chinese* window: these windows stand open in day time, because they do not give sufficient light; at night they are shut, to keep out gnats, bats, &c. In the lower story are few windows, and those look into the inner court.

NEAR some of the rooms is a little garden, of the size of a middling room. The doors, when opened, give sufficient light to these apartments; for the side towards the garden is quite free. The garden encroaches no farther on the court yard than the projection of the building. From the excessive heats, the doors are mostly kept open; but a *nanking* curtain is commonly hung up before them, with three pieces of wood plated with brass; one of which is at the top, one in the middle, and one at the bottom.

OUR hangings consisted of white *Chinese* paper, pasted to the wall. Though this paper is very smooth, yet lizards (*lacerta Chinensis*) run with such agility up and down the walls, that they can scarce be caught. In summer time

time they abound in the houfes, but in winter they difappear: they do no harm, but merely feek for their food, which is mill-beetles and other infects.

THE *Chinefe* padlocks are made in fuch a manner that many of them may be opened with one key; and therefore it is a proper precaution to bring fome from *Europe*.

THE company finds in every room a table, chairs, and a bed, with curtains of gauze, or blue *nanking*-ftuff.

You are obliged to draw your curtains quite clofe, to keep out *Mufquitoes*, a fpecies of gnats, which is very troublefome at night; and whofe fting is fometimes the caufe of incurable complaints.

HENCE the influence of different climates appears: for in our country the bite of a flea, and the fting of a gnat, are reckoned equal; but it is quite otherwife in *China*, though thefe gnats are the fame with ours.

IN each room is likewife a lamp, faftened to the roof by a long rope. The *Chinefe* do the fame same in their houses, though they have both white wax candles and others, which they call *Lapp-tiock*. These latter looked as if they were made of tallow; but, as I suppose, were made of the fruit of the tallow-tree. The outward layer of these candles, which is red and stiff, is called *Nan-cy* in the *Chinese* language.

SOME kept, on the outside before the windows, in a glass bowl, gold and silver fishes, called *Kamni-ko* by the *Chinese*.

THEIR colours shift like those of the finest birds. For their food, a species of plants was put into the water, the leaves of which resemble *Ceratophyllum demersum & Pistia stratiotes*, which is here called *Siu-yan-gai*.

OTHERS had, besides these fishes, several little trees in flower-pots, before the windows, such as are likewise cultivated in their nurseries and gardens; *videlicet*, a sort of low sweet orange trees, with a small fruit which is called *Gatt* here; moreover the *Lemt-yes* tree, which bears little round four lemons called *Na-mang* in *China*, and which are used instead of tamarinds, or common lemons, in punch, and
generally

generally before they are ripe. Besides these are the following plants:

Capsicum frutescens.

Thuya orientalis.

Lanfa, or *Leenfa Chinensium.*

Moquaifa Chinens.

Nyctanthes orientalis, wood of roses.

Celosia cristata, in the *Chinese* language *Lat-seo.*

Narcissus Tazetta, or *Chinese lilies,* which flower in January, and are called *Soifinn-fatt* by the *Chinese.*

THEIR culture requires little art; they only put so much coarse sand upon a tin plate as just covers it, and upon this they set the bulbs quite naked. These were sooner in flower when the bulbs were prevented striking downwards.

Gomphrena globosa.

Impatiens balsamina.

Ipomœa

Ipomoea Quamoclit, in *China* called *Kam-fan-fang*, which adorned the hedges without the city.

The tea-chests and porcelane-chests, and other effects which are to be taken home, are piled up on both sides of the yard. This yard is divided quite across by three arched walls: in some places of the yard buildings like coach-houses run quite across it, which are sometimes supported by arched roofs.

A FACTORY is mostly built in the following manner: near the entrance of the street of the factory, on both sides of the gate, is a little apartment, upon which are commonly some papers with figures like arms, and two round lanthorns of bamboo, covered with skins; for glass or horn lanthorns are quite unusual here. The gate of the factory is on the inside built over: directly behind it stands a high board almost as broad as the entrance, to hinder the people in the streets from looking into the yard or court, without being any obstacle to those who pass to and fro. In almost all corners are buckets into which people make water, which is afterwards carried upon the fields.

The

The foremost rooms on the sides look like kitchens, and have rails before them. Further on, quite acrofs the court, in the second story, is an open hall, with a sort of gallery, upon which is an altar covered with flowers and incense, provided with a gilt picture and a table. Behind this the yard is quite open in front, but on the sides are rooms both above and below. In the side roofs are here and there some lanthorns of painted gauze, in some of which they burn lamps at night. Before the side roofs, and on their sides, are little gardens, with bamboo trees, citrons, and plaintains, and other trees already mentioned. The wall about these trees towards the yard is made of brick, which, except the foundation, are laid like lattice work. Next to these gardens is an inclofed court-yard, and then an open one, with rooms and gardens for pleasure on the sides: the last of all is a hall in the second story acrofs the yard, having rooms on its sides, and another hall goes towards the water, which we fitted up for a dining-room. Below it is the kitchen, the watch-house of the sailors, and the lodging of the captain of the factory. The captain of the factory has a mate, who is to take care that the sailors and *Chinese* workmen do their business: and he notes down

down those people who come from or go to the ships with sampanes of burden. In the factories live the supercargo, the assistants, the pursers, the cooks, and other servants, during the whole time of their stay; and besides them, those who come occasionally thither from the ships.

THERE are continually some sailors, who watch with drawn swords in their hands, to hinder those from entering who have no right. They indicate the time upon the *Gungung*; and beat upon it as it were upon a drum with sticks, when dinner or supper is ready. Every thing is carefully kept in the factories, both effects coming from the ships, *videlicet*, money, lead, cloth, raisins, almonds, &c. and those which are to be embarked, as porcelane, tea, silk, and many other things, which are brought on board by the sampanes of burden, after some mandarins, appointed for that purpose, have weighed them, and stamped a seal upon them. In each sampane, loaded with these and other things, goes a mandarin and some armed sailors from the factory to the ship to guard them, lest the master of the sampane should defraud them, as often happens notwithstanding these regulations. The supercargo

cargo always sends a letter to the captain, or whoever has the command of the ship, with an account of all the boxes and packs, and the sailors bring an answer back. The flag of the factory stands on the water-side, and is hoisted on all festivals.

Our ships are obliged to have a *Fiador*; For that purpose one of the richest and most respectable merchants is generally chosen, who is answerable for all damages to the company; and in case an *European* should wrong a *Chinese*, must make up matters in the best manner possible, &c. Our *Fiador's* name was *Suqua*.

The name we give to the *Chinese* servants is *Kulier*. These wait at table in the factories, bring in the meat, wash the dishes, &c. clean the knives and forks, fill the lamps in the yard and rooms with oil at night, clean the vessels, and do the like business; which the *Chinese* valets de chambre look upon as trifling, in regard to sweeping the rooms, assisting in carrying the tea-chests, and other wares in and out, &c.

These, and a *Chinese* cook, are paid by the company. Besides these, every one, or several together, hire a *Chinese* servant, who is paid some dollars *per* month. This person buys every thing you want, and frequently by this means avails himself more than by his wages. Happy is the man who has not the misfortune of hiring a thief into his house; but often however it is the case.

THE city of *Canton* is the trading place of *China*, whence all the *European* ships fetch their *Chinese* wares, since the trade upon *A-moy* has ceased: the merchants came hither from thence. *Canton* lies in a province of the same name, under 23 deg. 8 min. north latitude, and 95° 30′ longitude, or 6 hours 22 min. east from *Upsal*; but 3 deg. 31 min. west from the meridian of *Peking*. One side of it lies on the banks of the river, from which one or more canals cross the suburbs. The houses are built on both sides close to the stone bridges which go over the canal; which, for this reason, is not immediately perceived. Both the old and the new city have the name of *Canton*: the latter is not fortified: the old town, which has been built many centuries, has high walls and several gates: each gate has a centinel, in order that no *European* may get in, except under particular circumstances, with the

leave

leave of people of note; in this cafe you are carried into the city in a covered chair, and thus you do not get a fight of any thing worth notice in the place. The centinels have whips inftead of mufkets. Three fourths of this fortified town (which, as we are told, is inhabited on one fide by the *Tartars*, on the other by *Chinefe*) is furrounded by the fuburbs. On the outfide of that part of the city which is open to the country, is a fine walk between the wall and the ditch. The plantations begin clofe to the ditches; they are moftly on low grounds, contain all forts of greens, roots and rice, and reach as far as you can fee. The dry hills ferve for burying places, and paftures for cattle.

THE city wall confifts of hewn fand-ftones, is covered with all forts of little trees and plants, *videlicet, Ficus Indica, Urtica nivea,* &c. and on the top of them are centry boxes; however, the watch is fo ill obferved, that ftrangers paffing by are often welcomed with fuch a volley of ftones that their lives are endangered; as happened to an *Englifhman* during my ftay. It is faid that on the walls are fome eight or nine pounders; at leaft it is certain, that at eight o'clock at night their report is heard,

heard. I had no opportunity of measuring the circuit of the city, but it seemed to me to be above a *Swedish* mile[x].

I know nothing of the inside of this city, except what report says of it; namely, that besides the merchants and ladies, it is inhabited by people of the highest rank.

Tsang-to, or *Tsan-tack*, is the principal person in this town, who has the whole command not only of the militia, but also of the province and the cities round about; and is compared to a viceroy by the *Europeans*. The inferior lords fall upon their knees before him: his retinue is magnificent, as we had an opportunity of observing when he honoured us with a visit.

Fu yenn is the next in rank to *Tsang-to* in this town.

Happa is the principal officer of the custom-house.

The high court of judicature at *Canton* has 17 other towns under its jurisdiction, one of

[x] That is, about six miles three quarters *English*. F.

which is of the second, and the rest of the third rank.

The suburbs of *Canton* (in which the *Europeans* live during the time they trade here) are much greater than the fortified city.

The streets are long, seldom strait, about a fathom wide more or less, paved like the court yards, with oblong sand-stones, (*Cos Chinensis*) without any gutters. The stones are full of holes, that the water may run off; for the town, at least a part of it, is built on piles. Nothing is more common than to see *Chinese* hogs, dogs, and chicken, about the streets, and in the houses: yet every thing is cleanly here, because poor people continually go about with baskets and gather up all the filth. I never saw any other animals, such as are usual with us, not even horses, though they are to be met with in the country: where also I saw buffaloes, which were kept off from the plantations (which have seldom any fence round them) by people appointed for that purpose. No carriage is to be met with in the city; and whatever is brought from one place to another, such as hogs, ducks, frogs, snails, roots, greens, &c. is all carried on

men's

men's shoulders in two baskets, hanging on the extremities of a pole.

Living fish were carried about in buckets; The *Chinese* keep them in the following manner in their houses:

The fish are put into large water vessels in the streets, but each vessel stands under a spout which comes out of the wall; out of which the water runs continually, but slowly, upon the fish: and for this reason they were always to be got quite as fresh as if they had just been caught.

Fish cut to pieces were carried about for sale on little tables, which hung on poles as above described: the same was done with bacon, and *Fdaufu*, a dish which is like our sweet cheese, but which was prepared of *Chinese* beans (*Dolichos Chinensis*).

Persons that carry any thing must continually be calling to the people that throng the principal street, *to clear the way.*

Palankin, or *Chinese* chairs, carried by two half naked *Chinese*, on the shoulders without

out ſtraps, were to be hired out of the city, at the rate of half a piaſtre.

Most of the houſes are built of bricks, and are in general as high as the aforementioned factories, but ſometimes lower. They contain merchants ſhops, working-places, and the ladies houſes, which are far removed from the ſtreets.

The ladies are continually confined; and in ſhops or working-places are only men, and perhaps ſometimes a blind beggar woman.

Some merchants have ſeveral ſhops in one houſe, and quite cloſe to one another, in a line; but beſides them ſcarce any other apartments. They leave their houſes at night, and go home to their ladies. In the outward ſhop they commonly have coarſe porcellane, ſuch as the *Chineſe* themſelves buy, a quantity of toys, and the like. This ſhop is quite open towards the ſtreet, ſo that the people that paſs by may ſee every thing in it. In the middle of it is an opening to another vault, filled alſo with porcellane on both ſides, but of a finer kind, and for the *Europeans*, who are here not ſo much peſtered with impudent *Chineſe*,

nese. Behind this is another for silks, velvets, and such like commodities. In some shops the next vaults have tea or other commodities of this kind. On great festivals these long, narrow houses are opened, illuminated and ornamented with artificial flowers and trees, which look as if they were the work of nature itself. The last vault is for the musicians.

In the porcellane street, which is the broadest in the whole town, are several of these houses, with many arches or vaults one after another, in which is nothing but porcellane.

The less merchants are satisfied with about two shops, one behind another; in the first of which, as just mentioned, is coarse porcellane, and in the other all sorts of other wares, as silk, stuffs, handkerchiefs, ribbands, cotton-stuffs, *Indian* ink, painted paper, tea, snuff-boxes of mother of pearl, tortoise shells (*cypræa*), fans, tea-boxes made of tutanego, or of copper, with a porcellane enamel, *English* knives, &c.

In the inward vault is a stair case to a gallery which goes above the outermost vault, and gets its light from windows towards the street.

street. They use it as a dining-room, or sometimes to work in, &c. In a place like this, the famous *Face-maker* was at work, who makes mens figures, mostly in miniature. *Europeans* often go to this man to be represented in their usual dress; and sometimes he hits them exceedingly well. The upper rooms above-mentioned, the floor, the partition, the lattice-work, as also doors, stair-cases, and rails towards the streets, are commonly all of wood. On the outside, before the shops and working-places, hang boards, on which the name of the merchant or tradesman is written, in large *Chinese* characters: on the sides are other boards, on which the wares are marked.

INSTEAD of ovens and chimnies, stoves are made use of here, which draw very well. The pots in which they boil rice and other meats look clumsy, as if they were made of cast iron; their shape was pretty much like the cup of an acorn.

PEOPLE of the same trade commonly live in the same street together. The factory street has merchants shops, joiners, japanners, and workers in mother of pearl.

THE

The porcellane street is known for its fine vaults, containing porcellane. In the other streets are a number of druggists, and apothecaries, flower-makers, dyers, umbrella-makers, book-binders, mirrour-makers, smiths, taylors, shoe-makers, distillers of samsu, stone-masons, and some goldsmiths. In the apothecaries shops (of which there are a great many) hung some stags horns on the cieling and walls, as also a number of dried plants, unknown in our country.

I never could observe that they mixed several things together, or that they sold any electuaries, essences, and the like; but only some roots, partly entire, partly cut in pieces. The people bought these medicines without prescriptions, and cured themselves as well as they could.

Yan-sam, or *Yan-som*, is the *Chinese* name of a root, which is to be got in our apothecaries shops by the name of *Ninsi* (*Panax quinque folia*, Linn.); every ounce of it costs at present 30 or 40 ounces of silver: the root is whitish, somewhat like parsnips, but scarce so large; it often divides into two stalks, in which the

Chinese

Chinese find the resemblance of a man, for which reason they have given it the aforementioned name. It is somewhat knobby, or as it were in rings; and so it is in the inside. It is hard; and the heavier the better.

YAN-SAM, or, as we commonly say, *Ginseng*, is not allowed to be imported into *China*, because it grows wild in that country. *Duhalde*, in his Description of *China*, Vol. II. says, that it grows in *Tartary* from 39 to 49 degrees latitude; that it was to be met with in fields surrounded with woods, as also in woods on the banks of rivers, on the roots of trees, and near mountains, but was never to be found in vallies, morasses, and open fields; and that the *Tartars* call it *Orhota*, that is, *Captain of the Plants*. When Father *Jartoua* undertook to make a map of *Tartary*, he described this plant; which is likewise, though seldom, found in *Setchuen*. In *America* it is called *Garentouges*, or human thighs. Notwithstanding the order against importing it, the *Europeans* buy that in *Spain* which comes from *America*, and import it privately; but I fear that they get scarce half what it costs in *China*. The *Chinese* are of opinion that the *West Indian* roots of *Ginseng* are not so good as theirs; for that

that reason they hang it over a boiling pot, so that it may sweat, and dry it afterwards. I never looked into their apothecaries shops, but they were always selling *Ginseng*. Both poor people and those of the highest rank make use of it. According to their opinion, it is an excellent remedy for a consumption, and other diseases, if they boil half an ounce in their tea or soup, every morning. In 1709 the Emperor gave orders to 10,000 *Tartars* to go in quest of these roots, and to bring as much as they could find; of which every one was to give two pounds of the best to the Emperor, and to sell the rest for the same weight of fine silver. In this manner the Emperor got 20,000 *Katye*, or *Chinese* pounds of *Yan-sam*, in that one year.

I WAS greatly desirous of getting some knowledge of the *Chinese* officinal herbs, and the diseases against which they are made use of. On this account I applied to those who were able to instruct me in this branch of knowledge; and offered moderate rewards: but it was absolutely impossible; for first I could form no idea of their inward diseases, as the people themselves are not able to give a clear description of them; and the mere names

names of diseases are as incomprehensible to us, as ours to them. When they grow sick, they go into the ladies apartments, which no stranger is allowed to enter. Secondly, their officinal plants themselves were unknown; and that the more, as none of them are to be met with in the apothecaries shops with the parts of fructification: and I could not, even for money, get one to shew me the place where they grew. It is probable they get them at a considerable distance; since, notwithstanding my walks about the town, I never found a single one in the places I was allowed to go to, such as gardens, environs of villages, hills, ditches, and rice fields. Thirdly, As soon as a *Chinese* observes you want to be acquainted with these particulars, he is either silent, or gives you a false account; as I have often observed from the different relations of several persons; which at last made me very loth to make any more enquiries. I finally considered, that the *Chinese* officinal plants would not thrive in our climate; that if any were of use in some diseases, we should be forced to get them from *China*, and so increase the revenues of its inhabitants unnecessarily, when we are already provided with a sufficient number of medicines. We have many plants in our country, which have not yet been tried in medicine.

The goldsmiths work pretty well, and commonly cheaper than in our country; but they do not think it inconsistent with their characters to cheat. In silver snuff-boxes, plates of lead have been found; not to mention other frauds. Their touch-stones nearly resemble an egg in shape, and were like our pebbles. Snuff-boxes are made of several sorts of stones, commonly called fluors, of mother of pearl, false agate from *Sumatra*, and of tortoise shells; some have *Japan* copper on the inside, in-laid with figures of silver. The *Europeans* get buttons, heads of canes, &c. made, in which manner part of the silver comes again to *Europe* after the *Chinese* have wrought it. Gold is not so much esteemed as with us, and is not so fine. Great quantities of gold are brought from *China* into *France* and other countries.

The joiners here make use of a less number of tools than ours do, but they are not so skilful as ours. For want of a bench, they sit down on the ground, put the board against the belly, and hold it only with the feet. Their hatchets, or *tu-pao*, are small, and somewhat excavated

excavated on the inner fides, but like our hatchets on the outward fide, and in the reſt of their fhape. They do not make uſe of hammers, but content themſelves with theſe hatchets. Their pincers are not at all like ours, for they confiſt of an iron a foot long, ſcarce as thick as a finger, and an inch broad; however one end of it is ſomewhat broader and thinner, in which are two or three holes; on the other end it has a quadrangular foot, which is an inch ſquare, and ſharp on the corners; on it a looſe quadrangular ring is hung, juſt fitting to the foot, ſo that the extraction of a nail is eaſily effected. [See tab. xii. f. 3.] Their whet-ſtones are of a fine ſand-ſtone, and were much admired by our carpenters. Their ſaws are like ours, but leſs; the whole frame is wooden. The handle of their piercers, and the piercers themſelves, are like thoſe which we employ to pierce iron, and other hard bodies. They work in many ſorts of wood, both hard and ſoft, which are no further known to us, than that the bureaux, draught, and cheſsboards, &c. which we bring to *Europe*, are made of them. The black ebony, which is *ghome*, is not plentiful here, becauſe it is brought hither from other places in the *Eaſt Indies*, particularly the *French Iſle of Maurice*.

Rose *wood* is heavy, red, has a fine smell, has black and light veins, and is very dear. A certain species of light-brown wood is much esteemed here, and the *Europeans* have chests made of it. All tea-boxes are made of a soft sort of wood, which cracks in the fire like firr; and, as it is used to contain tea, the *Chinese* call it *Tia-mock*, or the *Tea-tree*. The light-brown wood, of which *Europeans* get chests made for their cloaths, is sold pretty dear. I bought a chest of five feet long, two feet broad, varnished over, and plated with brass, to lay my cloaths in, for 100 dollars of copper. *Chess-boards* of rose-wood, inlaid with ivory and black ebony, were to be sold here.

SHAUPANN is the *Chinese* name of that sort of wood of which they make coffins, which are almost every where of an equal breadth, and therefore are more like our bee-hives [y] than our coffins: the sides and the lids of them are of planks of the thickness of some

---

[y] In *Sweden*, and in the northern countries, a bee-hive consists of a piece of fir-wood of about five or six feet length, excavated on one side like a canoe; and then a board is clapped before this long hollow, with a small hole in it, for the bees to go in and out. F.

inches:

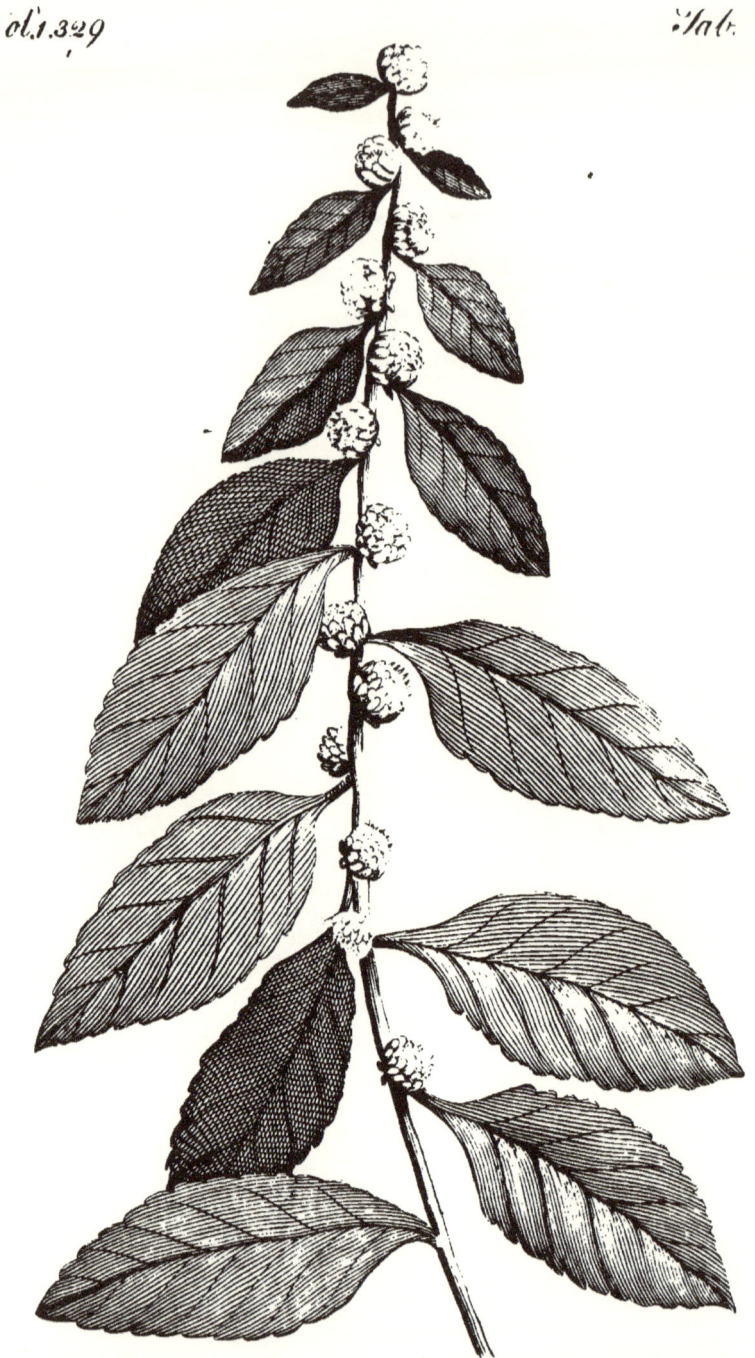

Carpesium abrotanoides.

inches: the bottom and the sides are likewise of planks. On the ends, which stand out a little, the boards are cut obliquely, and very sharp on the outward edge. The coffins are made so close, that no smell can come through.

THE Japanners have ready-made bureaux, tea-boards, boxes, &c. besides the work that is bespoken. These men, as well as those who work in mother of pearl, and the painters of porcelane, have little boys who are very diligent and active. That kind of varnished work which comes from *Japan* is reckoned the most valuable.

KILONG, or the blackish-brown thick varnish, which is spread with a broad stiff brush upon boxes, and other such like things, is very hurtful to the eyes. *Duhalde* says, that this varnish is made of rosin which exsudes out of trees growing in *Setchuen* and *Kiangsi*; the dearest varnish is said to come from the neighbourhood of *Kantcheou*, which is one of the most southern cities of *Kiang-si*. The rosin is gathered as soon as the trees are seven years old. They gather it in the summer nights; and to that purpose they make incisions in the tree, of which the lowest is seven inches from the ground, and the reft at the diftance of feven inches from each other, along the whole ftem. Under the incifions they put oyfter fhells, out of which they take the varnifh the next morning. See *Du Halde's* Defcript. p. 303. Any thing covered with this varnifh muft by all means be dried under cover, and not in the open air.

The dyers make ufe of brazil or *fernambuco* to dye purple, which is moft in fafhion here. Their other dying materials I never faw; though I have often been in their dying manufactories. I am of opinion that we can learn very little from the *Chinefe* dyers, fince there is fcarce any comparifon between the colours of their ftuffs and thofe of ours.

Those people who work in mother of pearl, have a quantity of counters, boxes, tea-fpoons, &c. to fell.

Here are barbers in plenty. Their razors are fmall, and fomewhat bent; they are well fkilled in their work. The hair is preferved, and employed to manure the ground.

RUBBING is ufual among the *Chinefe*, to put the blood in motion, inftead of bleeding. The people who do this bufinefs rub and beat the body all over with their clenched fifts, and work the arms and other limbs fo that their crackling may be heard at a confiderable diftance. Some young fellows follow this trade; they carry a chain with feveral inftruments on their fhoulders; among thefe inftruments are tongs, with which they make a noife like that of a Jew's trumpet, and give notice of their being at hand. They cut the nails with an iron which has the look of a narrow plane; as alfo the hair within the noftrils, and on the eye-brows, for fuch a trifle, that even the loweft rank of people are enabled to make ufe of them.

PORCELLANE comes hither from other places; fome is painted, and fome not. That which is painted here according to particular directions, or with names, or coats of arms, is very dear. The porcellane from *Nanking* is reckoned the beft, next to that from *Japan:* though a certain author fays, that the beft porcelane comes from the village of *Sinktefimo*. See *L'Ambaffade des Prov. unies*, p. 118. The

ftone

ſtone porcellane is the heavieſt, and its price the greateſt. *Duhalde* ſays, that this porcellane is only made in the province of *Kiangſi*, in the city of *King-te-ching*, which is ſaid to be a league in length, and to contain a million of inhabitants. Porcellane is a compoſition of two kinds of clay, one of which is called *Pe-tun-tſe,* and the other *Kaolin*; the latter contains ſhining particles, and keeps the whole together. They have lately found out a ſort of ſtone, or lime, which they call *Ho-a-khe,* and uſe inſtead of *Ka-o-lin.* [Their phyſicians give ſix parts of this ſtone with one part of powder of liquorice wood, to cool the blood]. The porcellane is glazed with *Chekao,* a ſpecies of ſtone like allum, or with *Ho-a-khe.* The *Chekao* is firſt burnt in an oven ; to make the blue colour, they take *Lapis lazuli*; and to the purple they add a kind of ſtones which they call *Tſin.* *Duhalde* ſeems to mean by it *Cobalt,* with which our porcellane is painted. See *Duhalde's* Deſcription of *China,* Tom. ii. p. 310, 312, 314, 324.

UMBRELLOS are made in great quantities, of black waxed paper and bamboo-wood, and ſold at two dollars in copper apiece.

BOOKS

Books are only stitched in white, and sometimes in gold paper. The leaves are thin and always double. The size is large octavo. No books of any other language than the *Chinese* are to be met with in the country: and in the suburbs of *Canton* are scarcely any others than almanacks: the paper is made of the inner bark of bamboo tree. See *Le Comte's Descript. of China*, p. 186. May not the bark of the juniper shrub, and of other trees, be of the same use? The mirrour-makers have some little pitiful looking-glasses. I was told of a glass-house in *Canton*, but never had an opportunity of going to see it. It is said, the importation of glass from *Europe* is forbidden. However, the *Europeans* often bring glass with them, and get roses or other flowers painted on them, as the *Chinese* are pretty skilful that way.

The shoe-makers have learned to make *European* shoes and slippers, and sell four pair for a piece of eight, or ten dollars in copper: but they are indeed not worth more; for they are sewed with cotton thread, and therefore, as soon as they are used in the wet, the seams part, and the soles and heels get loose. They are

are made of hogs leather, and often rough on both sides; the hair is burnt off with a red-hot iron.

TAYLORS offer their service as soon as any *Europeans* arrive, as almost every one wants waistcoats of satin, paduasoy, or taffety; for which the black colour is commonly chosen. All *Europeans* go here, as well as aboard, only in their waistcoats, with a white cotton cap, and a hat over it, carrying a stick in their hands. Coats are only made use of when one *European* visits another. The taylors commonly find the stuffs, and are paid for all together afterwards: a waistcoat and a pair of breeches of satin came to five tel, or seventy dollars in copper. The *Chinese* taylors scissars are small, but exactly like ours in every other respect. Their needles have round eyes, 100 of them cost a mes. Pins are not made here. Instead of the smoothing iron, they have a little pan, without feet of brass or copper, into which they put some burning charcoal, and rub the seams, or all that must be smoothed with it. Their silk buttons and button-holes are strong and well made. These taylors are often contented with worse silver than the *Spanish*. The ell which the taylors make use of is sometimes

longer,

longer, and that used in shops shorter, than it ought to be.

THE hatters twist all their hats, both for men and women, of bamboo. The *Chinese* never make use of other hats. They at first make their hats like a round mat, and beat them afterwards to the right size. Hats for women are higher than mens hats.

THE distillers of *samsu*, or the people who make the *Chinese* brandy called *samsu*, live likewise in the suburbs. This drink smells like the worst sort of common brandy, and does not taste much better. It is made of rice, and is by no means, as some imagine, the same as arrack, which the *Chinese* and we buy of the *Dutch*; because the cocoa-nuts of which arrack is made do not grow here, but only near the Line, in *Java* and other places.

THE *Chinese* make the *samsu* warm, and drink a tea-cup full at their meals. They do not use strong liquors to excess, unless some of them learn to drink from the *Europeans*. During my stay in *China*, I never saw a drunken *Chinese* among such a number of people. The heathens, who have no law naturally, do what
the

the law requires; but the chriftians are not afhamed to difhonour God by fome vice or other amidft the heathens.

The houfes of the ftone-mafons take up a whole lane, and perhaps more. They hew tomb-ftones and mill-ftones, the former of red and the latter of grey fand-ftone. The millers live in great numbers in a feparate part of the town, and make the rice-groats. They firft grind off the hufks by a wooden mill; they then ftamp the grains in a ftone mortar with a peftle, which is faftened with an iron pin to a wooden lever; one arm of which is weighed down, and then the peftle by its own weight falls upon the rice in the ftone mortar: this motion is continued till the work is finifh-ed.

Watch-makers are very much wanted here. The *Chinefe* buy large and little watches of the *Englifh*. In their fhops they have fometimes *Englifh* watches to fell, and fome-times at moderate prices, but moftly of the worft kind.

Perriwigs, gloves, bread, and coffee, are things which the *Chinefe* can do without; and for

for this reafon we find no places where they are made. They do not cut their tobacco, but fmoak the leaves fuch as they naturally are. Taking fnuff and chewing of tobacco are not yet in fafhion among them.

THE filk manufactures are as far off as the apartments of the ladies, whofe bufinefs it is to fpin and to weave. Their looms are level with the floor, and fo fituated that they may fit on them and put their feet into that part on which the loom ftands. I once came into fuch a place towards the ftreet, where a mat of bamboo was hung up inftead of a door. This occafioned an outcry from the perfon who ftood at the door; the dog received me as an enemy, and the female weavers left their work in a great hurry. The *Europeans* order their filks as foon as they arrive, and they get them ready a little before they fet off again. Old ftuffs are feldom bought, becaufe they are good for nothing when they return from fuch a long fea voyage. The filks are rolled or calendered between two fmooth ftones, whofe thicknefs is the breadth of the filks: the lower of thefe ftones is faft in the floor, and is like the concave fide of half a cylinder; the upper one fits into the lower, in the form of a half-

half-moon. The stuff is rolled upon a cylinder of yellow brass, and put between the two stones; then a fellow gets upon the upper stone, so that he has one foot on each side; and holding himself by a fixed piece of wood, thus with his treading he calenders better than four persons in our country are able to do it upon our inconvenient and dear wooden rolls. [See tab. xii. f. 4.]

COTTON is plucked asunder and made clean with an instrument which would be worth procuring: and though I ordered one, the *Chinese* was not so good as his word; and the same happened to me in many other things.

IN the markets, where the people every day run about like ants, they sell fruit, garden herbs, fish, bacon, &c.

A PAGODA, or idol-temple, is near one of these markets. In this they offer incense to their idols, which the *Europeans* call *yos*, from the *Portuguese dios*, and which are represented by one or more gilt pictures of several sizes, according as their saint looked when he was alive. The honours they bestow upon him are in consequence of his writings, or of any other

other services he has done to the public. These pictures, together with some foliage on the sides, are in the place of an altar table. Both upon the altar, and upon particular tables, are flower-pots, incense, and all sorts of meat and drink, such as fruit and the like; in particular large oranges [a], a species of fruit like sweet oranges, but much larger, and having a spungy peel of the thickness of one's finger. This fruit has an agreeable taste, is somewhat sourer than a sweet orange, and sweeter than lemons. They offer the same sacrifices in private houses; for every body has his own idol. A bell without a clapper hangs on one side, and a drum on the other side, before the altar. In other places at the entrance there are many areas and terrasses, but on both sides stand very tall figures of men. The pagodas have never any steeple. The roofs are ornamented with large dragons, lying length-ways along the walls. Rich people build pagodas sometimes, that their relations may be every day employed in burning incense, sacrificing, and other ceremonies, in commemoration of their saint. The priests are called *Vau-siong* by the *Chinese*,

---

[a] These are shaddocks.

and

and *Bonzes* by the *Europeans* [a]. They go with their heads bare and shaved, dress in steel-coloured silk coats with wide sleeves, which look like surplices, and wear rosaries about their necks. When they officiated on the festival of the lanthorns, they had red coats and high caps. Perhaps this was an order different from the former. Hundreds of bonzes sometimes perform their functions in one temple. The houses of these priests surround the pagodas, instead of a church-yard wall. They live upon the revenues from the legacies of their patrons, which afford likewise subsistance to the steward. Rice, which is their principal food, is boiled in a pot, which is fixed near the pagoda. They eat all together in a hall.

Trade is carried on here by the inhabitants and by the *Armenians*, and other *Asiatic* nations, besides the *Europeans*.

A quantity of foreign commodities, and of their own country, is annually exported from *Canton*, especially porcellane, commonly called *China* ware, which is used many ways. They bring it hither from the inner parts of

---

[a] The priests in *Japan* are likewise called bonzes.

the country, some painted, and some not. The *painted china* from Nanking is much esteemed. The *Japan china* is reckoned best. The *stone porcellane* is heavier, harder, and dearer than the common china. Du Halde says, that the finest comes from the little town of Kin-te-ching.

RAW *silk*, such as is clean and dry, does not rub off its colour; if well packed up in chests, is the best.

SILK *stuffs*, are of all sorts, of one colour, as well as of many, such as damasks, satins, paduasoy, taffeties, pelings, velvets, &c.

COTTONS, white, a piece commonly contains ninety-two *koabi*, or thirty-seven and a half *Swedish* ells, and are not in width above half such an ell. A piece costs two pesos duros, or about twenty dollars of copper, though some cost more, when the bottomry is reckoned in: a piece of their common linen, which is much finer, closer, stronger, and not bleached, contains 113 *koabi*, or seventy-one three quarters *Swedish* ells, and costs four piastres and an half. Quilts, cotton-tick at four or or five mefs; ſtockings, handkerchiefs, &c. are plentiful here.

But all theſe cottons are to be got at *Madras*, and other *Indian* trading towns, much ſtronger, and with more laſting colours.

Fine *chintz*, *Madras* linen, *Madras* handkerchiefs, &c. are likewiſe to be had at *Canton*; the *Engliſh* ſhips bring them to that place; but they are very dear, ſince they are ſecond or third hand goods.

Linen, made of other raw materials, ſuch as *Hannoes*, *Kantyoa*, *Chincao*, is to be got here at four kandarin, four kafs, an ell.

Umbrellas are here made in great quantities, of horſe bones, ivory, mother of pearl, tortoiſe ſhells, and bamboo.

The painting of this country, repreſenting men and their employments, trees, plants, flowers, fruit, birds, and the like, by their lively colours compenſate for the want of art [b].

[b] Some years ago the *Chineſe* were very defective in their drawings: but of late, ſince they have had opportu-

Flowers

OSBECKIA chinensis
kom kocang-Loaa or Goldrose feather

FLOWERS of paper, and filk ftuffs. Of the innumerable quantity of painted flowers which are to be had here, none are like nature; and either the leaves or the petals are mifreprefented. As for the animals, they feemed to me like horfes with birds feet, and men with claws.

JAPANNED goods are bureaux, fhrines, band-boxes, powder-boxes, and other boxes, tea-boards, tables, fnuff-boxes, &c.

GOLD is exported in great quantity to *France*, and other *European* places.

COPPER in bars. *Japan* copper is much employed to in-lay boxes of mother of pearl, and of other kinds. Tortoife fhell boxes are plated on the infide with fuch copper, gilt.

TINTENAQUE, or tutanego. See *Wallerius's* Mineralogy, p. 464. fpec. 32. is to be got in long pieces, each of five or fix pekuls, at the rate of three or four tel. It comes in

---

nities of feeing the performances of *European* artifts, they are much improved, and particularly in perfpective, with which they were before perfectly unacquainted.

great quantities from *Queda* and *Jahor*, on the *Malacca* coaſt, with the *Engliſh* country ſhips [c]. It is univerſally believed, that this metal when mixed with lead, is uſed to plate the tea-cheſts.

TIN comes in ſmall pieces from *Pegu* and *Jahor*.

LEAD is uſed for tea-canniſters, and to line tea-cheſts.

ALUM. The katty of the fine and clear ſort is ſold at two kandarin.

LAPIS *lazuli* comes from the north of *China*, and from *Tibet*.

BORAX, we uſed to buy annually of the *Dutch*, after it had been refined, as a thing abſolutely neceſſary for our goldſmiths. But probably we have already begun to refine it at home; which will enable us to be ſatisfied with crude *borax* for the future; which we can get from *Suratte* in our ſhips, with conſiderable gain [d].

[c] Country ſhips are *European* ſhips, going from *India* only to *China*, and to other *Aſiatic* places.

[d] The *Venetians* were the firſt that refined *Borax*, or *Tincal* as it is called before it is refined: ſince whom the

QUICK-

QUICK-SILVER is tried by squeezing it through shamoy, or any thin leather: and if the quick-silver is good it will leave nothing at all behind. Another way of trying it is, to evaporate some in a spoon over the fire: if it leaves a spot behind, it is looked upon as impure and adulterated.

CINNABAR is looked upon as not pure when it is in cakes, or ground. The best must be clean, of a shivery compact texture, of a shining crimson colour, very heavy, and in large lumps, of two or three inches thickness. It generally bears the same price as quick-silver.

INDIAN *ink*. The best comes from *Nanking*.

MUSK comes from *Tonkin* in bladders. The true musk burns with a flame when set on fire, which it does not when it is adulterated with goat's blood. *Du Halde* relates, that a *Chinese* who has musk about him may sleep in the fields without any fear of snakes.

Dutch, and of late the *English* have obtained the method, which is still a secret in few hands.

Sugar is to be got at a reasonable price here. Powder-sugar is prepared in the *French island*. Sugar-candy comes from *Cochin, China*, and other places. The whitest and clearest sugar-candy comes from *Chinkew* in loaves: a pekul of it was sold at six tel, and three mess. Loaf-sugar is not made in *China*.

Tea[c]. The *Europeans* learned to drink this infusion in the fifteenth century, and since that time have vied with each other in giving the *Chinese* the most money for this and other goods which are become fashionable: it grows both in *China* and in *Japan*, of which see *Kæmpfer's* Amoenitates Exot. p. 505. et seqq. where both the gathering and drying of the leaves are described. It likewise grows in *Tonkin*; but the best tea, according to *Du Halde*, comes from *Fokien*. We have as many names for tea as there are places where it grows; and different ways of preparing it; [f] though all the *Chinese* tea is said to be of one

[c] Tea in the *Chinese* language is called *Tia*, in *Fokien* it is called *Te*, and as the *Europeans* landed first in that province, that dialect has been preserved.

[f] It has been universally believed that all teas came from the same shrub, and are only distinguished by the different shrub.

Vol.1. 247   Tab. 13.

Tea	茶 Tja		f. lik
			f. six Catty kann
Honang-Tea	何南 há nam	春 hey	g. satt
		g. Heyson Tea kiän	g. seven Catty kann
Ankai Tea 3	安吉 an kaj	沃茶 tie the 10. Tie-Tea	h. gall h. eight Catty kann
Tao-kyon Tea 4	頭春 tao kjänn	成茶 sino tja 11. Sinolo Tea	i. k'au i. nine Catty kann
Congo-Tea 5	交吠 kong so	大失 tdaj sjó 12. Yams	k. siapp k. ten Catty kann
Soutchuen Tea 6	少軍 sou giäng	萬 tao 13.	l. jatt l. one Tale lá
		a. jatt a. a stekel daam	m. jatt seen m. one Mace sien
Linkisxim Tea 7	車心 linkis äm	b. jatt b. a Catty kann	n. jatt n. one Kandarin fann
Pekho Tea 8	白皮 pack há	c. sam c. three Catty kann	o. nji o. two Kandarin fann
		d. so d. four Catty kann	p. jatt p. one Cash lui
Bohea Tea 9	軍吏 mo ju	e. on e. five Catty kann	s. ts S. sa f. teh Kampf-amom t.17.

shrub. Tea is generally distinguished into brown and green, according as it tinges the water.

BROWN tea is *Honam Té*, or *Kuli-Té*, which grows in some places about *Canton*, and is drunk by the *Chinese*, but not by the *Europeans*: its taste being the least agreeable of any. [See tab. xiii. fig. 2.] The dried leaves are either yellow or brownish. The tea shrubs, which are sold in flower-pots here, scarce grow to the height of an ell. The flower consists of six white petals, of which the three lowest are the smallest.

AN-KAY is a coarse sort of tea, from a place of this name. [Tab. xiii. f. 3.]

age, gathering, and preparation. But Doctor *Hill* has lately discovered that the brown tea comes from the tea shrub with six petals, or flower leaves, which *Kæmpfer* has described, and represented: but that the green tea is taken from the tea shrub with nine leaved flowers. The former in *Linnæus's* Spec. Plantarum, Ed. ii. p. 734. is *Thea bohea*, and the latter *Thea viridis*. *Linnæus* distinguishes it, besides the flowers, by the longer and narrower leaves. Dr. *Schreber*. It is notwithstanding, very doubtful whether the plant of the green tea is really different from that of the bohea tea. F.

TE-BOHE, which we usually call *Bohca-tea*, is called *Moji* by the *Chinese*. This sort is brought to *Sweden* in greater quantities than any of the others. The best sort smells agreeably, and in a short time gives a brown colour to the water, and consists of leaves of one colour; if any black ones are among them, it is a bad sort. [Tab. xiii. f. 3.]

TAO-KYONN is the name of the best sort of bohea tea. [Tab. xiii. f. 4.]

KONGO, or as the *Chinese* call it *Kong-fo*, has an agreeable scent: its leaves are finer than those of *Té-bohé*; though it is scarce distinguishable from the best *Bohea*, except in price; for *Congo* is somewhat dearer. [Tab. xiii. f. 5.]

SUTCHONG, or *Sootchuen*, which the *Chinese* call *Saatyang*, or *Su-tyann*, is the dearest of all brown teas, and is most usual among our people of quality; as green tea is among the *English*. This tea gives a fine yellow green colour to the water, and has an agreeable taste; unless you put too much into the pot,
which

which spoils both taste and colour. [Tab. xiii. f. 6.]

PADRE *futchong* is the best tea that can be drunk: for even the best *Ruffia* tea, which comes by land by carravans to *Ruffia*, is not better in taste or scent. The leaves of this tea are large, yellowish, not rolled up, but expanded; and packed up in papers of half a pound each, like tobacco. If it is not taken great care of at sea, it is much altered for the worse.

LIN-KISAM is a sort of tea which hath narrow rough leaves, and foot-stalks. It is seldom used by itself, but mixed with other sorts. The *Chinese* can turn *Congo* into *Pecko*, if to the first they add some *Lin-kisam*. This may be compared with with what *Kæmpfer* mentions about the word *Zasanqua* [g]. [Tab. xiii. f. 7.]

---

[g] *Amœn.* p. 853. "*Zosanqua* is a less sort of *Tsubacki*, "has a simple flower, with five petals, many filaments, "and a pear-like fruit, with three grains, of the size of a "*Pistachio Kernel*; the grains are white and globose; the "leaves are prepared and mixed with tea, to give it a fine "smell."

BACH-HO

BACK-HO, or *Pack-ho*, is that which we call *Pecko*, which has leaves with dots. It is a mild tea, has a good taste, and is said to be the least heating of any. [Tab. xiii. f. 8.]

Of Green Teas, there are

HYSON, called *Hy-tiann*, or *Hi-kiong* by the *Chinese*. [Tab. xiii. f. 9.]

SINGLO, or *Sanglo*, is so called from the place whence it comes. The *Chinese* likewise call it *Sing-tia*. [Tab. xiii. f. 11.]

BING, or imperial tea.

TIO *tê* is rolled up like pease [h]. [Tab. xiii. f. 10.]

HYSON-UTCHIN, is distinguishable from the *Hyson skin* by its narrow and short leaves.

GO-BE' hath long narrow leaves.

THE *Chinese* likewise make *tea cakes*, which they sell very dear.

[h] This sort is rolled up between the hands in a rounder shape than the others. A smaller kind is called *Gunpowder tea*.

IT

It is almoſt incredible what quantities of tea are annually exported into *Europe* and other parts; and what innumerable hands are employed in ſo unneceſſary an article. The countryman muſt with great care plant and nurſe the tea ſhrubs; pluck every leaf in due time; ſeparate the new leaves from the old, and dry them with extreme accuracy. The green tea is ſaid to differ from the others only by conſiſting of young leaves, or by means of repeated dryings. But ſince ſome ſort of brown tea likewiſe conſiſts of tender young leaves, the afore-mentioned reaſon is not probable. I imagine the difference ariſes from the plates on which (according to their own accounts) the tea is dried. It is not unlikely that green tea is dried on copper plates, and the brown on iron plates: which is the more likely, ſince green tea occaſions purging, which ſeems to be the effect of verdigreaſe: but brown tea hath the contrary effect. At laſt when the merchant has got the baſkets of tea, at a low rate, from the country people, he muſt often take care of it for years together; and is always uncertain when or at what price he ſhall ſell it. When the *Europeans* have fixed upon a place where they will make their bargains, they empty the
baſkets

baskets (but let it be noted I am now speaking of *Bohea tea*, for the finer sorts are sold in chests); and if any bad tea is found in these baskets, it is separated from the rest. The good tea is then packed up in new chests, the weight of which is deducted; and these chests are marked, and lined with lead in the inside. A *Chinese* gets into these chests, and treads down the tea as it is emptied out of the baskets: this is very hard labour; and throws the treader, who is almost naked, into a profuse perspiration [i]. Though great care is taken to prevent any thing from coming into the tea, yet it is hardly to be avoided: and sometimes their feet are wounded and bleed. But the tea has already passed through so many dirty hands, that those who use that drug have no reason to be disgusted with this last mark of indelicacy in the package [k]. As soon as some

---

[i] This disgusting circumstance remarkably attends the bagging or treading of hops into their bags. Nor are the circumstances regarding the treading the wine-press, or of sugar or raisins into hogsheads or barrels, very delicate; yet such kind of package is unavoidable.

[k] The veins on the feet of some *Chinese* are very strong, and run in extraordinary directions. The bamboo sticks, upon which they carry tea chests and other heavy things, make deep impressions on their shoulders.

of the chefts are packed by a number of *Kuleers*, or *Chinese* fervants, they are pafted over with paper, and carried out of the warehoufe to the factories, where they are weighed by the *Chinese* cuftom-houfe officers, in the prefence of the interpreter, and marked red with a ftiff brufh, or with a wooden ftamp. Some poor people are fatisfied with the leaves of *Rhamnus Thea*, which they put into their clayey water inftead of tea, to make it more palatable. In the account of the *Dutch* embaffy to *China*, it is related that the *Chinese* make ufe of a fpecies of mofs inftead of tea.

SOYA, or the *Tyong-yao* of the *Chinese*, (*Dolichos Soja* Linn.) the *Japan Soya*, is better and dearer than the *Chinese*. For its preparation fee *Kæmph.* Amœn. p. 839. and likewife *Soja Dolichos*, *Flor. Zeylan.* 354. It was fold the katty at three kanderins.

CAMPHIRE is fold here unrefined at a good price. If it is to go far, it muft be well packed up in a tintenaque. When camphire is packed near tea, it fpoils its fmell and tafte. A *Chinese* told me, that the camphire tree was to be found near *Canton*, (*Laurus Camphora* Linn.) and that it was called *Tyong-fio* ; he alfo began to tell me in what manner the camphire or *Tyong-noao* of the *Chinese* was extracted from the wood by boiling; but as soon as he understood that this tree was unknown in my country, I waited in vain for further information. I desired him to shew me a branch of it; but he answered that the leaves were already fallen off, and that it was not to be distinguished: but what he endeavoured to hide from me may be read in *Kæmpher's* Amœn. p. 770.

RICE (*Oryza Sativa*) is the daily bread of the *Chinese*, and grows in such plenty here, that both *Europeans* and other nations provide themselves and their countrymen with it at a very low rate. If there is a famine in the country, the people run by thousands to *Canton*, where they can get their livelihood better, and may live upon rice groats for two stivers (1*d*.) a day. For on the sea shore no other grain is in use.

RHUBARB, in the *Chinese* language *Tay-hoang*, is sold the katty at two mefs, and sometimes less. If we are to believe the *Chinese*, no rhubarb grows about *Canton*. But I saw in one part of the town quite fresh roots drying in the sun; which therefore could not come

come a great way off. *Du Halde* tells us, that the best rhubarb grows in *Setchuen*. The marks of its goodness are, that it is dry, old, and as it were marked with oriental characters. The *Chinese* doctors never use rhubarb by itself [1], but prescribe it always fresh, and mixed with other medicines. They cut the root into slices and put it into a cullender over a boiling kettle, that it may imbibe the steam of the boiling water. These slices are then exposed to the sun for six hours together: this is nine times repeated. The *Portuguese* at *Macao* boil it in water, and drink it as a stomachic [m].

CHINA root, (*Smilax China*) by the *Chinese Long-fan-tao*, ought to be heavy, and not pierced by worms: it is very cheap here. In our ship we only threw it in between the chests of tea, and thus brought them to our apothecaries shops. It grew near the river, on dry hills, where the wind can blow freely.

[1] The Jesuit *Martini* died of half an ounce of rhubarb. See *Bayer's* Muf. the Preface, p. 23.

[m] *Bayer's* Muf. the Preface, p. 24.

GALGANT,

GALGANT, *Galangal,* or *Radix Galangæ* (*Maranta Galanga*) is likewise an agreeable root. It ought to be red, and not eaten by worms. It is used, like *China-root,* to fill up the empty spaces in the ships, between the tea chests.

INDIGO is sold here: but the best comes from *Biana* near *Agra* in the *East Indies.*

MOTHER *of pearl* is plentiful here.

THE *Chinese* sell their goods even in *Java, India, Japan,* in the *Philippines,* and other *Asiatic* isles. They export not only their own goods, but also those which they have got from the *Europeans,* to supply their wants and those of others.

GOODS from *Europe* are silver, lead, thin cloaths, scarlet cloth, blue, black, dark, and violet woollen stuffs; flints, pistols, guns, blades of swords, watches, wines, raisins, bottles, and other glass, *ginseng* [n], &c.

[n] *Ginseng* is a *Chinese* plant, but it grows likewise in *North America,* on plains in shady places, and was fre-

THE *Chinese* get many commodities from several parts of *Asia*; and in particular,

Parrots,

Ivory,

Tortoise shells,

Asa-fœtida.

PINANG, or *Areca Catechu* Linn. is a fruit which looks like a nutmeg in the inside. Our East Indiamen begin to bring *areck*. from *Suratte* to *Canton*. A quarter of one of these nuts is wrapt up in a betel-leaf, and covered with lime of oyster-shells. In *India* it is looked upon as a mark of ill-breeding not to eat *Pinang* before you speak to a man of quality; and you will think yourself neglected if he does not likewise treat you with the same.

THE *Chinese* keep the shells of the *areck-nuts*, and make a decoction of them against dysenteries, &c. It is likewise reported that

---

quently gathered for the *Chinese* trade in the neighbourhood of *Quebec*. See *Kalm's* Journey through *North America*, 1749, the 7th Aug. Mr. *Osbeck* mentions it under the *Chinese* merchandizes. F.

they communicate to each other by means of *Pinang* lascivious medicines, their antidotes, and the leaves of *Obcat goena*, together with other poisons. Old *Pinang-nuts*, made round and polished, put during one night into water in which some snake-tree wood has been soaked before, are sometimes given for *Piedra del Puerco*°, as *Rumph.* says.

BIRDS nests[p] are a scarce and dear dish: they look like little dishes, or like half the rind of a lemon; the best are white and clear, almost like isinglass. They grow tough like a

---

° *Piedra del puerco* is a concretion found in the *cystis fellea*, or gall-bladder of the *Malacca Porcupine*, which, when soaked in water for some hours, impregnates it with a considerable bitterness; although the *Piedra del puerco* loses scarcely a grain of its weight. This infusion is used in *India* as a cordial in malignant putrid fevers, and in the jaundice. The high price of these *Piedras del puerco*, which sometimes amounts to fifty pounds sterling apiece, has caused that they are frequently counterfeited and adulterated. See *Kæmpfer's* Amœn. Exot. p. 395. F.

[p] *Nidus avis* is the name they bear in our apothecaries shops. *Yenova Yenika*, vulgo *Yens*. Nidus halcyonum, vulgo nidus avium, pro obsoniis ad coquinas expetitus. Nidos hos rupibus oceani orientalis affixos parant hirundines marinæ, domesticis multo majores ex holothuriis mari innatantibus materiam decerpentes. *Kempf.* Am. p. 833.

piece

piece of leather: they are got at *Borneo, Java*, the *Molucca Isles, Cambogia,* and *Cochin-China*. These birds are said to build their nests of little fishes on the rocks in the sea, and to belong to the swallow kind. A slimy juice is said to issue out of their bills, by means of which they fasten their nests to the rock: it is also related of them, that they make use of the slime swimming in the sea, to make all the parts of their nests much in the same manner as swallows do with clay. Their nests are taken after the young ones are flown q.

SANGUIS *Draconis*. The goodness of its colour is tried upon white paper.

SAGU,r or *Sago*, from the *Molucca Islands, Java, Sumatra, Jahora,* and *Borneo*. White *Sago* is more scarce, and must be of a different sort.

COSTUS *dulcis* (*Costus Arabicus* Linn. Mat. Med.) or *Putchuch*, is a root usual in our apothecaries shops. It ought to be clear, and smell like violets.

---

q *Du Halde's* Descript. of *China*, 8° tom. ii. p. 201.

r This is the *Malaic* Name; in *Java* it is called *Bulum*, and is made of the pith of the *Cycas circinnalis* Linn.

SPICES;

SPICES; videlicet, *Pepper* (*Piper nigrum*); *Long Pepper*, (*Piper longum*); *Cubebes* (*Cubeba* Linn. Mat. Med. 526) *Cloves* (*Caryophylus aromaticus*), *Cardamum* (*Amomum cardamomum*), come from *Cochin-China, Cambogia,* and *Siam.*

STICKLACK from *Pegu:* The gum which quite covers the sticks is clear and high coloured. The lack from *Vizapatnam* is not so good.

GUMM *Benjamin,* or *Benzoin,* comes from *Sindi,* and the *Spice Islands,* in large chests of 50 or 60 pounds weight, packed up in mats. The best looks like white marble. There is likewise a coarse kind, which is black and soft: it is packed in chests.

CAMBOGIA, *Gamboge,* or *Gum-gutta,* of a high yellow gold colour, from *Cochin-China, Cambogia,* &c. in bundles.

SANTAL (*Santalum album*) is sweet-scented, and comes from *Suratte,* where our *Swedish* ship the *Gothic Lion* (the first that ever came to that place from *Sweden*) bought, in 1750, some of this wood for seven tell, and sold a great deal of it at *Canton:* the pekul at 13 tell.

tell. The *Chinese* make use of this wood instead of incense. They take the saw-dust of it, and glew it to a stick, light it, and put it before their idols, or in any place where they would have an agreeable scent.

KOBI, or the *Chinese* ell, is about fifteen *Swedish* inches long. It is divided into ten pann, and each of them into ten kanderin. The taylors ells are commonly longer, and their length is sixteen inches two-thirds. These ells are commonly made of bamboo.

EVERY thing either received or given out is weighed. However, *Spanish* money has a fixed price; and a piastre is valued at seven mes, and four kanderins. At *St. Helena* it is taken for five shillings. The *Chinese* puts his stamp upon the piastre, the more easily to avoid taking false ones, which are sometimes made of tin or copper, plated over with silver. For want of small coin, a *Chinese* has, besides the weight, a pair of sciffars about him, with which he cuts the silver money in pieces, and either gives or receives such pieces on buying of goods. These sciffars, which are very thick, they call *Kiapp-chin*. When a *Chinese* wants to cut a piece of silver, he puts it between the sciffars scissars, and knocks them against a stone till the pieces drop off.

KAS, which the *Chinese* call *Lai,* is the only current coin which is struck in *China,* and is equal both in size and value to our one-sixth oere silver coin. This coin is made of yellow brass, and round; hath a quadrangular hole in the middle; the edge is plain, but its sides are marked with *Chinese* characters.

DATCHIN is their larger weight, with which they weigh by pekul and katty.

LAY-TANG is a less weight, with which they weigh little things.

A PEKUL, or *Idaam* as the *Chinese* call it, is 100 katti, or 139 lb. $21\frac{7}{16}$ half ounces, $\frac{17}{32}$ [s] *As,* victual-weight; but is generally reckoned equal to 142 *Swedish* grocers pounds.

A KATTY, or *Chinese Kann,* which is 1 lb. $12\frac{11}{16}$ of half ounce, and $\frac{20}{32}$ *As,* contains 16 tel.

A TEL [t], which the *Chinese* call *Lea,* has ten *mes,* about 14 dollars of copper coin.

[s] The smallest *Swedish* weight.

[t] The *English* write it tale, the *Portugueze* taël. It contains 100 *French* sous, or $2\frac{3}{8}$ half ounces, and 12 *As, Swe-*

A MES [u], by the *Chinese* called *Hane*, contains 10 kanderin.

A KANDERIN, or as the *Chinese* call it *Fann*, is 10 kas.

A KAS, or *kash*, is the smallest coin which is used in every part of this country, and its value is about ⅙ ocre silver coin; though *Du-Halde* mentions several less, which perhaps may be used in particular places, and be necessary only on particular occasions.

The *Chinese* count thus:

Yatt [w] *Ydaam*, a pekul. [Tab. xiii. fig. *a*.]

Yatt Kann, a katty or catti. [Tab. xiii. f. *b*.]

Nghee kan, 2 ditto.

Samm kan, 3 ditto. [Tab. xiii. f. *c*.]

dish victual weight. See Memoir of the *Swed*. Acad. of Sciences for 1750, p. 110, the *Swed*. Edition.

[u] The *English* write mace, the *Portugueze* maz.

[w] *Yatt*, or *Yett*, is one.

Tſockan, or *ſa kan*, 4, (*Tſin*, *Tſi*, *Tſoe*, or *Tſey*, is 4.) [Tab. xiii. f. *d*.]

On kan, 5. This is liſped through the teeth, and leaves one to gueſs whether it muſt be *un*, or *n*, or *œn*. [Tab. xiii. f. *e*.]

Lock kan, 6, [Tab. xiii. f. *f*.]

Satt-kan, 7, [Tab. xiii. f. *g*.]

Patt-kan, 8, [Tab. xiii. f. *h*.]

Kau-kan, 9, [Tab. xiii. f. *i*.]

Siapp-kan, 10. [Tab. xiii. f. *k*.]

Siapp Yatt-kan, 11,

Siapp-ngee, 12.

Ngee-ſiapp, 20.

Ngee-ſiapp-yett, 21,

Sam-ſiapp, 30,

Tſi-ſiapp, 40.

On-ſiapp, 50.

Lack-ſiapp, 60,

Iſat-ſiapp, 70,

Patt-

Patt-fiapp, 80.

Kau-fiapp, 90.

Yett-pa, Ye-pa, or *Ghee-pao,* 100.

Ye-pa-yett, 101.

Ye-pa-ngce, 102.

Yatt-tfin, 1000.

Sam-tfin, 100,000.

Siapp-pack-tfin, 1,000,000.

Yatt-leo, a tel. [Tab. xiii. f. *l.*]

Yatt-fane, or *Siane,* a mefs. [Tab. xiii. f. *m.*]

Yatt-fann, a kanderin. [Tab. xiii. f. *n.*]

Ngee-fuen, or *fann,* 2 kanderins. [Tab. xiii. f. *o.*]

Yatt-lai, a kas. [Tab. xiii. f. *p.*]

SVAN-PANN, or the *Chinefe* accompting-board, is oblong, divided into two equal parts, and has little beads, which are moved backwards or forwards on wires, of which there are fometimes more or lefs, fometimes 25 on each fide. One fide of each of thefe beads

fignifies

signifies one, but on the other it stands for five. If you count by thousands, 100, or 20, &c. the first row on the right is one, the second 10, the third 100, the fourth 1000. If the *Chinese* knew how to reckon with cyphers, they would do their business very quickly, since all their weights, measures, and money accompts, are decimals; *videlicet*, when I have 464 kanderins, I immediately see they mark four tel, six mess, and four kandarins.

The inhabitants of this country, whom we call *Chinese*, are quite white, excepting those who are tanned by the sun. Most of them look alike; they have short noses, small eyes, short black eye-brows, a broad face, great ears, and black hair, which the men always shave off, having a tuft at the top of the head, which grows as long as it will, and is made up into a broad stiff plait. In this manner the *Chinese* have worn their hair ever since the *Tartars* began to reign over them. They formerly let the hair grow on the whole head, which we see the *Chinese* in *Batavia* do still. Old men, who have few hairs, make their plait more conspicuous with ribbands, lest at first sight they should be looked upon as criminals, whose hair is cut off, if we may believe
their

their own accounts. The men let their beards grow, and divide them into several locks. The *Chinese* are some of them greater and others smaller in size than we are. In conversation they are civil: in their demeanor gentle; in social life diligent, having genius for trade in particular: but they are likewise talkative, inquisitive, loving to take presents; are obstinate, proud, and suspicious. They sit upon their feet, for want of chairs. When they meet one another, they lift up their hands; but touch neither hat nor cap, and do not move their feet, but bow a little, saying, *Hoaw, Hoaw*,[x] which is a friendly salute, with which they wish all manner of good to each other. The lower sort of people kneel down before men of high rank, and shew them their submission both by words and gesture.

THE *dress of the men* generally is as follows: They wear two wide coats of silk or cotton, the lower of which is white, but the upper purple or black; they are like our long nightgowns, and have no lining, stiffening, buttonholes, folds, and facings; they are buttoned

---

[x] *Good, Good.* A repetition of the positive makes their superlative, as in the *Hebrew* language.

before with little round gilt buttons, which are at a distance from each other, and catch into little strings, fastened a little inward, and this makes the coats to be double upon their breasts. They do not quite cover their feet. The sleeves are so wide and of such a length as to be sufficient to cover the hands. Their breeches are wide and white, and are laced about the body, and about the knees. The stockings are thick, embroidered, and made like boots, of a dark-coloured silk-stuff; people of quality have the edges and clocks of the stockings embroidered with gold or silver; sometimes they are fastened to the shoes, sometimes not; their shoes are like slippers without heels, but without quarters, and a white sole as thick as ones finger; they are as it were chopped off before: the upper leather is embroidered: every thing belonging to them is of hog's leather, and sewed with cotton yarn. The workmen who are frequently exposed to the sun, particularly peasants and fishermen, cover their heads with hats of bamboo, whose brims are of different colours. They use caps; some of which look like an inverted funnel, with a button at the top. They are covered with a tuft of raw red silk, which is fastened at the top, and hangs down loosely to the bottom

bottom of the cap. None but men of high rank make ufe of thefe caps. Others wear caps of black filk, with brims of velvet: fometimes the whole cap is made of velvet, with or without tufts of red filk, in threads, which hang at the top; and in the middle is a button of gold, precious ftone, amber, glafs-fluor, or even fomething lefs valuable, according to the difference of rank and fortune of the wearer. No one is allowed to cloath himfelf above his rank. Some men of high rank diftinguifh themfelves from the reft by the badges of fome orders, which they carry on their breafts: others carry behind in their caps two fquirrels tails; and others diftinguifh themfelves by the value of the button on their cap. But a *Chinefe* is never feen to wear a wig, cravat, fleeve buttons, gloves, garters, knee buckles, and buckles in the fhoes; and feldom walks with a ftick. Inftead of thefe things, their tobacco-pipe, tobacco-bag, and purfe, hang down to the knees by long ftrings. In winter they frequently put on thirteen or fourteen garments one above another, or get them lined with furs. Inftead of muffs they carry a live quail (*Tetrao coturnix*) in their hands. The poorer fort of people are content with a little coat of cotton, with wide trowfers, and

with

with caps of bamboo leaves; they go barefoot, and most of them are half naked. It is a very common thing to see small boats full of naked children, and of half-naked parents, who have no other habitations than these on the surface of the water, and live by thousands by fishing, picking up old rags, dead hogs, or whatever else is thrown from the ships.

Labourers are obliged to pare their nails[y], but people of quality let them grow as long as they will; keep them very clean and transparent, and at night put little cases of bamboo on them.

The dress of the ladies is little known to me, since ladies of fashion always keep in their houses. I saw, however, a head-dress at the goldsmith's, which was twisted of a coarse silver-wire, and looked like a little basket; in it were fastened pieces of red cloth, to heighten the lustre. Their round silk fans are well known. They can scarce walk, on account of their little feet. As this inability

[y] Very long nails are a token of elegance, and shew that the wearers are arrived at a thorough pitch of genteel helplessness.

for

for walking is a mark of gentility, people of rank prefs the feet of their daughters from their very infancy in iron shoes. It is said that this was a punishment on the female sex, for attempting to betray their husbands in an irruption of the *Portuguese*; but they look upon this as an injurious report, which cannot be proved. Common women are every day seen, particularly in the boats, and they are dressed like men, in a coat and trowsers; but they do not shave their heads; they tie their long hair together in a knot at the top of their heads; and fasten it with a great long silver bodkin. The hair of the unmarried women is cut on the sides, and hangs round the head about an hand's breadth. To paint the face, is universally the fashion. Tobacco is used only for smoaking; but its use is very general with both sexes: and women are frequently seen in the boats at the helm, with their children at their backs, and a tobacco pipe in their mouths. The mothers, who always educate their own children, tie them to their backs, that they may not be troublesome to them in working: and as the children often knock their noses against their mothers backs, it is probable that this is the cause of their broad noses, which are a general characteristic of this nation.

nation. The children are adorned with silver rings about their hands and feet, and with medals hanging on their breasts. Their parents tie a gourd, or a large fruit which the *Chinese* call *Po-o* (*cucurbita lagenaria*) which is shaped like a bottle, to their childrens backs, that they may not be drowned in case they should fall into the river. The business of the women in general is to take care of the children, the kitchen, weaving, and spinning. The elder children must help to carry the younger on their backs. The men help to wash.

THE eye is every where struck with the populousness of this healthy country, in which the people chuse rather to want, than to seek a plentiful subsistence elsewhere. They are allowed but little more navigation than what they can carry on by their inland canals. Their foreign trade is chiefly to *Batavia*, and some places adjacent. An *Englishman*, whose men were run away during his stay in *China*, could with difficulty get so many *Chinese* sailors as were necessary to navigate his ship to the *East Indies*; though he assured them he would send them back by the first opportunity. The streets are as full of people here, as if there was a fair every day, at leaft during the ftay of the *Europeans* in this country, which is from *July* to *February*.

In *China* are faid to be 58 millions of inhabitants, all between 20 and 60 years of age, who pay an annual tax. It is reported that many were ftarved to death this year on account of the bad crop, and that great numbers were come from different provinces to get their livelihood here. Notwithftanding the induftry of the people, their amazing populoufnefs frequently occafions a dearth. Parents who cannot fupport their female children, are allowed to caft them into the river; however, they faften a gourd to the child, that it may float on the water; and there are often compaffionate people of fortune who are moved by the mournful cries of the children to fave them from death. *Le Comte* relates, that in the conqueft of *Nankin* by the *Tartars*, women were fold in bags, and he who had bought an old woman, caft both bag and woman into the river [z]. The boys which cannot be brought up by their parents are educated at the expence of the public.

[z] *Le Comte*, p. 301.

The language of the country has nothing in common with any other; it has no alphabet, but as many characters and different figures as they have words; which have different significations according as they are differently pronounced, and have different accents; *videlicet*, *Tchu* signifies a master, a hog, a kitchen, and a pillar. *Le Comte* shews that by the pronunciation only they make 1665 words quite different from each other out of 333. He is reckoned very learned among the *Chinese* who knows half their words; for they have 80,000 characters [a]; and for this reason the *Europeans* think it impossible to learn the *Chinese* language any other way than by abiding many years in *China*; and they likewise look upon it as unnecessary, since they can avail themselves of the *French*, *Portugueze*, or *English* languages, which the *Chinese* servants employed in trade have learned; though they have a particular dialect, and think that he does not speak well who does not intermingle *English*, *Portugueze*, and *Dutch*. Some of the *Chinese*

---

[a] It is said that the emperor *Koambi*, 4300 years ago, introduced the characters; and afterwards wrote himself astronomical, arithmetical, and medical treatises. *Le Comte*, p. 189.

servants

servants speak *Swedish*; we likewise saw a man who had taken the Roman catholic religion in *Siam*, where he had been taught Latin, which he spoke readily. This man's name was *Thomas Tya*, and he related that he was born in *Nanfiong*, a place ten days journey from *Canton*. It is the more difficult for a foreigner to learn the *Chinese* language, as there is a mixture of nations here, who all distinguish themselves by their dialect, beside the eastern *Tartars*, who speak their own *Mantcheore* language. In *Tonking*, *Cochin China*, and *Japan*, they make use of the same characters as in *China*; however, a *Chinese* does not understand their languages.

Sometimes the names of animals correspond with the noise which these animals make; *Miaa*, a cat, &c. The composed characters likewise deserve some attention; thus *Tsai*, which signifies a *misfortune*, is composed of *Miane*, a house, and *Ho*, fire, since they can image to themselves no greater misfortune than that of a house being reduced to ashes. We can by no means pronounce some words so well as the *Chinese*, because to my knowledge the teeth of their upper jaw stand out forwards a little: on the contrary,

they

they are unable to pronounce all the *Swedish* letters, but pronounce *b, d, r, x, z,* like *p, t, l, ſ, ſ;* they do not speak alike, and pronounce a great many of their words with a singing tone. When they are heard speaking to each other, one would frequently be induced to believe they were quarrelling, in particular when they shake their heads, and when they speak very loud, which is the case on ship board, and in other great companies; where they far exceed the clamour of our poorest pot-houses.

PAPER is made of the inner bark of bamboo (*Arundo bambos*); it is not at all like our paper, except in colour. Their sheets are as large as four of ours. On one side it is as smooth as glass, but not on the other; and for this reason they always lay their leaves double, and always write or paint on one side only, and from the right to the left, from top to bottom. The *printing paper* is as thin as an egg's skin, for which reason the letters show through it. The fine paper which comes to *Europe* with the tea is common enough. A sort of writing paper stronger than the common writing paper, and which is bought by the name of *Macao paper*, is to be had here;

it

it may be written on with ink, and in my opinion is to be preferred to any *European* fort, especially for drying plants. The *Chinese*, who neither make use of pens nor of our ink in writing, but write with hair pencils dipt into *Indian* ink, can very well do with thinner paper. Instead of an ink pot, they make use of a small marble table with elevated borders, of the size of one's hand; this serves to mix the *Indian* ink, which, being dissolved in water, gathers in a little hole at one end of the stone.

Books in all sorts of sciences are to be had here, stitched in thin white paper; but none in a foreign language. The size of their books answers to that of our royal octavo. All their books are printed with wooden plates, in the manner that the manufacturers in *Europe* print cottons.

Their observations on the heavens and earth, and their history, are remarkable on account of their antiquity [b]. Their morals are looked upon as a master-piece; their laws are considered as excellent maxims of life; their medicine and natural history are both of them

[b] According to their accounts, they go as high as the times of *Noah*.

founded

founded on long experience[c]; and their husbandry is admired for the perfection it has risen to. But the want of the true knowledge of the Supreme Being is an imperfection which outweighs all their other knowledge.

The religion in *China* is pagan; but by their own accounts, there are almost as many sects as persons among them: for as soon as a *Chinese* expects the least advantage from it, he is without any consideration to-day of one religion, to-morrow of another, or of all together: however, there are three principal sects, of which we have an account in *Du Halde's* Description of this Empire.

The first principal sect is called *Tao-tsa*, and their founder *Daokiun*. Its followers endeavour to disengage themselves from every thing which tends to disquiet the rest of the soul, to

[c] This is proved by their *Pent-sa-o*, or books of plants, which were wrote by little and little. The emperor *Shinnongs* made a beginning with it, and described 360 medicinal plants, in three volumes. Afterwards several things were published concerning natural history, all which was at last reduced to 16 classes by *Li-khe-tchin*; who likewise added their use in physic, and their other uses. Of this see *Du Halde's* Description of *China*.

live

live free and void of cares, to forget the paſt, and not to be in apprehenſions for the future. They have fictitious ſpirits, which are independent of the Supreme Being, and among theſe they comprehend ſome of their ancient kings. They look upon it as a folly to procure another perſon's happineſs, and loſe their own reſt by it. They brag of a preſervative againſt death, leſt the remembrance of it ſhould cauſe them trouble. They think to get their wiſhes fulfilled by the aſſiſtance of the evil ſpirit. The emperor *Fou-ti* drank ſeveral times of their pretended draught of immortality; but he at laſt found he was as mortal as others, and pitied his own credulity. The heads of this ſect are very learned, and live in towns in fine houſes. Numbers of people come to them out of the adjacent provinces, and fetch remedies for their diſeaſes; and by the way get them to tell them the fate of the remainder of their lives; and the principal man gives them a paper full of particular letters, which they pay for very thankfully. This ſect has decreaſed or increaſed according as the court has favoured or neglected it.

THE ſecond and moſt common ſect, are the *Fo*, or *Fo-é*. The emperor *Ming* introduced it in the year 65 after *Christ's* birth, having dreamed of, and recollected an opinion of the great *Confucius*, that the Most Holy was to be found in the western countries. He, therefore, sent to enquire for him in *India*; and his people meeting with the idol *Fo*, or *Fo-é*, they believed they had found the true worship, and brought this idol to *China*, and together with it those tales which fill the *Indian* books. This infection began at court, and soon took root in the provinces, and afterwards spread through the whole empire. Their religion consists in not killing any living creature, for they believe that the souls of their ancestors transmigrate into irrational creatures, either into such as they liked best, or into such as they resembled most in their behaviour: for which reason they never kill any such animals; but while they live feed them well, and when they die bury them with splendour [d].

[d] Mr. *Des Guignes*, in his *Histoire des Huns, des Turcs & des Mogols*, is of opinion, that the religion or sect of *Fo* is originally the Christian religion, perhaps corrupted by length of time so far as to admit these absurd tenets. Perhaps the decay of his own religion was the only foundation he had for this opinion. F.

LE COMTE gives the following account of that which happened to himself: "I once was called to baptize a sick man 70 years old, who lived upon a little pension, which the emperor bestowed on him. When I came to him, he said, I am much obliged to you, for you will deliver me from a great punishment. I replied, This is not all; baptism not only delivers a man from hell, but it also leads to a happy life. I do not understand you, said the sick man, and perhaps I have not expressed myself plain enough: you know, that I have for some time lived upon the emperor's bounty; and our bonzes, who are well instructed concerning what happens in the other world, have assured me, that I shall be obliged out of gratitude to serve the emperor after my decease; and that my soul will undoubtedly animate a post-horse, to bring the posts to court out of the provinces. They exhort me, therefore, when I shall have assumed my new form, to do my duty well, and take care not to snort, nor to kick, nor hurt any one. They further exhort me to trot well, to eat sparingly, and to be patient, in order to move the compassion of the gods, who often

"often change a good animal into an human
"being, and make a great lord of him. I
"own this thought makes me shudder, and I
"cannot think of it without trembling; every
"night I dream of it, and sometimes when I
"am asleep, I think I am saddled, and already
"start at the first lash of the rider's whip;
"after this, I awake in great trouble and
"anxiety, uncertain whether I am a man or
"a horse. But alas! what will become of
"me, when I am to be a horse in reality! I
"have therefore taken this resolution: It is
"said, that those of your religion are not ex-
"posed to this misfortune; but that with you
"men remain men, and will be such in the
"world to come. I beseech you, receive me
"among you. I know it is difficult to live con-
"formable to your religion; but if it was
"even more difficult, I am however ready to
"embrace your faith, and at any rate to be a
"Christian rather than a creature void of
"reason." This sect particularly prohibits
pride, uncleanness, and drinking of wine.
They acknowledge a God, who dwells in
heaven, sees every thing, rewards virtue and
punishes vice; for which reason, if I made a
doubt of what they said, they answered with
great emotion, that I being a priest should ask

*Yoss*ᵉ in heaven if it were true or not. Yet they have a very limited knowledge of the Supreme Being; for being asked who was the Creator of heaven and earth and of every visible thing, they said it was a great Lord. If they were further asked, whether he was yet alive, they answered no, he died some years ago. However, their priests, in their morning, evening, and other prayers, and when they sacrifice, bowed three times to the ground, as if the Trinity was not unknown to them ᶠ. They are greatly afraid of the evil spirit, and believe, that if he was not withheld by a superior Power, he would be able to do as much mischief as he pleased; for which reason they pray to him to spare them. They have a num-

---

ᵉ This is a name they have learned from the *Europeans*, by which they mean *God*; but in the *Chinese* language he is called *To-en*, heaven, &c.

ᶠ It is from these and the like feeble hints that the party of unbelievers have got so frequent opportunities to ridicule the sacred doctrines of the Christians. Such is the argument of the Trinity doctrine discovered even among the *Tibetans*, by a late learned writer, and which he deciphered from an idol with three heads, on a paste coin, with some *Tibetan* characters: which his friend so well acquainted in the *Hibernian* antiquities gave out to be an old *Irish* Inscription. F.

ber

ber of tales ready to support the truth of this opinion. They sometimes pretend to see in their rooms small lights which on a sudden grow very large, together with many other things which they attribute to the devil. They believe that the dead come back, and that the deceased husband visits his surviving wife, and the dead wife her husband. This is the reason why at every little alarm in the night-time they are afraid of spectres; and I myself have often seen how fearful they were. But they likewise believe every human being has his angel, who attends him during his life and after his decease. They reckon the sun, moon, and deceased great men, such as kings and the like, among their Gods.

The third sect consists of those philosophers who ground themselves upon the writings of *Confucius*, and the disciples of *Memcius*. *Confucius* [g] was born in the year 551 before *Christ's* birth, in the province of *Canton* in the city of *Kiosian* [h]; his works are highly esteemed, and on account of his excellent morality deserve to be read by those who would embrace the

[g] From *Cun* a peacock, and *Su* the sun.
[h] *Boie's* Journal, p. 79.

good

good and reject the bad. They are printed at *Canton*, and a part of them at *Goa* in *India*, in *Chinese* and *Latin*, under the inspection of the *Sicilian Intorcetta*, subscribed by 16 *Roman* catholic fathers, in the year 1676. *Kircher* promised to publish this philosophy with the commentaries upon it, which he had translated into Latin at *Rome*; but soon after the writings of these philosophers were published in Latin at *Paris*, 1687. The editors of this edition were, *Intorcetta*, *Herdtrich*, *Rougemont* and *Couplet*. However, this edition little differs from that published at *Goa*. A greater book of the writings of this philosopher was that which *Couplet* had with him, which has been published by *Aymon*, after it had been corrected by the most learned members of the society, and some *Chinese*. *Franciscus Noel* published, anno 1711, at *Prague*, the six *Libri Classici* of the *Chinese* empire [i]. The philosophers of the sect of *Confucius* endeavour to persuade the people that the creation and government of the world are effected by material causes, not to mention other unreasonable maxims with which they dishonour their Creator.

[i] *Baieri* Præf. Muf.

The *Roman* catholics have, by means of the jesuits and other learned men, converted many *Chinese* to their faith; but are now expelled the country, after having experienced the vicissitudes of favour and persecution; all except those who were allowed to stay in the empire (though not at court) in order to teach mathematics, and are, it is said, only about 20 in number. Others hide themselves in desarts, or in distant villages, waiting for the recovery of the liberty of teaching their doctrine.

The *Chinese* priests, who in their language are called *Wo-aw-siong*, pay their morning and evening worship in those idol temples which we call *Pagodas*. They are daily clothed in grey coats reaching down to their feet, with very wide sleeves. About their necks they wear a large string of beads. Their heads are every where shaved. In this dress they appear at the above places by hundreds, and go in pairs, one after another, several times round the altar, at which they sometimes stop, and with a low voice repeat their service, which they call *Wo-aw-siong-lam-king*: at which they sometimes fold their hands, and sometimes hold them up to heaven. This they continue for an an hour together, during which time they look at nobody. During service several *Chinese* instruments are played upon, at certain times. Sometimes they fall down three times with their faces to the ground, burn incense and sacrifice. They sometimes go about in the town and sacrifice in the houses, and on that occasion their dress is a little different. They do not marry, and eat neither flesh nor eggs. The chief priest of the whole empire is called *Wo-aw Siong Tao*. The people go into the *Pagoda* on certain festivals only, when they bring their sacrifices; but during service they stand at the doors, and look in through the rails. However, every body says his morning and evening prayer besides, both in the houses and in the boats, kneeling before their God; in the latter they light on this occasion a trough, or *Chinese* boat, which they call *Lintkyee*, of gold or silver paper, which they throw into the water; because, according to their opinion, it will turn into gold or silver if it is thrown into the sea when it is burnt during the music of the *Gungung*.

They have four holy feasts every year; among which is the lanthorn feast, which will be described hereafter.

The parents of a boy marry him sometimes when he is yet a child, and even before the children are born; in this case, two men whose wives are with child agree, that if one gets a son and the other a daughter the children are to marry one another, whether they be born with defects or become maimed afterwards, whether they be handsome or ugly. Or if a man has a little son, whom he would gladly see married, he goes to the father whose daughter he thinks most fit for his son, strikes a bargain with him about the daughter, and settles the day of his son's marriage. 'Till that day the bridegroom does not see his bride, but must be content with the choice of his father. The bridegroom receives his bride at his house door, and delivers her to his mother, or to some other women in the house, while he treats the men in another room. If he does not like his bride he may send her home again, but the father-in-law keeps the money which was paid for the bride. Before the *Chinese* give their daughters in marriage, they teach them to respect their fathers and mothers in law, to live peaceably with their sisters in law, to honour their husbands, to teach their children, to be compassionate towards their servants, to take care of their filk work, to be fparing, temperate, diligent, and patient, not to love pratling, nor to meddle with any thing which does not belong to their houfewifry. If they get a fon, they make great feafts, and treat fuch of their friends as have congratulated them on this account, and have made fome prefents. The third day, when the child is to be wafhed, the ceremony is ftill greater; they then in particular eat painted eggs (which are prefents of the grand-mother), comfits, and other prefents. If a man attains to 40 years of age and has no children, he may marry more wives than he has already, to prevent the extinction of his family, provided he is able to maintain them. He may ufe them as he pleafes, and fuffers no punifhment if he kills his own wife in anger.

NUPTIALS are likewife celebrated in the decked boats, which on this occafion are orna-mented as well as can be imagined, both with-in and without. They put little banners upon the deck of the boat, and hang it round with crowns, flowers, and fruits made of paper, and in the night-time lanthorns are placed on it. During this, feveral mufical inftruments are heard, in particular the *Gungung*, which is used on all occasions.

If a woman suffers herself to be deflowered, she is carried into the market by her superiors, as soon as it is known, and sold to the highest bidder; these are bought to be servant-maids for life, at the price of 100 dollars copper money, sometimes more and sometimes less.

Thieves and other offenders are punished with bamboo lashes, which punishment may be compared with the gantelope.

The malefactors are laid on the ground, and beaten with switches of split bamboo wood; and the *Chinese* ell being made of the same wood, a stroke with it is very ignominious in the eyes of a *Chinese*. I likewise saw another way of punishing a thief; a board was hung on his neck, and his hands were put through two holes in the board, and were screwed fast into them. He was carried about the streets in this posture for two months together, and was obliged to wait for his further punishment: behind the thief went one who was very probably the beadle, holding up money in both hands, undoubtedly to shew the people (who
come

come from all the streets) what the fellow's crime was.

ALMANACKS, or *Tong-sioc* of the *Chinese* [k], were sold in those streets where fruits were exposed to sale. The derivation of the word seems to denote, that they formerly may have carved their chronologies in wood, as we on our *Runic* sticks; for wood in the *Chinese* language is called *Sioe*, or *Si-e*. Three thousand almanacks are annually printed for each province. They are either smaller ones, or greater historical ones. I bought one of the latter sort for eight kandarin, about 12 stir. It was for the year 1752, or the 17th year, which they call *Daat sing kan long siapp sat miang*, or the great emperor *Kang-long's* 17th year, counting from the accession of the present emperor to the throne; for the *Chinese* begin a new period at the beginning of every emperor's reign. This year was to begin with them the fourth day of *February*. The 12 months are marked with large letters at the top of every page in the almanack; each day takes up a line, and in this is marked every thing which may be successfully undertaken on that day;

[k] *Bayer* de horis Sinicis. *Petrop.* 1735, 4to.

which are the best days for building, fishing, travelling, sowing, offering, bargaining, marrying, &c.

The first month hath	30 days.
The second,	29
The third,	30
The fourth,	29
The fifth,	29
The sixth,	29
The seventh,	30
The eighth,	29
The ninth,	30
The tenth,	30
The eleventh,	29
The twelfth,	30

Accordingly their year hath 354 days.

The 11 days which are wanting are supplied every third year, which has 13 months. An example of this is the present year 1751.

The *Chinese* divide the day into 12 hours, beginning at midnight; accordingly an hour of theirs is equal to two of ours.

In each town is a tower, and on it an hour-glass, with sand or water, by which the hours are divided.

Days and nights in this latitude being continually equal, we often longed for a thing which we do not take any notice of at home, to wit, the agreeable change of unequal days and seasons.

Soldiers are seldom seen, though the army is said to be very numerous. Those which I saw, had only sabres, and their dress was not distinguishable from that of the other *Chinese*, except by their caps which were like those of grenadiers.

The *Chinese* bought arms of the *Europeans*, especially old muskets and guns, at a very moderate price, and they sold their air guns of yellow brass.

According to *Du Halde's* account, the *Chinese* knew nothing of the management of cannons before the year 1621, when they got three cannons from the *Portugueze* at *Macao*. In the year 1636, when the roman catholics were severely persecuted, and the *Tartars* made inroads into *China*, the government had notice that the jesuits could shoot with guns; father *Adam-schall* was desired to assist them; however,

however, he excused himself with his unexperience in those matters. But *Ferdinand Verbiest*, a *French* jesuit, and president of the mathematical tribunal, very successfully fired 130 cannon shot, for which the emperor allowed the free exercise of his religion.

HUSBANDRY, especially agriculture and gardening, are in a most flourishing state; but as the *Chinese* sow and plant such herbs and trees as we can scarcely maintain in our hothouses, our observations must be less advantageous than if they made use of the same plants for their food as we do. Their emperors have always shewn great regard for agriculture and planting, and even put their own hands to work. *Du Halde* relates that the emperor *Yao* (who, according to the accounts of the *Chinese*, lived about 4000 years ago) once asked his courtiers whom he should appoint his successor? upon which they proposed his eldest son: but the emperor knowing that his son's disposition would prevent him from being a good prince, offered this dignity to one of his most faithful ministers, who excused himself, and proposed a young country fellow, who in his opinion was most able, on account of his fidelity and prudence; for as

he

he was able to command his paffions under a bad father, unnatural mother, and quarrelfome brother, fo he would likewife have fufficient ftrength of mind to direct the helm of an empire. They fay that he really afcended the throne, and that during his reign he took great care of husbandry, made feveral canals for the convenience of the country, and wrote feveral books on agriculture. His fucceffors have always contributed more and more towards the improvement of the country: in particular the emperor *Ven-ti*, who lived 179 years before the birth of *Chrift*. He affembled his council, and confulted with its members how his fubjects, after deftructive wars, might be moft ftrongly induced to practice agriculture. Their refolution was, that he himfelf fhould give them a good example. Accordingly he himfelf began ploughing, and the queen planted mulberry trees. This is looked upon as the foundation of a great feftival which is held every year in *China*. The emperor goes into the fields in fpring, and ploughs fome acres to encourage the countrymen; the nobles who accompany him have each their bufinefs; one prepares the facrifice, another makes the fpeech which the emperor is to deliver on this occafion; another

erects

erects the tent in which the emperor is to eat; and another gets 40 or 50 old venerable peasants together, who are presented to the emperor; the younger ones direct the plough, lead the oxen, and get the corn ready which is to be sowed. The regard of the emperor, and of the greatest lords, for agriculture is such, that when deputies are sent to the governors, the emperor always enquires in what condition agriculture is. The governor of *Peking* often visits the fields, and is greatly rejoiced in case he finds all in a good condition. The emperor *Cang-ti* particularly favoured countrymen; he ordered the governors annually to send in an account of what was most remarkable, because he intended to reward the diligence of the husbandmen with peculiar honours, so that they should be dressed like the king's servants, visit the governor of the city, sit down in his presence, and drink tea with him; and after their deaths be handsomely buried, and a decent monument erected to their memories.

THIS nation prepares its food in the most simple manner: rice, which they make use of instead of bread, and which is their principal food, they boil in water, letting the water

run off, and eating the fwelled rice quite
warm. The people in the boats feat themfelves about the pot, each has a large tea difh
of coarfe porcellane, into which they put the
rice with a fpoon. They hold the tea difh to
their mouths with the left hand; and between
the two firft fingers of the right hand, they
hold two flender fticks, almoft a foot long, with
which they cram one difh full after another
into their mouths.. Between this they eat a
bit of fifh, bacon, or a reddifh fruit like figs,
but longer, and almoft every where equally
thick, called *Ay-qua* or *Kea* by the *Chinefe*;
befides this they alfo make ufe of a fort of
greens, which they eat out of another faucer
along with the rice. The workmen in the
factories feat themfelves in the yard in a circle,
after each has filled his pot out of a great tub,
which ftands by and is full of frefh boiled
rice: this is eaten in the fame manner one
pot full after another, along with the other
victuals. Thofe who are fomewhat higher in
quality make ufe of tables and chairs; but
have neither table-cloth, knife, fork, or
napkins; but handkerchiefs fupply the place
of the latter. Knives are unneceffary at table, fince they eat no bread. Fifh, bacon,
&c. are cut into little pieces, and put upon

the

the table like the greens, in tea dishes, or little pots, that every one may take what he likes best. Spoons are of use. Their meat has no sauce, nor do they make soups, or the like. Two little sticks for each person, and some tea dishes or pots with meat cut in pieces, make the whole arrangement in a collation. They drink either tea without sugar, or a wretched sort of brandy called *samsu*, during their meals. And with this they treat one another, so that no one drinks off his own cup, but each carries his cup to the other's mouth and lets him drink, and the other returns this civility with his cup of *samsu*. They make no compliments before or after meals. They eat hastily, and take three or four good meals a day. Their provisions are not dear, and it is said a workman may maintain himself upon two stivers a day, (1*d*.) at least one who lives upon plucking of tea leaves will scarce be able to get more a day.

Pork and fish are the common food the *Chinese* eat with their rice. But flesh is less usual; the most uncommon is beef, then goat's flesh and mutton, next rabbits, &c. hares and venison I have never seen. It is said the *Chinese* like horse-flesh, dogs, and rats.

Frogs,

FROGS, called *Kopp-na* by the *Chinese*, are sold here in every street. They tie them together with a thread about their bodies, and carry them alive in baskets; and they are the dainties of the *Chinese*, though they are little different from our common frogs, as appears from the following description:

RANA (*Chinensis*) *palmis tetradactylis fissis, plantis hexadactylis digito indice reliquis longiore.* The *paws* have four distinct *fingers*, which are almost of equal length; but the second and fourth is a little shorter: on the feet are six joined toes, these are palmated: the first and third are equally long; the fourth is shorter; the fifth still shorter; the sixth, or innermost, the shortest; but the second the longest of all. The body is warty at the top, with streaks of black brown; white below: the throat is white, speckled with black: the belly is white, without spots, except on the sides: the eyes are black, the irides yellow gold: the fore and hind legs blackish yellow, with whitish spots on the outward side. The [i]*palmæ* and [k]*plantæ* are flesh-coloured, and inclining to black. I here am put in mind of what I read in the *Turkish Spy*, *Lond.* 1748, vol.

[i] Paws.   [k] Feet.

vol. iii. p. 167. viz. that the *French* in 1646, began to eat frogs and mushrooms, being pressed by hunger.

BUFFALOES (*Bos Indicus*) are used to plough with, and foreigners buy them to kill. These oxen are generally wilder than ours; however I ventured through the midst of a whole herd of them. They are generally grey, their hams almost strait, somewhat angulated. A buffaloe costs at present 10 tel, and a calf two tel and five mess.

THEIR goats are (as far as I could see) no way different from ours.

THE sheep of this country have little horns, and short tails, which are one lump of fat, and oblong. These sheep are no bigger than the *Swedish* sheep, but grow so fat on the dry *Chinese* mountains, that mutton tastes better here than in any other place in the world: and they likewise sell dearer than in any other country. A sheep costs here 15 plates, and sometimes more. At present it is sold at four tel and eight mess, which is thought very cheap. In a climate which is so warm, where wool is not wanted, and cotton and silk are plentiful, they are less necessary.

THE

THE *Chinese Swine* (*Sus Chinenfis*) are already so well described[1] that I can add nothing. They are generally either black or white. They propagate more than ours, and are cleanly; for which reason they are kept in houses like dogs. They also sometimes go into the streets, but never wallow in dirty places; however, I have been told by one of our husbandmen, that when they come to *Sweden* and see the uncleanness of our swine, they sometimes take to the same manner of living. The *Chinese* hams are much esteemed by the *Europeans*. The katty is commonly sold for one mess, or a piastre apiece, which is nine dollars and six ocre copper money; but they are very little, and what they want in weight is made up by a piece of string to which the ham is fastened. The goodness of the hams doubtless depends upon the manner of salting and smoaking, but likewise much upon the food of the animal, by which they get a better taste, and more flesh. It is more agreeable to nature to allow the animal during its fattening some moderate exercise, than

[1] *Linnæi* Iter *Westrogothic.* p. 62, and Iter *Scanicum*, p. 72.

to confine it in a narrow ftye; in which, though they get more fat, yet it is not fo good; and who knows whether it is not more unwholefome?

CHICKEN of feveral forts are to be met with here, and are fold at fuch a price, that a pound came to about 10 ftivers. But here, as well as in every other tranfaction with the *Chinefe*, you muft take care of being cheated. One of my countrymen can teftify this, who buying fome chicken, the feathers of which were curioufly curled, found in a few days time, the feathers growing ftraight, and that his chicken were of the moft common fort. The *Chinefe* had curled the feathers up like a wig, a little before he was going to fell them. This is an inftance of a *Chinefe* who fpares neither time nor pains if he can only gain money, whether by fair or fraudulent means.

EGGS were fold at three ftivers apiece, (two *cas*.)

THE *Chinefe* goofe is not unknown to us (*Anas cygnoides β. orientalis*); fome had yellow bills, but they are ufually black. Compare with this *Linn.* Iter *Weftrogoth.* p. 145.

THE

THE *Chinese quails* (*Tetrao Chinensis*) have already been mentioned as being used instead of muffs by the *Chinese*. We bought several females to make into pies on our voyage. We gave three kandarin apiece for them. The cock quails are larger, dearer, and more scarce.

CONUS (*Chinensis*) *striis transversis retrorsum imbricatis*, called *Ha-ing* by the *Chinese*, is a sort of almost round shells; the animal of which is taken out, put into water, and sold in every street by the name of *Ha-in-yo*.

As the *Chinese* live mostly on roots, fruits, and pot-herbs, the country hereabouts is almost all garden. Besides rice, sugar-canes, and *Chinese* potatoes, I have observed the following sorts:

PEASE of several kinds are sown here, and likewise two species of beans, which are not usual in our country, for they require more warmth than our climate affords. I have perfected some however in *Sweden* by a hot-bed. One sort is called by the *Europeans*

CALLVANSES

CALLVANSES (*Dolichos Sinensis* [m]). They are planted on dry hills, and are treated like dwarf kidney beans. They do not grow high, and therefore do not much want to be supported; this however is done in some places, and especially where they stand in the open fields, which have no hedge or fence round; nor are fences necessary, as the cattle are always kept in the pastures by herdsmen. These beans are of the smallest kind, and are quite white, except the germen, which is black, but white in the middle. The *Europeans* buy them in great quantities, and make use of them in their return from *China* instead of pease. They have thin husks, and are very palatable. A katty, which answers to a pound we use for grocery, was sold for two kandarin, or about three stivers.

LACK-TAO [n] is the *Chinese* name of another sort of beans, or rather pease, which are much less than our wild vetches. The plant itself grows like the former, upright, and

[m] *Dolichos* (*Sinensis*) caule erecto ramosissimo, pedunculis erectis multifloris, leguminibus pendulis; Chinensibus *Tao*.

[n] Phaseolus Max. Mungo Persarum.

wants

wants no support in case it is not too much exposed to the wind. It is treated as the former. With these pease they feed the parrots. Among the many seeds which I brought to *Sweden*, was a kind of small green pease, which was so nicely eat up by the worms at my arrival, that nothing but the husks were left, which served as a nidus to the little beetles, with which they were almost filled. They were doubtless stifled in the paper into which I had put the pease.

FDAU-FU, or *Tou-fu*, which has been mentioned page 218; was sold by pieces in several places. The *Chinese* shewed me a sort of small pease, which they call *U-ang-teo*, and of which cheese is said to be made, though the name gives reason to conjecture that it has been made from *Tao*, which are the *Chinese* beans, or *Callvanses*.

LING-KAMM, or *Leng-ka* among the *Chinese*, (*Trapa natans**) is a fruit which looks like two horns put together, and has a kernel in the middle. It was sold in the shops which we should call hucksters, and eaten by poor

* Trapa bicornis, Vid. Plum. Icon. T. 67.

people. I saw in one place a very small tea pot, whose handle was made of this fruit.

KAMM-KATT is the name of a sort of small lemons, which are not much larger than cherries.

AYQUA, see page 297.

SAMM-NIM is the name which is here given to an oblong, yellow, sourish fruit, with five deep furrows (*Averrhoa Bilimbi*) which has the quality of lemons, but is sooner spoiled. The *Chinese* make a conserve of this fruit, because it then becomes more palatable. I have been told that it is called *Kala-mang*.

LEMTYES (*Citrus medica*). With this compare page 208 [p]. Though the *Chinese* are forbid to sell punch prepared with the juice of *Lem-tyes* to the men on board the ships, yet

---

[p] The *stem* is round, somewhat rough, ash-coloured, with pale streaks. The *boughs* grow in no particular order, are expanded, bent backwards, and have seldom any thorns. The *young shoots* have strait thorns, which are very sharp, and stand either alternately or in the corners of the boughs. The *leaves* are alternate, lanceolato-oblong, petiolated, somewhat emarginated. The *petioli* are sharpened, and of an equal breadth.

they

they hand many a bowl full through the port holes; but sometimes the sellers have the mortification of not being paid for their forbidden goods, and the buyers get dyfentaries or other bad difeafes; for the juice which is taken before the fruit is ripe for this purpofe, is very unwholefome. The trees which are fold in pots are feldom above a yard high, and looked like lemon trees. A hundred of thofe fruits were fold for one ftiver and a half.

HERE are two forts of *China oranges* (*Citrus finenfis*). The firft is that called the *Mandarin-orange*, whofe peel is quite loofe, and the *Chinefe* call them *Kamm*, and it is the beft kind. The peel of the other fort fits clofe; it is called *Tiang*, or rather *Kang*, the better to diftinguifh them from oranges.

HERE alfo are two forts of *Lemons* (*Citrus decumana*) See page 150, which are called *Tao* by the *Chinefe*. The firft is round, and its name is *Lo-yao*; and the fecond, called *Hanyao*, is long, and is ufually offered as a facrifice to their idols.

REINETTES, and other forts of apples, are eaten in the country; but I doubt whether they grew about *Canton*.

LAT-YEE is the *Chinese* name of a fruit, which is here eaten with tea. This fruit taftes almoft like a fort of our plumbs, and looks like large gall-apples, covered with a brownifh, thin, and warty fkin.

LANG-AN is lefs than *Lat-yee*; they have a fmooth fkin, and fweet pulp, as in the *Lat-yee* q.

PLAINTAIN tree, (*Mufa paradifiaca*) fee page 151, is called *Tfeu* by the *Chinese*. When the yellow fkin is pulled off, which muft be done by the fingers without a knife, that the iron may not alter the tafte, the fruit itfelf is as foft as dough, and of an agreeable fweetnefs. It is believed that *Adam* after his tranfgreffion in paradife covered himfelf with the fpreading leaves of this plant r.

MANGO (*Mangifera Indica*) is the name of that fruit which is in *China* fold by the name

q An Cuffambium? *Rumph*. lib. i. p. 154. T. 57.

r The *Plaintain tree* has flowered for the firft time in the year 1755, in the *Upfal* garden, and has alfo brought forth ripe fruits.

of *Quaimao*, and in the *Javanic* language is called *Po*.

GUAYAVA (*Psidium Guajava*) is likewise eaten here [1].

ORIENTAL *Mustard* (*Sinapis orientalis*.)

PACK-LA are *Chinese olives*.

TAMARINDS, (*Tamarindus Indica*) in *Java* called *Sunda assa*: but the tree and fruit are called *Thampahou*.

GOURDS, *Melons*, and *Water-melons*, which are red on the inside.

LECK of two sorts, viz. *Tsong*, and *Lofra*. The katty is sold for two *kanderin*.

RADISHES. A *kanderin* is the price of a hundred of these roots.

LONG *turneps*, at one stiver and a half the hundred.

[1] The inhabitants of *Java* call it *Nyamba-cuneng*, *Rumph.* I. p. 141. T. 47.

CARROTS of the white sort were not very good. The *Chinese* pound of them was sold for four stivers.

GNAO, or *Laen-gao* (*Nymphæa Nelumbo*) is a sort of white roots of the thickness of carrots, but longer, articulated like a bamboo-stick, and hollow in the inside. Poor people eat them raw, but they are not very palatable. They are planted in a moist clay ground.

O-O-TAO are roots so called by the *Chinese*; they cannot be eaten raw, because the acidity would prevent the action of swallowing. None of us *Europeans* would taste them.

BAMBOO *roots* (*Arundo bambos*) is what we call *Asia*, when preserved with salt, vinegar, leek, and *Guinea* pepper (*Capsicum*). This is the only root of all those above mentioned which we make use of. A pot of *Asia* is sold here for eleven dollars copper money.

PRESERVED *ginger*, or the *Kaong* of the *Chinese*.

DRY

DRY *ginger*. This is valued at six stivers per pound.

FANN-SIO, or *Fay-sio* [t], the *Chinese* potatoes, grow with long tendrils, which they extend along the ground. They are multiplied either by planting the tendrils which are cut off in the ground; or by cutting the roots as we do. These potatoes are quite different from ours, and seem to be natives of a warmer climate, for they never flower in *China*, so that they would hardly grow with us, though they are more palatable, and perhaps more wholesome than ours. They are planted in the dry sandy fields, at a distance from each other, manured with human dung, and kept clean from weeds, which rule is observed in all plantations. A hundred *Chinese* potatoes were sold for about one stiver and a half.

TDAI-SIO [u], or *Yams* (*Dioscorea alata*) is a dry root of different shapes, about as big as

[t] This plant is, to my certain knowledge, the *Spanish* potatoe, *Convolvulus batatas*, Linn. or *Convolvulus radice tuberosa esculenta minore purpurea*, Sloane Cat. Mill. Dict. ii. c. fr. *Kalm's American* voyage, Part II.

[u] The stems wind to the left, and arise between leaf and stalk. The leaves are opposite to each other, cordato-

two fifts, sometimes larger, sometimes less. In many places of *India* it is used instead of bread. The katty was at present sold for a kanderin and two kas. These roots are planted like the potatoes on high places, about half a yard asunder, and a quarter of a yard deep. They grow ten months; and when such a root is taken out, it weighs some pounds. In winter they keep them in sand. Before they are planted, the rotten parts are cut off; and before they are eaten, they are put into water, that their bitter taste may in part be extracted. The lowermost joint of the root is pentagonal, the next hexagonal, the third heptagonal, the fourth tetragonal, which I observed in those roots which I planted in pots, and took with me to *Sweden*; which grew very well. If they bear so great a change of climate, they may very likely in time be inured to our air and short summers, and be of no small advantage to our husbandry.

Sivv, *Chinese* truffles [x], are carried about for sale in the streets.

sagitated or heart-shaped, though almost like the head of an arrow, pointed, and have three strong nerves.

[x] Confer. Siooro tubera esculenta. *Kæmph. Amœn.* p. 832.

CHINESE

CHINESE *cabbage* [y], is very like our white cabbage. Among all the cabbages which we bought for our ship I did not see one head but they were all in flower. This makes me doubt whether the white cabbage, which in our country requires more than one year before it arrives to fructification, may not by the warmth of this country blossom the first year, instead of forming heads.

CELERY and *Spinage*, which is here called *Bout-say*.

CONVOLVULUS *reptans*, by the *Chinese* called *Or-say*, was sold to our men instead of spinage, but is, in regard to genus, totally different from the true spinage. This creeping *Convolvulus* grows spontaneously every where, in ditches, and low places: of the true spinage I only saw the seeds. We daily eat of the new fashioned spinage, without suffering the least inconvenience. This may give us a hint to make use of our common *Convolvulus* in the

---

[y] *Brassica Chinensis* or as the *Chinese* call it *Kay-lann*: the leaves of the calyx are alternately narrower. Another sort, which the *Chinese* call *Pack-se-a*, with a bulbose root, is sold here likewise.

fields,

fields, which is very like this *Chinese* spinage, instead of true spinage.

The leaf of a kind of pepper called *Betel* (*Piper betle* Linnæi) is wrapt about the nuts, which the *Chinese* are continually chewing.

Chinese *mushrooms* [z]; of these the katty, or pound, is sold at *Canton* for two *mes*, but they took four kanderin more per katty when they brought them on board the ships.

Here is no other water than that which is taken out of the river. For six hours together the salt water is brought up into it by the tide, and during that time its water is by no means drinkable. And though the water required for common uses is taken during the six hours of ebbing, yet it is somewhat brackish and muddy. Thus the people here, for want of good water, are obliged to boil the bad, and to mend its taste with some tea.

The *Chinese* always drink tea without sugar or milk. The fresh *Honam*, or *Canton* tea, which is not agreeable to other peoples palate, is most usual in town. They make use of no

---

[z] Agaricus Chinensis, cfr. Fungus, *Kæmph.* 832.

tea-pot, but only a tea-kettle, which they put into a wooden veffel, to keep it warm the longer; but the poor have none but thefe wooden veffels, without any brafs or copper kettle in it.

CHINESE *brandy*, (*Skee-et fa oa*) which we likewife call *famfu*, is never drunk except at meals, and inftead of tea. It is unneceffary here to hang up figns to denote the houfes where fpirituous liquors are fold; for the difagreeable fmell of the *famfu* is a fufficient guide.

THE *Chinefe* wine, which our *Eaft India* traders call *Mandarin* wine, is fqueezed out of a fruit which is here called *Paufio*, and reckoned the fame with our grapes. This wine was fo difagreeable to us, that none of us would drink it. The *Eaft India* fhips never fail taking wine to *China*, where they often fell it to confiderable advantage. The *Xeres*[a] wine, for which at *Cadiz* we paid 13 piaftres an anchor, we fold here at 33 piaftres an anchor. But in this cafe you ftand a chance of having your tons fplit by the heat during the voyage. I have fince been told, that in 1754, the price of wine was fo much lowered at *Can-*

[a] Sherry.

ton, that our people could with difficulty reimburse themselves. The *Spaniards* send wines to *Manilla* and *Macao*, whence the *Chinese* fetch a considerable quantity, especially for the court of *Peking*. The wine of *Xeres* is more agreeable here than any other sort, on account of its strength, and because it is not liable to change by heat. The *Chinese* are very temperate in regard to wine, and many dare not empty a single glass, at least not at once. Some, however, have learned from foreigners to exceed the limits of temperance, especially when they drink with them at free cost.

BEER, and *small beer*, is not brewed in this country: all the strong beer which is sold at *Canton* comes from *England*, in very strong casks.

ARRACK is well known among us, since the use of punch has been introduced. This liquor comes from *Goa* and *Batavia* to *China*, but is not, as some have related, made in *China*, of rice alone. It might sooner be imagined that it is made of *Areca*, since this tree is called *Araquero* by the *Portugueze*. If *Arrack* was distilled of rice, the *Chinese* (who have

have such plenty of rice) would, without doubt, take this advantage from others, and keep it to themselves. These people do not want industry. But to make *arrack*, not only rice, and sugar canes, but likewise cocoa-nuts are required, as I have been told by a person that comes from *Batavia*. While a sufficient degree of heat is wanted in *China* for the *Cocoa-tree*, its inhabitants will be obliged to fetch *arrack* from those countries where this sort of palm grows spontaneously; among which *Goa*, on the *Indian* coast, and *Batavia*, on the isle of *Java*, are the most noted. The *arrack* from *Goa* is weaker, paler, more scarce, and commonly dearer, because that place is the furthest off. The *arrack* from *Batavia* is like *French* brandy, but is so variable, that sometimes it is but half as strong as at others, though the price continues the same. For this reason the buyers ought to provide themselves with an instrument, which by its rising or falling shews how strong the *arrack* is. Our *East India* traders buy the *Batavia arrack* from the *Dutch* ships, and the *Goa arrack* from the *English*; but in *Suratte* it may be had at first hand. A liggar of *Batavia arrack* was sold from 44 to 50 piastres; and a quart of it came to 12 dollars of copper money,

money, instead of six plates, which it was sold at about two years ago. The duty upon *arrack* is three dollars of copper money *per* quart. The company has lately begun to carry *arrack* to *Sweden* on its own account; all was conveyed before by private persons, under the name of provision for the voyage. It is known to almost every one how punch is made; but, that it may be observed for the future where it is made to its greatest perfection, I will mention the true proportion of its constituent parts[a]. To a quart of boiling water, half a pint of *arrack* is taken, to which one pound of sugar, and five or six lemons, or instead of them as many tamarinds as are necessary to give it the true acidity, are added: a nutmeg is likewise grated into it. The punch which is made for the men in our ship was heated with red hot iron balls which were thrown into it. Those who can afford it, make punch a usual drink after dinner. While we stayed in *China*, we drunk it at dinner in-

[a] If the *English* reader should be inclined to smile at seeing a receipt for punch so gravely introduced, let him consider that it proves the simple and abstemious life of the *Swedes*, and how little they are acquainted with those luxuries so common to the rest of *Europe*. F.

stead

ſtead of the wine which the company allowed the firſt table.

The *Chineſe* drink no coffee, except with the *Europeans*, though the berries might be procured from *Java*.

Turkish *tobacco* (*Nicotiana ruſtica*) which has the colour of our dried *tobacco*, is univerſally ſmoaked in *China*, both by the old and young. Their pipes are long and black; the heads are very ſmall, have the ſhape of the cups of acorns, and are made of white metal. They very often ſmoak while their tobacco pipes hang on a ribband on one ſide.

Blindness is eſteemed the infirmity of this country. Authors relate, that many *Chineſe* are blind; but I have not obſerved it. It is true, they may ſtay in their houſes; but in the ſtreets I never ſaw more than three or four blind old beggar-women, and one or two blind children, among ſo many thouſand people. It was lucky that I found ſo few, as a ſtranger could elſe ſcarcely paſs. For a blind old woman comes with a wooden diſh in her hand, and cries, *Lou-taya Tſlaves-lamma*; if ſhe then catches a ſtranger, by the directions of the

other

other *Chinese*, she hangs with all her might about his feet or body, and cries, with an agreeable look, *Palata, Senior* [b], which signifies *Money, Sir*, and does not loose her hold till she has been satisfied. Some are of opinion that the eating of rice is the occasion of blindness. Perhaps it is the effects of the steam rising from the hot rice. But why should not the same happen in other places of *India*, where the same food is made use of? It may be ascribed to many other causes. The husbandmen, who have a great deal of business with human dung, may have their eyes hurt by it. The japanners too may be injured by the strong varnish, which affects the eyes worse than horse-radish. The strong smoak arising every evening from their perfuming chips, may likewise contribute to it. I once asked a *Chinese* about it, and he told me that the washing with warm water, which they do every morning, was the cause of it. But none of the causes can be considered as universal, for most of the blind people are, according to the accounts of the *Chinese* themselves, born blind. And in this case, the cause is to be looked for in the mother.

[b] From the *Spanish* words *Plata Señor*.

FEVERS

FEVERS, and other diseases usual in our country, are likewise not unfrequent here. But those who have had an opportunity of being better acquainted with the sick in this town, are better able to describe their distempers. It is said that a consumption is in this country cured by a glue of asses skin, called *Okeeao*. This glue has a very bad taste, and you either take a piece of it into your mouth, or dissolve it in tea.

WOUNDS and sores are the worst disorders here. Poor people who are plagued with them, must not only suffer the greatest pains during the great heats, for want of surgeons; but must likewise carry their disgrace about them; and only cover themselves with mats, when they are obliged to go about the streets.

WOOD is seldom or never made use of, but coals supply its place; and their consumption is so much the greater. There is no occasion for a fire in the rooms, except in the most rigorous cold, or on account of sick people. On this occasion the room is warmed by means of a little stove, which is set in the middle of the room. These little stoves are

VOL. I.   Y   extremely

extremely convenient, and deserve to be made known universally in our country. Some of our company took such stoves with them to *Gothenburgh*, as models for those who might want to know their construction.

There is no occasion to fear any beasts of prey; but the men have assumed their ferocity, and assault strangers frequently with stones and insults. Murders are seldom heard of: but a *Chinese* makes very little of stripping people to the shirt. I here will add an account dated at *Canton*, *November* the 7th, 1747. " Captain *Congreve* being happily ar-
" rived at *Canton*, with the *English* ship *Onslow*,
" took a walk upon the *French Island* (an isle
" near the road where the *Europeans* anchor),
" where he was soon attacked by some *Chinese*.
" They took, without much ado, all his money,
" gold, silver, and buckles; they cut the gilt
" buttons off his coat, and he would hardly
" have preserved his finger, if he had not
" pulled a ring off with all his might and
" given it them. After he had been quite
" stripped, he returned to his boat. But the
" next day, being *Sunday*, he armed his boats,
" and landed in the same isle with sixty of his
" men, who had fixed their bayonets, and
were

"were provided with four small cannons: he
"marched his men before *Wam-pu*, a town in
"this isle, and began to fire. The inhabi-
"tants were immediately put into the greatest
"confusion, and the principal mandarins im-
"mediately came to him, to desire him to
"cease the attack, being very willing to give
"him satisfaction. The captain told them,
"that he had been stripped the day before,
"and now was come to revenge himself and
"other people who had been insulted by
"those rogues; that he would not cease till
"satisfaction should be made him by the pu-
"nishment of the malefactors. During this
"time, the robbers were searched for in the
"town, and four of them were apprehended,
"who, in the presence of the captain, had
"their hands and feet tied together, and were
"sent to *Canton* to receive further punish-
"ment [c]."

PLAYS were acted *gratis* in the streets. A scaffold is built quite across the streets, here and there, but commonly at the corner houses, from one corner to the other. The

[c] A like example see in Lord *Anson's* Voyage round the World, p. 360, &c. *D. Schreber.*

scaffold is about six yards above the ground, so that any one may with ease pass under it. It is closely covered with boards, and chairs are placed on it for the actors and musicians. The players generally wear long gowns, and sometimes are dressed like harlequins. The inhabitants are no doubt better pleased with their singing, bawling, and mimickries, than the *Europeans*, who are used to see their own theatrical entertainments much more skilfully conducted. These plays are acted in the beginning of autumn, both in the streets on account of good success in trade, and likewise in houses after meals, to inspire the guests with mirth. The spectators sit upon the roofs or in the windows, those excepted who stop in the streets while passing. The *Chinese* play at cards sometimes; but their cards have a different form from ours, and have but half their breadth. They likewise play at another game which requires a great deal of thought, and goes on very slowly, and is managed with two stones, which are moved on a board, somewhat after the manner of chess.

THE children play at night with their birds, kites, and butterflies of paper, which they send up into the air.

September

September the 8th, 1751.

TO-DAY, being the fifteenth Sunday after Trinity, I preached in the factory in the suburbs of *Canton*, and some *Chinese* came to hear me. In the afternoon I passed the river in a boat, and landed at the little town of *Holam*, or *Honam*. Here was a large pagoda, or *Chinese* place of worship (if there are not several one above another); round about it were built houses for the priests and their stewards. Between the shore and these houses is a broad way, or great space, surrounded with large high trees, which were called *Leean-see*. At the entrance stood two gilt images, somewhat bigger than life. On the sides lay large blocks of wood, which were intended for the imperial palace at *Peking*.

My company sat down at the uppermost *Pagoda* and eat some water-melons, but I had a greater inclination towards the plants that grew hereabouts; for which reason I went to the other side of the house. Here I was met by a *Chinese*, who offered me a filled tobacco pipe; but, on my refusing to accept of it, he took hold of my coat, and endeavoured with all his might to take my knee-buckles. I at last got rid of this fellow, who, however endeavoured to do me a favour in return, and set a number of boys at me, who pelted me with sand and pebbles. I was therefore obliged to join my company, and give over my amusement. In the mean while I had found the following plants:

Mirabilis odorata, which grew in the same situation as nettles generally do in our country.

Convolvulus hederaceus.

Scirpus glomeratus.

Nymphæa Nelumbo, growing in a ditch in the yard, which was dry.

NEAR this place was a garden, but neither entreaties nor money could procure me an entrance. We saw *Lemon* trees, and the *Nymphæa*, through the door. We went to the house where the surveyor of it lived. Here was a little gilt human figure, on an altar, which was one of the *lares* of this *Chinese*. We were well received in his room: and he immediately ordered a dish of tea without sugar, and a tobacco-pipe to be given us, but did not desire us to sit down. We were afterwards presented with two sorts of fruit, which

in

in their language are called *La-tyce* and *Long-an* [d], and which have already been mentioned. We went further on to the right, into a little wood, confifting moftly of *Bamboo* trees, of which our light *Bamboo* walking-fticks are made, which we get from the *Chinefe*. The wood is light and exceeding tough, for which reafon it is more ufed than any other fort. The *Chinefe* cover their boats with it, and build their warehoufes, called *Bancfhals*, near *Wam-pu*, for the *European* fhips, of that fort of wood; and their own houfes are partly of the fame. It fupplies them with fticks to carry any thing upon, for chairs, beds, tables, rails, fails, angling-rods, hats, cafes for guns, fans, weavers combs, painting-brufhes, bowers, fpouts, and troughs for cattle; in which latter cafe, the wood is fplit afunder. Thefe *Reed-trees* are of all fizes, from the bignefs of a quill, to that of a yard round, and more; and many yards long. The tree flowers, as the *Chinefe* fay, every fixtieth year only [e]. It appeared to me that there are two forts of this tree in this country: one grew on the hills, no

---

[d] The leaves of this tree are palmated, and have eleven lanceolated *laciniæ*, fmooth at top, and downy below. The flowers grow in clufters, and have five filaments.

[e] In the year 1754 I got fome flowers from *China*.

higher than about two yards, and is very ramose and full of spines [f] ; and the other in lower places, as high as eighteen feet, and without spines [g]. We went through the little wood of *Bamboo* trees, and came to a high even spot, where the *Chinese* buried their dead.

Some coffins stood above the ground, and were put close to the trees like bee-hives. They occasioned a stench, which made me keep off. In this manner they bury those whose kindred is either unknown, or who come from very distant parts.

In the burying-place I found

Euphorbia neriifolia, which is used for hedges.

Solanum diphyllum.

Hibiscus ficulneus.

Frutex baccis albis, foliis obverse ovatis.

Nyctanthes hirsuta: the *calyx* is cylindrical, sexfid, with equal *laciniæ.* The *corollæ* have

---

[f] Arundo arbor spinosa, *Rumph.* iv. p. 14. t. 11.

[g] Arundo arbor fera, *Rumph.* iv. p. 16. t. 3. cfr. Gron. Flor. orient. 22, 23, *Rauwolf.* iter. p. 97.

eight oblong pointed *laciniæ*, which are shorter than the tube: the filaments are short: the *antheræ* are oblong, and longer than the filaments. The leaves are elliptically lanceolated, frequently oval, undulated, opposite. The flower stalks stand between the leaves and stem, (*axillares*).

Curcuma Chinensis.

Gratiola Virginica.

Citrus aurantium.

Clematis Chinensis: it has many characteristics in common with the *Clematis vitalba*; but the leaves are narrow, lanceolated, and the flowers smaller.

Achyranthes Chinensis: the calyx is double, and longer than the pentapetalous corolla, which it includes: the exterior calyx, or flower-cup, is less and bifid; the interior quinquifid: the flowers grow at the top of the stalks, in clusters: the flower-stalks proceed from the corner of the leaves: the leaves are lanceolated, opposite, venose, smooth: the stem is red.

Achyranthes lappacea, fol. oppositis.

Carpesium abrotanoides.

Sida spinosa.

Polygonum

Polygonum Chinenſe.
Vitex Negundo.
Poa Chinenſis.
Poa tenella.

In ſhady places:
Canna Indica.
Caſſica ſophora.
Hedyſarum Gangeticum.
Apluda mutica.

Panicum arboreſcens, which grew out of the wall, is a ſort of graſs of an odd ſort; for it grows to ten or twelve feet high, and is very ramoſe.

As night advanced, we were obliged to return to *Canton,* for which reaſon I reſerved my amuſement for another day.

PHALÆNA *atlas* Linn. is one of the fineſt moths which can be met with [h]. I found ſome of them in a merchant's ſhop: they were all alive, upon a branch of the *Nerium*

---

[h] Cfr. Petiv. Gazophyl. nat. et artis, decas I. t. 8. f. 7. Papilio Indicus maximus, Valentini Muſeum, ii. p. 168. t. 54.

Oleander,

Oleander, and suffered themselves to be carried on it to the factory, where I stuck them upon pins; but the windows being open in the night, a bat came in and eat them all but the wings. However I got some afterwards in a little box of insects, which the *Chinese* bring to sell. These boxes were made of *Tya-mock*, and other coarse wood, without covering, and lined with paper. Such a box full of butterflies, the *Chinese* sold at half a piastre. In the box were about ten or twelve sorts, but many of each sort. In their shops are no *Hemiptera* except *Cicada Chinensis*, nor any *Coleoptera* except *Buprestis maxima*. Perhaps it is the opinion of the *Chinese*, that other insects do not strike the eye so much as butterflies. I seldom found any but butterflies in the fields; but it is probable that others may be met with in spring, though they were not visible in the other seasons of the year. The butterflies which were exposed to sale in the afore-mentioned boxes were:

Papilio Helena.
——— *Deiphobus.*
——— *Dissimilis.*
——— *Similis.*

Papi-

Papilio Tryphe.
——— Agamemnon.
——— C. Aureum.
——— Orythia.
——— Pammon.
——— Aonis.
——— Leucothoë.
——— Demoleus.
——— Troilus.
——— Paris.
——— Midamus.
——— Mineus.
——— Euippe.
——— Almana.
——— Plexippus.
——— Chryfippus.
——— Philoctetes.

The 10th of *September*.

THE weather was fine and clear, such as it had been for some days past.

THE fruit of the *Avicennia tomentofa*, which by our apothecaries is called *Anacardium orientale*, was brought hither in a *Swedifh* fhip from *Suratte*. This fruit in bulk and hardnefs equals a nut, but is blackifh, and fomewhat compreffed, and contains, inftead of a kernel, a thick black juice, with which names are written upon cotton, ftuffs, and handkerchiefs, as with ink, though it does not flow fo well. The letters are covered while wet with quick lime, which makes them laft in wafhing, and prevents them from hurting the ftuff.

I NOW longed to fee the country without the town, and fome of my fellow travellers honoured me with their company. We had fcarce paffed through the principal ftreets of the fuburbs, but a croud of boys gathered about us, who perhaps looked upon us as ambaffadors from the moon, or fome fuch odd animals, whom they were obliged to attend out of the city with an univerfal clamour: the croud continually increafed, and particularly in the *Miller's-ftreet*, in all the houfes of which, on both fides, rice is pounded and ground. Little ftones, fand, and dirt being thrown at us, we made the beft of our way out

out of the suburbs, to get rid of our disagreeable retinue.

We left the city with its wall on the right, and saw on both sides of the road only ploughed grounds, or great narrow clay fields, covered with rice, *Nymphæa Nelumbo*, and *Sagittaria bulbis oblongis*[1]. The last mentioned plant is just like our *Swedish* arrowhead above the ground, it only grows larger, which may be owing to the culture; the roots of the *Chinese* sort are the size of a clenched fist, and are oblong, and the *Swedish* are round, and not much larger than pease.

We change the quality of the ground by draining the water, and other arts, till we make it agreeable to our few sorts of corn; but the *Chinese* make use of so many plants for their subsistence, that they can scarce have any sort of ground, but what will fit some one of them. Thus they do not improve the

[1] The *Chinese* call it *Succoyee-fa*. It is larger than ours: the stem and the flower-stalks are hexagonal, and pretty strong: the leaves have eleven red nerves, of which the middle ones are ramose on both sides: the leaves under the flowers (*Bracteæ*) are oval-pointed: the flowers are umbellated, and commonly thirty-three in number.

field

field for the feed, but chuse the feed for the field. *Rice* (*Oryza sativa*) grows under water: *Nymphæa* and *Sagittaria* grow in water: *Sugarcane* (*Saccharum officinale*) and *Potatoes* (*Convolvulus Batatas*) want a less moist soil. If it is still more dry, it will do for *Yams* (*Dioscorea alata*). *Indigo* (*Indigofera tinctoria*) and *Cotton* (*Gossypium herbaceum*) grow on the highest mountains. If a mountain should happen to be too dry, it serves for a burying-place. But if a soil be ever so wet, the *Chinese* have a plant that grows in it, and serves for food to men. If we could not imitate the *Chinese* in our tillage; yet we might manage the pastures in the same manner. Let us suppose a piece of ground whose situation will not afford so much fall to the water as to let it run off: now no meadow is so wet but *Poa aquatica* grows on it; which we fetched out of other countries, till we discovered this excellent grass in *Westgothland*, in ponds, rivers, and the like places. No hill is so dry but *Festuca ovina* grows well on it. For want of money, and the workmen necessary to work in the ponds, a poor farm may be greatly improved by a simple imitation of nature; namely, if the husbandman brings such plants upon his meadows as will fit each soil, this

would

would make up what is wanted, and take up the place of such plants as we should like to get rid of.

But let us proceed on our road, where we saw hedges of *Euphorbia Nerii folia,* or *Fuyong-sa,* here and there twisted along with *Ipomæa quamoclit,* which, with its fine red flowers, would be an ornament even in an arbour. We have likewise found our *Swedish* hops (*Humulus Lupulus*) climbing over the hedges; and likewise *Periploca Græca,* whose flowers seem to be of velvet in the inside.

At last we found a burying-place, where the bones of many of our countrymen rest, as the epitaphs shew. This mountain lies on the right as we come from the town, near the road, without any enclosure, like a common. It is said to be half a mile distant from our lodgings. I found in this burying-place the following scarce plants:

Cassia procumbens.

Crotalaria juncea.

Celosia argentea.

Achyranthes aspera.

And

Cassida nigra, oblonga, fasciis duabus transversis testaceis, punctis quatuor ad basin.

ON our return we met three *Chinese*, who desired money; but their demands not being complied with, they attacked us with great stones; I in particular was in danger, being somewhat behind my companions, in quest of plants. I found

TORENIA *Asiatica:* the *calyx* is pentagonal, erected; its five segments are lanceolated, narrow, and shorter than the *tube* of the flower: the *corolla* is lanceolated: the upper *lip* is almost entire, and reflected: the lower lip has three *laciniæ*, and is bent downwards. The *filaments* are four, shorter than the *corolla*, two of them are even shorter than the tube of the *corolla*, they are fastened in pairs in the lower lip, the two upper ones have a sterile excrescence by their side: the *stylus* is filiform: the *stigma* is bifid: the *capsula* is long, and seems to be unilocular: the seeds are numerous: the flowers are axillar: the leaves are oval, emarginated, opposite, and have very short stalks.

This plant likewise grows in the rice fields, in the *Danish* island. It may serve now as a monument of the discoverer Mr. *Torcen*, and remind his friends of their loss.

We met a *Chinese* burial. We were then sufficiently protected. There were wooden idols in the procession. First and foremost went two *Chinese*, with little banners; next were the pipers and other musicians, who sometimes sounded their instruments. Behind these, the idol, a gilt human figure, was carried in a palankin; it was followed by the coffin, which was carried on a pole of bamboo. The mourners had white handkerchiefs about their heads. When they have let the coffin down into the grave, they lay a couple of stones upon it, and besides that, for the subsistence of the dead, and for the reconciliation of the idol, they put rice, fruit, tea, money, &c. by him. At night they likewise perform all sorts of musick in the boats, and row up and down the river in them.

Wives and husbands only mourn 49 days, or seven weeks, for each other. No *Chinese*, and much less a foreigner, can be buried in the

the town. I once asked a *Chinese* whether, at least, people of the highest rank were never buried in the town? Is this, said he, with a sneer, your custom? And I answering in the affirmative, he proceeded to say, What honour can this possibly be to the deceased? We bury our dead in the free, blooming fields, and erect a stone by the side of their graves, on which all their remarkable actions are inscribed, that every body may read them. If we should bury them in the houses, they would be noisome to their children, and their merit would, as it were, be buried with them.

THE *Chinese* graves are made on the side of hills, and look like ice-cellars. They are elevated on both sides with stones. Instead of the door stands a stone, on which the epitaph is hewn in large *Chinese* characters.

September 11th.

I HAD a mind to have a nearer sight of the *Moorish Pagoda* (*Delubrium Mauritanum*), which is at a good distance from the *European* graves: for this reason I left the town by the same road we had taken the day before, in company

pany with Mr. *Braad*, whose attention to all that is curious is well known, and two other gentlemen. On the road, a *Chinese* covered only with rags ran after us, and desired *Kam-sa-a*, or alms. We did not mind him, but went on as fast as the great heat would allow; but he came nearer, and pulled one of us by the coat, and would not leave his hold till he had money given him. We did not know how to act; for though we could have made him depart, we were afraid that by his cries he would bring hundreds of the *Chinese*, who were every where working in the fields around us; to whom we could not have proved our innocence, since none of us understood the language. When we were in doubt what we should do, another *Chinese* came and lashed our follower about the legs with a whip, which made him cry out exceedingly, and jump into the rice fields, where he was up to the knees in mud. This man called himself and his comrade officers of the government; he afterwards accompanied us to the *Pagoda*, which lay upon a high mountain, and its inside was somewhat different from that of the *Chinese* temples. Having observed all the trees that were planted hereabouts, we made haste back. In the hurry we found no other

than

than the trees which have already been mentioned before, except the *Plaintain* tree (*Musa Cliffortiana*), which was now fully in blossom.

Going down the hill I observed the *Té-limm*, or *Melastoma octandra*, on both sides of the road. This little plant is an ornament to the most barren hills, by means of its red flowers, which stand open during night, at least a long while after sun-set, while others are closed to escape the nocturnal dews, which would injure the tender parts of the flower. Its description is as follows:

The *calyx* is urceolated, or cylindrically oval, covered with stiff, short bristles, and includes the *germen*; its segments are quinquefid, equally brown, and downy, except the five lesser ones in the incisions: the *corolla* is pentapetalous; the petals are obovated, and fastened to the inner margin of the *calyx*, whose segments they surpass in length: the eight *filaments* are subulated, inflected, and fastened to the *calyx*: four of the *antheræ* are equally broad and erected; the other four are sterile and hamose, and longer than the filaments; they are all inflected when they are not yet evolved: the *pistillum* is longer than the *stamina:* the *germen* is almost round (*obrotundum*): the *stylus* is pointed and bent at top: the *stigma* undivided: the *seed capsula* is an almost round urceolated berry, which is black without, but red within, and is surrounded by a setiferous *calyx*. The *seeds* are numerous, very small, almost in form of rings, and dispersed in the berry. The *plant* is bushy: the *root* is ramose, creeping: the *stalk* is round, and lies on the ground: the *leaves* are oval, a little emarginated, trinervous, opposite, and petiolated: the *flowers* are on the top of the branches. I found another plant here, the flowers of which, by a cursory view, was like the preceding; though it is quite different from all the other *genera:* in the natural order it is like the *Lysimachia*, and the *Chinese* call it *Komm-Heyong-loaa*, or *Feather of Goldroses*. Sir *Charles à Linné*, thinking that my labours deserved some remembrance, has thought fit to call this plant *Osbeckia Chinensis* [See Tab. ii. f. 1, 2. 3.]. The whole plant is sold in the apothecaries shops; they boil it together with old *Kuli-Tea*, and drink the decoction in colics. In strains and swellings it is used in the bath. The following are the characteristics of the plant;

THE

THE *root* is woody, and sometimes consists of a little knob with branches, but sometimes it has no knob; it is perennial, and sometimes shoots into a number of stalks: the *stalk* is quadrangular, of the thickness of a pack-thread, seldom exceeding half a yard in length, generally ramose, and sometimes like a little bush. The branches, which are quadrangular and somewhat hairy, are commonly opposite, and single, or not divided. On the top are commonly two flowers, surrounded with four leaves, two of which are short, but longer than the flowers: the leaves are opposite; each couple is about an inch or more from the other, and the nearer to the flower the further asunder. They are somewhat obtuse in young plants, and about an inch long; but in old ones they are longer, and run sharp: those which grow at the bottom of the branches are frequently as long again as the others. They have most of them no *petiolus* or stalk, and are lanceolated sometimes, yet narrower; almost every where of equal breadth; have entire margins, are covered on the upper side with stiff hairs, which lie down, and have some thin down on the under side only, on the margin, and upon the three veins, which run almoſt the whole length of the leaf, in a ſtrait line. The *calyx* is monophyllous, campaniform, or bell-ſhaped, quadrifid, with four oblong, ſharp ſegments, which are ſomewhat downy on the out ſide; in each inciſion is a *ſquamula*, with hair on its margin. The *corolla* conſiſts of four upright, oval, red petals: the *ſtamina* are eight in number, narrow, inflected, and, together with the petals, faſtened to the *calyx*: they are the ſame length with the *calyx*, and are accordingly ſhorter than the petals: the *antheræ* are upſtanding, oblong, and end in a point which looks like the *calyptra* of a moſs. The *piſtillum* has an oval *germen*, a narrow and bent *ſtylus*, and a ſhort entire *ſtigma*: the *capſula* looks like a little pot, runs narrower towards the bottom; is quadrilocular, and on the outſide covered with the tube of the *calyx*. The *ſeeds* are numerous, ſmall, and in a microſcope look like little worms, which lie in a circular form.

COMING down the hill between the rice fields, we ſaw, in a field which was partly covered with water, *Impatiens Chinenſis*, which, if taken particular care of, might be made to adorn

adorn our windows with its fine red flowers, in the same manner as its relation the *Balsamines*.

Towards the city we found a species of small bushes (*Cryptanthus Chinensis* [k],) of the size of gooseberry bushes, which had white double flowers. The leaves are as large as those of the *Rose-mallow*, cordated, obtuse; their margin is unequally serrated; they are somewhat rough at the top, but smooth below, and have at least eight pretty large veins. The flowers grow in bunches, at the top of the branches.

Our companions, who joined us without being asked, called themselves government officers; and having reminded us of their rewards, put their whips into their pockets. We desired them to accompany us as far as the factory, where we would pay them; but they refused, and left us.

---

[k] With opposite leaves. The bush bears a great resemblance to a *Blackberry* bush.

September 12th.

AMONG the hay which was given to our cow in the factory, I found the following scarce graffes, which would adorn the *Hortus ficcus* of an *European* botanift:

Nardus articulata.
Agroftis Indica.
Panicum crus Galli.
——— *Diffectum.*
——— *Patens.*
——— *Brevifolium.*
Andropogon Schœnanthus.
——————— *Ifchæmum,* and likewife
——————— *Fafciculatum.*
Hedyfarum lagopodioides.

THE *Chinefe* needs not make hay for his cattle, for they may run all the year in the paftures. He does not want cows at home, for he can do without milk, butter and cheefe. He does not want horfes, for he either goes on foot, or is carried in a chair. Thus can a *Chinefe* employ all that time in agriculture, which

which in our country is spent in improving the growth of grafs, and in the hay harveſt. But he is obliged to have continually a perſon with his cattle, in order to prevent their doing any damage in the plantations; for, if they are ſurrounded with a thin hedge, it is too weak to be capable of keeping off unruly oxen. All other fences are unuſual in *China*, though perhaps a little ſpot within the hedge may be ſurrounded with a wall of common pebbles.

THIS day I returned on board, to look after the ſick.

THE *French Iſland* is an iſle in the river of *Canton*, which is reckoned to be two *Swediſh* miles from that place. The *Chineſe* name of the iſland is ſaid to be *Som fo-ang*. It has the name of *French Iſland* becauſe the *French* ſhips have their *bancſhal*, or warehouſe, on it. Near it is the place where the *European* ſhips ride at anchor; and when the ſailors have a mind to divert themſelves on holidays upon *Chineſe* ground, they go hither, becauſe they are, in ſome meaſure, ſecure from the inſults of the *Chineſe*. The love of plants likewiſe drew me thither, as to a place where for ſome

days

days I could not want new objects. I could here meet with nothing that decorates our *Swedish* soil. Trees, herbs, birds, insects, nay the earth itself, was a new sight in my eyes. On this island (for so I call it, though I have never been far enough on the other side of it to know whether it is one, or whether it is joined to the continent) are two steep mountains toward the river, with horizontal stages, or terrasses, like steps, on their sides, on which indigo, cotton, and *Chinese* potatoes, were planted. On the lowest terrasses, on the side of the *bancshall*, are several graves of our countrymen, *Danes*, and *Englishmen*, who died here some years ago, as the inscriptions on the tomb-stones show. For each corpse which is interred here, we pay one tel, four mess, eight kanderin, to the *Chinese*. Somewhat higher is a *Chinese* burying-place; and at the top grow fruit trees, such as *Lang-ann*, &c. and the *Chinese Pine* (*Abies Chinensis*).

The *soil* on the hills consists of a reddish sandy earth, which by the great heat often cakes, and forms a friable sand-stone, excepting the surface, which is kept loose by dung and vegetable earth. In these hills are great and small quarry-stones, some of which are like

like cryftals, but opaque, and of the colour of coarfe writing paper. The higheft hills feldom produce any thing befides fome dry graffes and trees, and thefe but very fparingly. This is the reafon why they are ufed for burying-places, or they let cattle graze upon them; but, thefe excepted, it is very difficult to find a place which is not ufed for gardens, plantations, or ploughed land. Cattle are kept here, but in fmall numbers; but what dung is loft by this means, is fupplied by another kind of manure before mentioned; and befides that, by bones, afhes, hair, men's beards, and many other things, which we make no ufe of. The *Chinefe* never fail carefully to gather the bones (which are elfe thrown into the river) from the *European* fhips. I have been told, that they burn them, and extract a lye from the remainder, with which they wafh their cotton ftuffs, which are always whiter in *China* than we can make them; and for this reafon we ought to try the experiment.

THE *Cotton plant* (*Goffypium herbaceum*) was now in bloffom, and had fruit. It is annually fown in the high grounds, and commonly in

rows,

rows, which are at half a yard's diſtance from each other.

THE *Indigo plant* (*Indigofera tinctoria*), by the *Chinese* called *Tong-am*, or *Va*, is annually ſown in high places, and is in flower almoſt at the ſame time with the *Cotton*.

AMARANTHUS *triſtis*, or the *In-ſcy* of the *Chineſe*, likewiſe grew here. I have been told, that its leaves are uſed inſtead of Cale.

SOLANUM *diphyllum* likewiſe, but very ſparingly.

SUGAR *cane* (*Saccharum officinarum*), the *Chineſe* name of which is *Kee-a*, was planted in rows between the hills. The plants were tied together, to prevent their bending to the ground. They were above a fathom long, but I could neither at that time nor afterwards diſcover its flowers. *China* therefore is not the place whence it originally came from, which muſt be a far warmer climate.

RICE (*Oryza Sativa*[1]) is by the *Chineſe* called *Waa* while it is yet in the ground, but

---

[1] From this account we may judge of the poſſibility of ſowing rice in *Germany* with advantage.

Wo-ko.k

Wo-kock when it is not yet pounded. The rice groats before they are boiled are called *Mahee*, and when they are boiled they go by the name of *Fann*. Rice is at first sown in *April* in high places; when it is grown half a yard long, it is dug out of the ground, and tranfplanted in rows upon a deep clay ground, in fo low a fituation, that it is always laid under water by the tide for fix hours together, and then is left dry for fix hours next following. Accordingly rice requires a natural ebbing and flowing, and a warm climate. If this were not the cafe, it would be worth while to plant it on our fhores. The ground on which it grows is called paddy-ground by our people who go to the *Eaſt Indies*, and confifts for the greateſt part of a blue clay, which looks brown at top from the different manures. The *Chineſe* make ufe of a kind of dung which we reject, to manure their rice fields and other fields with, though not very plentifully: it occafions a great ftench upon the grounds in dry places; but in the rice fields is fo tempered with, or wafhed away by, water, that it is but little regarded. The dung is brought to the innermoft bays of the water, in order that when it runs into the land every part of the field may have its fhare. When the water

cannot

cannot overflow the field, this inconvenience is remedied by water machines, but mostly by two *Chinese* who stand near the water, and water the ground with buckets. To each of the ears of the bucket they fasten a string, and stand opposite to one another, each twisting his cord together: they then sink the bucket into the water, and when it is full each pulls at his string, by which means the bucket is both drawn out of the water and overturned by the rope that was twisted together and untwists itself; and by this means the water runs over the higher rice fields, which cannot be overflowed. Ditches are scarce observable in the rice fields; but there are little canals, in order to enable them in harvest time to get between with their boats, and carry the rice from them to the high places, in order that it may be dried, after that they have paid the tythe in the custom-house. This species of corn bears very plentifully here, but costs a deal of labour. The bread which is baked for the *Europeans* (a katty or pound of which at present was sold at four kanderin two kas) is not made of rice, but of wheat, which, together with rye and barley, is said to grow further up in the country. When the *Chinese* mix rice flour with it (which they often do unless

Rhamnus lineatus.

unless you take great care) it renders the bread heavier and less palatable. About the hills we met with several scarce plants, and among these were:

Polygonum barbatum, by the *Chinese* called *Ka-yong-maa.*

Polygonum orientale, in the *Chinese* language *Yong-maa.*

Rhamnus lineatus, inermis, floribus hermaphroditis, foliis ovatis integerrimis multinerviis. [See Tab. vii.] A bush which till now has escaped the notice of botanists. It often grows to the height of a man, and is remarkable for its small and beautiful leaves, which are of a yellow-green colour below, and have red veins: the *antheræ* are black.

Valeriana Chinensis.

Hedysarum triflorum.

Nardus ciliaris, in high places.

Viscum baccis rubentibus. Kampf. Amœn. 785.

Convallaria Chinensis, foliis linearibus, corollis sex-partitio. This species of *Lily of the Valley* is a medium between *Scilla* and *Convallaria.*

It grows below and along with *Canna Indica*, in shady places.

On the road I found:

Torenia Asiatica. And in poor ground,

Lawsonia inermis.

Melastoma Malabarica, with fine red flowers.

Hedysarum Hedcrocarpon.

Urena lobata.

Aira seminibus hirsutis, aristis terminalibus flore longioribus.

Scirpus (*Chinensis*) *culmo triquetro subnudo, spicis ternis sessilibus terminalibus, involucro diphyllo reflexo*; a species of grass with long narrow leaves, one of which, next the ear, is much longer than the rest. In *Van Reede's Hort. Malab.* tom. xii. p. 71. t. 38. is a print of it, under the name of *Motte pullu.*

Ixora coccinea, by the *Chinese* called *Kanlong-fa,* or *Emperor's flower,* is a shrub, or small tree, which grows every where hereabouts on the hills, a yard high; but has the finest red flowers, in bunches at the tops of the branches. I made the following remarks

remarks upon it: The fegments of the *calyx* are obtufe: the tube of the *corolla* is very long: the *filaments* are very fhort, inferted in the incifions of the *limbus*: the *antheræ* longer, pointed and inflected: the *germen* is very fmall, and fomewhat fhorter than the *calyx:* the *ftylus* filiform, longer than the tube: the *ftigma* pretty thick: the leaves are oppofite, oval, without incifions, almoft without ftalks, and fmooth. On account of thefe magnificent flowers this fhrub has got a place in the *Chinefe* gardens, where it grows higher than a man's head. I here am put in mind of the many fine flowers which grow fpontaneoufly in *Sweden*; which, if they were transplanted into gardens, would look better than many of thofe which we get as ornaments from the moft diftant places.

Between the ftones on the hills, grew,

Nauclea orientalis.

Spermacoce verticillata. The *antheræ* are oblong and upright: the *piftillum* is longer than the *corolla*: the *germen* is fmall: the *ftylus* hairy: the *corolla* is rolled downwards: the *leaves* lanceolated, oppofite, with nine nerves, and gibbose: the *flowers* grow verticillated.

Near the rice fields the following plants were in blossom:

Verbesina prostrata.

——— *calendulacea.*

On the hills were:

Polygala ciliata.

Lycopodium varium.

——— *nudum.*

——— *cernuum.*

Polypodium cristatum.

——— *Barometz.*

Jungermannia Chinensis. Dill. Musc. 64. f. 4.

Lichen Chinensis, or *Lichenoïdes glaucum perlatum, subtus nigrum et cirrhosum,* Dill. Musc. 147. t. 20. f. 39.

Agaricus Chinensis, stipite albo, spithomeo, pileo lutescente.

Trichomanes chinense

Blechnum occidentale.

Trichomanes Chinensis. [Tab. vi.]

Of Infects I found:

Cancer oryzæ, a small kind of rough crabs, which crept about the rice fields.

SOLANUM *Indicum* grew by the graves. On this spinose plant I found a grub, which I kept and fed in my hut till its third change, which was into one of the *lepidoptera* kinds. The wondrous changes of these little creatures may inspire us wretched men (who are justly compared to worms in Holy Scripture) with the sublimest thoughts. The grub in its first state was reduced to creep over its little world with just as much trouble as we creep on earth and seek our subsistence, frequently with the greatest fatigue: how many needless journeys do we take, and to how many dangers are we exposed! one worm does not spare the other on the road. And as the grub in its next change into an *aurelia* enters into a dark house, in which it loses every sensation of former pleasures; thus we descend into the obscure grave, where we rest the appointed space: but when
the

the grub has staid its proper time in its narrow lodgings, without any nourishment, it at last appears, by its third change, in its true perfection and splendor; often enriched with the most glorious colours. This gives an excellent hint, that the grave shall not for ever hold our bodies; but that at last, at the general resurrection on the last day, we shall be cloathed with splendour and glory.

Larva Solani Indici. It is smooth: together with the head and tail, it is of the length of a span, and of the thickness of an eagle's quill. That articulation which contains the head has a great black line on the sides: the mouth is large: the *antennæ* are thickest at bottom, white, with blackish-brown tops, and two black rings. The three pair of fore legs are black, have claws, are dotted with white, and are placed at the first, second, and third articulation, beginning at the head. The five pair of hind feet are fastened to the seventh, eighth, ninth, tenth, and tail articulation; they are shorter, truncated, green, and have as it were short bristles at their extremities; the fourth, fifth, and sixth articulations have no feet. The body is green below: the sides have nine black spots: the equilateral triangles
(of

(of which one furrounded the other), which ftand on each articulation between the fourth on the back and the tail, are fhaded with green, yellow, and blue, (the loweft is yellow) and dotted with black. The tail is fharpened in form of a horn, and confifts of many joints.

THE *Croton febiferum* was the food of another kind of *larvæ* or grubs (*Larva feneftrata?*); which, the next night, changed into *aurelias*. The *larvæ* were green, with many rows of blue fpots. Of their change into moths you will have an account the 3d of *February* next year. On the road I found, befides the *Caffida cinerea*, a *Swedifh* infect, the *Coccinella feptem-punctata*, which feems to have been brought by chance from *Europe* as it were in exchange for the *Blatta orientalis*.

The 14th *September*.

THE hoppo, happa, or firft infpector of the cuftoms, (fee p. 216.) whofe bufinefs in particular it is to meafure the newly arrived *European* fhips, came to us to-day. He fent his own ftairs, covered with red cloth, before him, by which he was to afcend into the fhip; and afterwards

A a 4 came

came in a great sampane painted with red, accompanied by some musicians, to entertain him in his passage. In his train were, besides his servants, beadles and soldiers, who had each their badges; some had feathers in their caps, others had sabres at their sides, one had a belt hanging from his shoulder, another held the umbrella over him while he got on-board. After he had seated himself, he ordered two of his attendants to measure the length and breadth of our ship with a rope: this admeasurement came very high in price to us; for by his own decision our ship was obliged to pay 600 piastres, or about 6000 dollars of copper, for duty. He, in return, presented the ship, as usual, with two live oxen, eight bags of flour, eight pitchers of *Chinese* wine, &c.

BOTH on his arrival and at his departure, 16 canons were fired off.

The 15th of *September*.

A CHINESE *shining insect* sat on the ceiling of the great cabbin, and gave a considerable light in the dark.

It

It was the *Cantharis Chinenfis* (*Lampyris Chin.* Linn.) *thorace & elytris teftaceis, apice nigris.* The *thorax* and the *wing-cafes* are highly marginated: the *fcutcheon* is black: the *wings* are black: the *feet* are blackifh: the laft ring of the *abdomen,* or belly, is of a brownifh-yellow; but the laft but one is white below, and this is it which fhines like fire in the night time: the two rings next to this are blackifh: the *breaft* is brownifh-yellow.

September 17th.

As I landed at the *Bancfhal,* I again faw the *Gobius pectiniroftris* and *niger,* which I have already defcribed, page 200 and 201.

CYPERUS *odoratus.* The ftalk of it is triquetrous, but round near the root; with a fhort, even, obtufe leaf, which furrounds the ftalk towards the bottom.

The 18th of *September.*

TO-DAY the firft *Chinefe* boat came on-board with porcellain in chefts, and bales for the company's company's account, and ten *Chinese* boys who were to splice cables.

The 22d of *September*.

After I had preached and administered the sacrament, I was tempted by the fine weather to make a little excursion on the *French Island*, where I found the following plants in flower:

Barleria cristata, [Tab. viii.] by the *Chinese* called *Abliey fa*, is a shrub which exceeds three yards in height. The stem is so weak, that it cannot stand upright without a support. Its flowers are blue, and fall off easily: the tube of the *corolla* is bent: the *filaments* are fastened to its lower part; two of them are very short, and two almost as long as the *pistilla*, besides a barren one: the upper lip of the *corolla* is broad and oval, the lower is quadrifid, with long sharp points.

Chinese Gourds (*Cucurbita Chinensis*) grew here and there spontaneously; and in other places they were supported near the houses by little sticks, or shrubs.

Barzeria cristata?

Convolvulus Pes capræ, a plant with thick leaves, whose stalks lie on the sea-shore, which is ornamented with its red flowers.

Urena Chinensis, caule erecto, floribus majusculis, grew at the foot of the hills.

Verbena nodiflora, with its flowers, hung from a wall not far off the shore. I found it no where else. It is one of those plants which shew how much *America* is like *Asia*; for it is to be met with in both.

Pa-kock-fa, or *Morinda umbellata?* grew on the shore, together with the *Periploca Græca*. The flowers of the latter are an ornament to our hot-houses, on account of their velvet colour.

Mussænda frondosa, is a shrub which the *Chinese* call *Kaulimang*. It grew some yards high, and, on account of the weakness of its stem, it likes to lean on other trees. It spreads its boughs over the *European* graves. The following is its shape: the *calyx* is monopetalous, divided into six parts, and bristly: its *laciniæ* are long, narrow, and pointed: the *mouth* (*faux*) *of the corolla* is hairy: the *limbus* of it is expanded, horizontal, sexfid, with pointed *laciniæ*: the *filaments* are commonly

five

five in number, sometimes six, and even seven, all very short, and fastened about the middle of the tube. The *antheræ* are erected, of equal breadth; many times as long again as the filaments, and touch each other at the *limbus:* the *germen* is almost round: the two *stylufes*, which are joined together, are thread-shaped: the two *stigmas* are simple: the *stem* is round, hairy, brownish: the *leaves* are opposite, lanceolated, petiolated, not divided, reflected, have five nerves, and are downy, particularly below. The *flowers* sit close together at the ends of the branches; they are yellow, and have sometimes oval, white, petiolated *bracteæ*. The *seed capsule* is oblong, unilocular. The *seeds* are numerous and very small. It grows near the shore among the *Zanthoxylum trifoliatum*, and in other places.

The 23d of *September*.

ANOTHER boat with porcellane came to our ship. The air was fine.

KAY-PO-Y, *Diodon ocellatus* (*Tetrodon ocellatus* Linn.) is one of the finest fish I ever saw, but so poisonous that whoever eats of it generally dies

in

in two hours time. The *Chinese*, who affirmed the fact, seeing me take the fish into my hands, earnestly desired me to wash myself, adding that it is forbidden under some great penalty, to be sold among other fish. It is very like to the *Tetrodon lagocephalon*, and is able to blow itself up, which makes its fore part look like the breast of a cropper pigeon. Yet it differs in some things from the last mentioned fish, as in the number of rays in the back-fin, which is seldom found to vary in the same species: the same likewise happens to it sometimes with respect to the other fins; not to mention the colour, and some less constant marks, which however, upon the whole, distinguish it pretty well from all other fishes.

This fish has an *operculum branchiostegum* on each side: the dorsal-fin is single, directly opposite, the anal-fin is oval, and has fifteen rays: the *pectoral-fin* has eighteen divided rays. It has no *ventral-fins*. The *anal-fin* is oval, and has eleven rays: the *tail* is truncated, and has eight ramose rays: the two last fins are moveable according to the fish's inclination. The *body* is globoso-oval, with a skin over it. Its length is scarce a quarter of a yard. The *back* is green: the *line on the sides* is bent: the

the green colour of the back goes a little below it, but further down it is white. The breast and the belly are covered as it were with thick threads, or white pipes, which are best observed by stroking the fish with the hand upwards from the belly to the head. Behind the pectoral fins ran two brown-yellow spots from the back, and a circle of the same colour surrounded the dorsal-fin: the spot in the circle is black. The *head* is somewhat flat, and oval: the *mouth* round and small: the jaws are equal, and consist of two flat bones. In the midst of the mouth two *teeth* are visible, which are covered with moveable lips: the *tongue* is somewhat round: the *eyes* are small, naked, and round: the *pupil* in the eye is black: the *irides* are yellow: the nostrils are small, and close to the eyes. The fish was taken in the river at *Canton*; and a civil sailor, who was present when the *Chinese* caught it, gave it to me.

The 25th of *September*.

FINE weather.

A LITTLE bird, which was a good singer, was shot about the rice fields, whither it resorted ed to feek its livelihood among the rice. It was,

Lanius Schach, or the crested red or russet butcher-bird, *Edw.* 54. Its shape is as follows: the *bill* is short and narrow, the *upper jaw* is the longest, it is sharp and bent at the point. Near the head it has seven or more bristles: the *lower jaw* is spotted: the *tongue* is lacerated at the point: the seven *tail feathers* are long, but the middlemost are longer than the rest: its forehead is black, and about the eyes there is the same colour. The *wings* are black at the top; but below, and in particular on the inside, they are whitish, and outwardly quite white: the *head*, the neck, and the fore-part of the back, are ash-coloured: the hind part of the back, and the *uropygium* are red: it is red mixed with white at the top. The thighs are covered with down: the legs and feet are naked, and blackish. It has three fore-toes; and one hind-toe, which is as long as the middle fore-toe.

The 27th of *September*.

GENERALLY clear weather.

I crossed over in a *Chinese* boat to the *Danish Island*, which the *Chinese* call *Tsiangliao*. This is an island without woods, only separated from the *French Island* by a stream; but is exactly like it in regard to the quality of the soil, and has, like the former, hills, cultivated vallies, and rice fields in the low places by the river side. There is seldom any thing planted on the hills, since it would be burnt up by the sun, and the cowherds keep the cattle upon them. In some places were *Chinese* graves, towards the river of *Canton*; but here we saw *European* ones.

I here met with the following natural curiosities:

Coccinella quadri-pustulata? the foremost spots near the head are rhomboidal, but crossways; the hindmost are round points, on whose sides are little atoms, scarce visible to the naked eye.

Andrachne fruticosa. The *male plant* has no *calyx*. The *corolla* is bell-shaped, reflected, divided into six parts, and green: its *laciniæ* are very short, and the extreme edge as it were emarginated. The *female* plant has no *calyx*;

it

Clerodendrum fortunatum.

it has a *germen*, three *styli*, and six *stigmas*: the *capsula* is almost round, has six partitions with six *seeds*. The leaves are oval, smooth at top, and downy below. Both male and female plants are shrubs.

Clerodendron fortunatum [Tab. xi.] grew by the *European* graves; and has not yet been described by any botanist. The plant smells like musk, by which it distinguishes itself from all other plants growing near the graves. It is called *Hatag-nang* by the *Chinese*: the *calyx* is monophyllous, angulated, red, divided into five parts, and persistent: its *segments* are oval, pointed, of the length of the tube of the *corolla*, but broader than it. The *corolla* is monopetalous, quinquefid: the *upper lip* is trifid, rolled up: the *lower* bifid, bent downwards: the *filaments* are inserted in the mouth of the *corolla*; they are bearded below, and longer than the *corolla*; two of them are somewhat shorter than the others: the *germen* is oval: the *stylus* filiform, and shorter than the *filaments*: the *stigma* pointed and bifid: the *drupa*, or stony fruit, stands together in couples, is green, and surrounded with the *calyx*. The *plant* is ramose, about one foot high, and smells like musk. The *flower stalks* are axillary, and each bears several flowers.

Gerardia glutinosa. [Tab. ix.]

Ruellia ringens grew every where in the water on the shore, and was above half a yard high. It distinguishes itself from the *Ruellia antipoda*, which generally grows along with it, in the following particulars: the *calyx* is monophyllous, cylindrical, quinquefid, with small lanceolated *segments*. The *corolla* is monopetalous, ringent: the *tube* cylindrical: the *faux* inflated; the *opening* bifid: the *upper lip* bifid, and reflected: the *lower* deflected, trifid, dotted in the inside (like the *corolla* of the *Scutellaria*); the four *filaments*, of which the two lowest are the least, hang on the lower lip: the *antheræ* are sagittated, and erected: the *germen* is oblong: the *stylus* is filiform, longer than the filaments, and bent near the top: the *stigma* is undivided, and pointed: the *capsule* is oblong, narrow, trilocular, and contains only eight flat seeds. The *root* is big, and repent: the *stalk* round, erected, simple: the *leaves* are opposite, petiolated, lanceolated, smooth, and somewhat carnose.

Cyperus

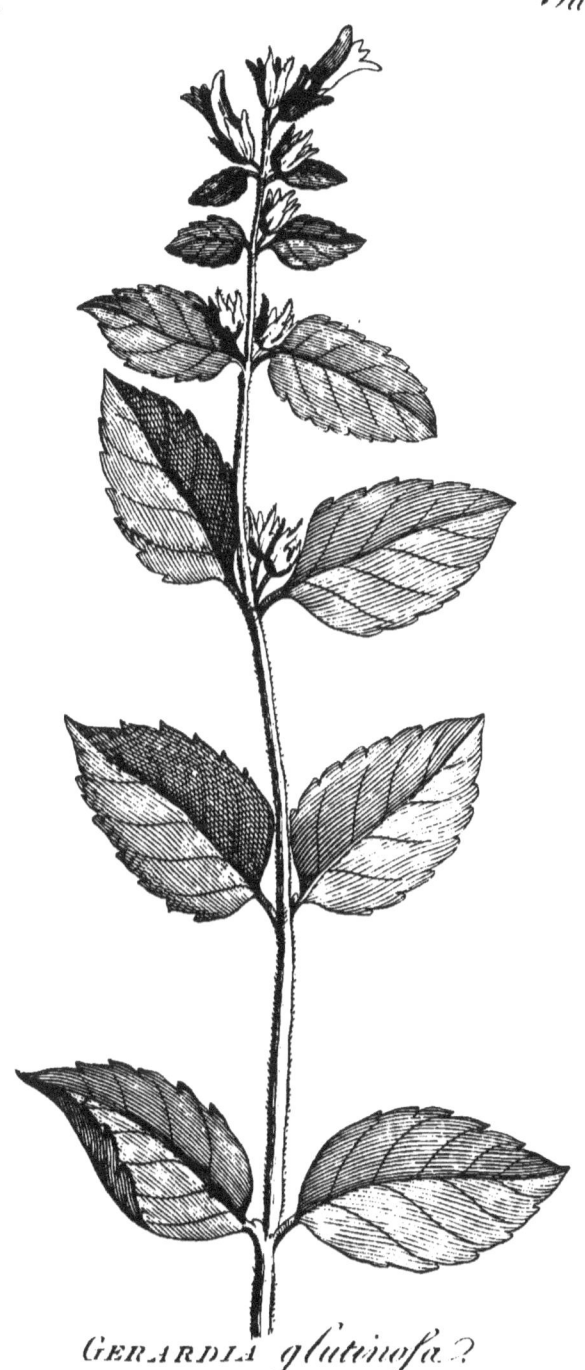

Gerardia glutinosa?

Cyperus Iria?

Cyperus dichotomus?

Onoclea sensibilis, or *Filix Indica polypodii facic*, Menz. pug. [Tab. x.]

Pange-ka (*Columnea? Chinensis*) is the *Chinese* name of a plant which is here plentiful along the river side; and generally grows in the water, together with the afore mentioned plant, and has an agreeable smell. It is with difficulty ranged under any of the *genera* yet known, as appears from the following description: the *calyx* is double; the interior one is diphyllous, very small, with pointed leaves; the superior *calyx* is quinquefid, with narrow lanceolated segments, which are shorter than the tube of the *corolla*: the *corolla* is monopetalous: the *tube* is cylindrical: the *faux* bearded: the *limbus* quinquepartite: the *laciniæ* oval: the incision between two of the *laciniæ* on one side is less deep than on the other; and on this lean the *pistillum* and the *stamina*, and are surrounded with a beard: the four *filaments* are filiform, two of them shorter; they stock together in pairs: the *antheræ* sit on the sides, and are small: the *germen* is ovated, or egg-shaped: the *stylus* filiform: the *stigma* in some manner represents a hat (*subcapitatum*) and is bent downwards: the *capsule* is oval, and contains many *seeds*. The plant has a *stalk* which lies on the ground, is round, thick, carnose and hairy: the *leaves* are oblong and serrated: the *flowers* are axillary, and likewise grow on the tops of the branches, and are of a blue colour: the *foot stalks* are rough. This plant grows on the banks of the river.

Justicia purpurea adorned the *European* graves. This plant too has hitherto escaped the notice of botanists. The *Chinese* call it *Happ-key-lee*, or *Happ-key-sa*. The *calyx* is double (which distinguishes it from the other species of *Justicia*), monophyllous, cylindrical; the exterior ends in four teeth, the interior in five bristles; the latter is shorter, is covered by the exterior, and includes the *germen:* the *corolla* is monopetalous: its *tube* cylindrical: the limb ringent: the *upper lip* oblong, broad towards the point, trifid; and the *lower lip* small, of equal breadth, and revolute towards the point: the two *filaments* are fixed to the incision of the *corolla*, they are subulated and bearded towards the inside: the *antheræ* are oblong and erect: the *pistillum* is of equal length

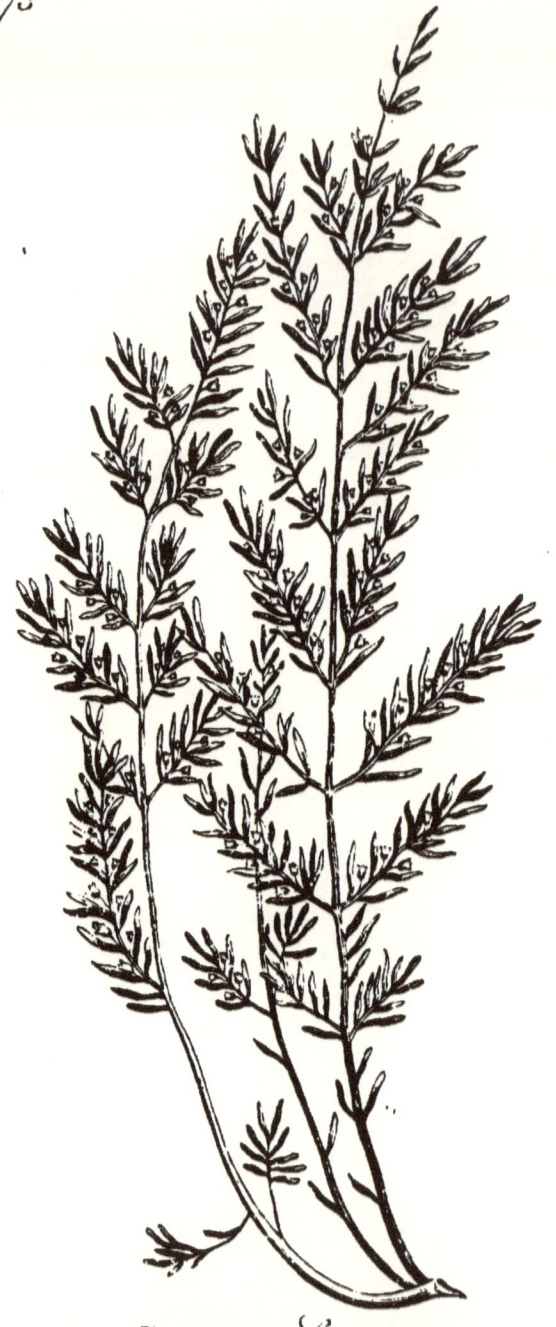

BAECKEA frutescens.

length with the *stamina*: the *germen* is egg-shaped and small: the *stylus* filiform: the *stigma* undivided: the *stalk* is almost round, very ramose, about a foot long: the *branches* are axillary, they are thicker at the place where they are inserted, and dichotomous: the *leaves* are oval, petiolated, run sharp at both ends, are smooth, and entire: the *flowers* are red, and form at the top and on the sides spikes scattered without order (*spicæ sparsæ*): the *bracteæ* are lanceolated. This plant, which looks like *Galeopsis tetrahit* is an ornament to the graves of the *Europeans*, since I have not met with it any where else.

Bæckea frutescens [Tab. i.] is a little shrub, which grows above a quarter of a yard high, looks like *Mugwort*, and smells agreeably. On my return I put some of it into my box, which preserved my cloths from *tinias*, or moths. The *Chinese* call it *Tiongma*. This was the first time that it was carried to *Europe*. It is described in *Linn. Species Plantarum:* its flowers are small, white, and smell somewhat like primroses.

NEAR the hedges the following plants were in flower:

Bryonia

Bryonia cordifolia.

Hedyfarum pulchellum.

——— *triquetrum*: *Kafong-fo* in the *Chinefe* language. It grows to a man's height, and is very ramofe.

Sigefbeckia orientalis, by the *Chinefe* called *Chimag*, was fupported by another fhrub near the water, which was called *Fo-kay*.

Volckameria inermis on the fhore.
N. B. I counted five *ftamina* in this fpecimen: the flowers were white.

Katong-qua, a fhrub. The *corolla* is quadrifid, has four *filaments*, and a *piftillum*: the *leaves* are fhaped like a heart, and thick. It twifts round other plants.

Conyza hirfuta, by the *Chinefe* called *Kylatfoy*.

Panicum glaucum.

Kay-in has four *filaments*: the *piftillum* is longer than the *filaments*: the *flowers* are blue: the *leaves* are lanceolated, and woolly on the under fide.

Ophiogloffum

Ophioglossum scandens, by the *Chinese* called *Ka-yin-scy*, winds about other plants.

Rhus Chinense (or, as the *Chinese* call it, *Monkhi*) was in flower about the graves.

Rhus Javanicum, germine rubro, which the *Chinese* call *Tay-sha*.

Pteris semipinnata, by the *Chinese* called *Ka-lao*, (S. t. 3. f. r.)

Waltheria Indica. Its flower is yellow, the leaves are woolly, reflected.

Rhamnus Thea, or poor man's tea, is a shrub which grows a fathom high, and whose leaves are like those of the common tea; but the flowers belong to the first order of the fifth class of the *Linnæan* system of plants. They are very small, and rest on the top of the branches, which are again sub-divided into lesser boughs. The poor make use of its leaves instead of tea; but in this place it served as a hedge. The *Chinese* call it *Tia*.

Min tao, Dolichos scandens floribus cæruleis magnis.

Panicum alopecuroideum.

On the shore grew:

Alcopecurus hordeiformis.

Cyperus haxpan, or *Cyperus litorum echinato capite.* cfr. *Ily Mullu,* Hort. Mal. 12. Tab. 175. grew by the river side.

On the hills grew:

Ocimum gratissimum.

Bartramia Indica. In the *Chinese* language *Hongfa-mo.*

The creeping *Convolvulus hirtus,* with its yellow flowers, by the *Chinese* called *Taqua.*

Cynosurus Ægyptius.

Ischæmum aristatum.

Helicteres angustifolia, by the *Chinese* called *Kay-ma,* which has hitherto not yet been found.

BESIDES the eatable roots which I have already mentioned, another sort is planted here, which is quite white, and is of the size of a pigeon's

Helicteres angustifolia

pigeon's egg, and by the *Chinese* is called *Fy-shin*. The plant is *Arachis hypogæa*.

We likewise saw three sorts of birds, which we met with in other parts of this country.

Ley-kao, which kept together in flocks.

Chinese black Ravens, with white necks.

Grey-spotted Chinese Magpies, which they call *Datt-sow*. And likewise

CHINESE *Locusts* (*Whom-ma*), or *Gryllus viridis, capite acuminato, obtuso, ense adscendente.*

October the 3d.

The cold northern winds now coming killed the gnats, which had hitherto been troublesome.

The 6th of *October.*

Fine clear weather.

After I had preached, I went to the *French Island* in a *Chinese* boat; where, besides the

plants

plants already mentioned, I found the following along the river side.

Mimosa Chinensis, inermis, stipulis foliolo longe majoribus, semicordatis. The *leaves* are seven or eight pairs: the *foliola* are numerous, lanceolated, but at the bottom more obtuse. It distinguishes itself from others of its kind particularly by the large semicordated *stipulæ,* which are fixed on the *stem* and surround it. I did not see the flowers.

Lichen (Euphorbiæ) foliaceus, pulverulentus.

Aralia Chinensis is a tree about two yards high, forms a crown, and is almost every where covered with thorns. Even the principal rib of the leaves (*rachis*) is thorny: the leaves are decomposite.

Hedysarum biarticulatum.

Senecio divaricatus.

Cacalia incana.

Aster Indicus.

Poa angustifolia, on high fields.

Convolvulus reptans, or wild spinage, on low places between the rice fields, in the road, but never in dry places.

The

The tree *Long-ann*, whose fruit the *Chinese*, as aforementioned, eat with their tea, grows on the summits of the highest mountains, and its size is that of a middling plumb-tree. Its leaves were devoured by a sort of grubs, of the following shape:

The grub is white, oblong, bristly, powdered: it has eleven articulations besides the tail, each of which has six bristles: the last articulation is blue on both sides, and longer than the three first: the fourth articulation has middling bristles; and the three first are the shortest. It has three pair of fore-feet, and four pair of hind-feet, which last are stronger, and have three joints: the tail has two prominencies, and its sides have a red ring, but at the top it is covered with a blue powder.

The 8th of *October*.

FINE weather: sometimes rain.

THE grub which I found the 13th, on the *Indian Nightshade* (*Solanum Indicum*) and which had been in the *aurelia* state for some days, changed into a *sphinx*. It was but a bad specimen;

cimen; but as far as I could see, it was *sphinx atropos*, the same with what we had already caught in sailing by *Java*. See page 133.

The 11th of *October*.

THE Captain of the *Gothic Lion*, Swedish East Indiaman, Mr. *David Shierman*, invited me to go to *Canton* in his sloop; which offer I accepted with pleasure. We passed the custom-houses, and only shewed the colours.

SOME jugglers came to the factory, and offered to amuse us with their slight of hand. They suddenly brought living snakes before us, and restored little land-tortoises to life, &c. The whole trumpery was contained in an old ragged carpet, which they spread on the floor.

The 12th of *October*.

I THIS day took a journey in a *Palankin* [a] for two *mase* and five *kandarin*, about half a *Swedish* mile up the country (about three *English* miles), to see the funeral of the *Dutch* supercargo

[a] *Kiao*, Bay. Mus. lib. i. p. 48.

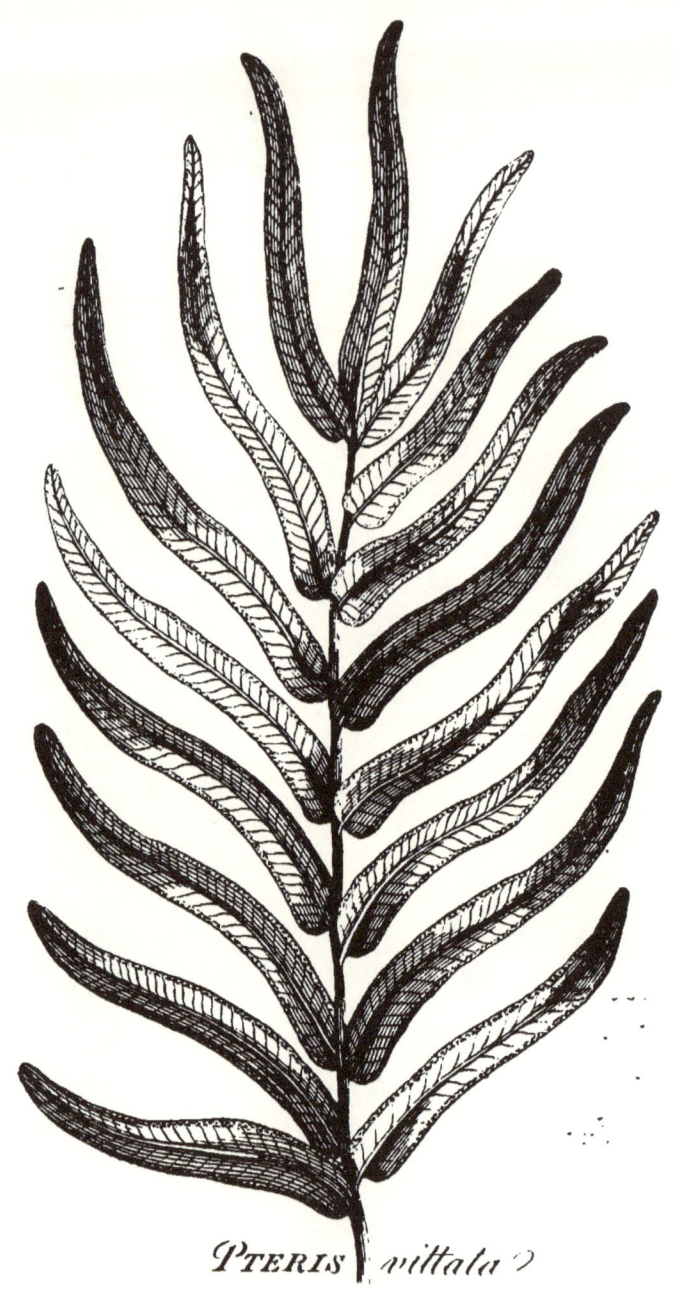

Pteris vittata

supercargo *Roberts*, who died the second of this month, in the 54th year of his age. All the captains and supercargoes were invited to come at two o'clock in the afternoon, and to follow the corpse to the aforementioned burying-place. On going thither I saw the following plants, which covered the old walls of the city.

Pteris vittata. [Tab. iv.]

Barleria cristata. Its blue flowers were in several places the ornaments of the wall.

Ficus Indica, with round *figs*.

Urtica nivea, which I have seen no where but on the walls of *Canton*.

Convolvulus reptans covered the graves, where some boys were met together with fishing-rods in their hands. They made use of a kind of large *dragon-fly* (*Libellula Chinensis*) as a bait. I understood they were catching frogs, but had as yet tried their luck in vain. It is happy for us that the art of fishing is not risen to such a pitch of perfection as hunting; for then fishes would be as scarce in our lakes as deer are in our woods.

Justicia procumbens grew on the road.

A GOOD way out of town, on the right of the high road, I arrived at the *European* burying-place, which was on a hill without any fence, or diftinction from the other hills. The infcriptions on the tomb-ftones are not all legible, on account of the rubbifh lying on them: however, I could fee that *Swedifh* captains and fupercargoes had died in this country. The corpfe which was now to be buried was carried by fix *Dutch* grenadiers. The proceffion followed in *Palankins* without order. The *Chinefe* merchants who were here prefent, mourned with white, long, cotton handkerchiefs, which were tied as the ribbands of an order, over their common clothes. This fort of mourning was diftributed to all the reft by the young widow of the deceafed. She was born at *Batavia*, and had accompanied her hufband hither, but got admiffion into the fuburbs of *Canton* with much difficulty. The people in this country are very fingular, looking upon foreign ladies as not much better than contraband goods.

A BLACK tomb-ftone was laid upon the grave, on which an infcription to the memory of the deceafed was engraved in great white letters

letters in *Dutch*, mixed with some *Latin*. On this occasion people of all nations were assembled together.

THE *Chinese* had erected tents about the tombs, and diverted the funeral procession with their rope-dancers.

The 13th of *October*.

AFTER I had a second time preached in the factory, the remainder of the day would not allow of any trip out of town; and for this reason I only walked about the neighbouring streets, to see whether the *Chinese* had any curiosities in their shops, for they make no distinction with regard to *Sunday*. I found a sort of linen somewhat rough to the touch, which was said (together with another very common brown stuff) to be made of a kind of bark. This linen was very white, and as narrow as the afore-mentioned *Canton cotton-linen*; but it was neither cotton nor linen.

FLAX is so rare a commodity in the East, that many have judged with great probability, that the

the fine linen of the rich man, Luke xvi. 19. was no more than our common linen.

ABRUS *precatorius Linn. Syst. Nat. Ed.* 12. (in the third edition of the *Spec. Plantar.* Linnæus calls it *Glycine Abrus*) is a sort of little red peafe, with a black spot, which were sold in the chandler-shops. I bought some for a low sort of coin; but some children seeing me buy them, gathered about me and desired me to give them some, which I did, and was glad to get rid of them in this manner: I was told, that they could buy fruit with them; that they were valued as the lowest coin, and used in weighing gold.

A SORT of *musk*, which the *Chinese* call *Wadnamm*, was kept in great bladders, and sold much cheaper than in our country.

[b] BUPRESTIS *maxima, Mus. Reg. Succ.* 82. a fine green insect, which the *Chinese* had dried, and fastened leaden wings to it (which were so painted as to make them look like butter-

---

[b] The *Bupreftis max.* is a species of the *coleoptera*; and must make a strange monster when disguised by the wings of the *lepidoptera*.

flies),

flies), was to be fold in the vaults among other trifles.

THE next day I again returned on board the ſhip; but the miniſter from the *Gothic Lion*, Mr. *Toreen*, went to town. When two ſhips are at *Canton* at the fame time, one chaplain generally officiates aboard the ſhips, and the other in town.

The 18th of *October*.

PACK-FANNY is the *Chineſe* name of a long, tranſparent, white fiſh, which is caught in this river, and being dried is boiled and eaten. It is *Albula Chinenſis*, and has the following characters: the fingle *dorſal-fin* oppoſite the *anus* is low, right-angled, and has 12 rays: the *pectoral-fins*, ſomewhat below the head, are oval, and have 10 rays: the *ventral-fins* are in the middle of the fiſh's length, and are wedge-ſhaped, and have eight rays: the *anal fin* is in ſome meaſure articulated, and has 26 rays: the tail is furcated: the body is of the length of a ſpan, and is white, tranſparent, and without ſcales: the head is narrow, lanceolated: the *operculum branchioſteg.* conſiſts of two scales: the jaws are almost equal: the teeth are sharp, fastened in the jaws, and bent backwards: the eyes are placed on the sides, and are almost round: the body, as far as the ventral fins, is almost round, but lower somewhat broad.

RHAMNUS *œnopolia*, is by the *Chinese* called *Kog-ne-imm*. On the leaves I found a *larva hirsuta, luteo, cœruleo, fusco et albo, variegata*. Its *antennæ* are long, like the hair of a whisker, black, but blue at the bottom: the head is brownish-yellow, like lattice-work: the articulated back is dotted yellow and white: between the third and fourth row of dots are two white hairy tufts. Twelve pair of (blue) *elevations* had black hair on the sides, some (white ones) on the tail excepted. The three pair of fore-feet are brown, the four pair of hind-feet likewise, and besides these is a pair under the tail. The *larva* is about an inch long, and of the thickness of a small goose-quill.

CONYZA *Chinensis* grew among the stones on high places. And also

Eriocaulon sexangulare.

Oldenlandia umbellata.

Mollugo

Mollugo pentaphylla.

Ammania baccifera.

Urena procumbens, floribus minoribus, a little tree with a very low stem, whose boughs hung round about on the ground. I only found a single one of this kind, and that on the summit of a mountain. At first sight its fructification looked like that of our *agrimony.*

A PLANT like the *Bromelia* stood near the water; but I could not ascertain it, as the fructification was wanting.

OF such plants as are good against scurvy I found none growing spontaneously in *China*; nor one with a cruciated flower (*Tetradynamia*). Indeed I did not hear of any body here who had been much incommoded with the scurvy. But in those countries where this disease is common, anti-scorbutic plants grow in plenty, especially on the sea-shores; that the sailors, who are most afflicted with this distemper, may, as soon as they land, have the necessary remedies at hand. Thus we may see in every place the clearest marks of the all-wise dispositions of our great CREATOR; and the more we consider nature, the more we are led to the knowledge of him, who is the LORD of the univerſe.

THE harveſt time now came on, for which reaſon the *Chineſe* aſſembled in great numbers, to mow their rice, carry it home, and dry it in convenient places.

THE ſailor, who ſome days ago fell from our ſhip into the river, and had been by the rapid ſtream carried immediately to the bottom, was now found floating on the water, as commonly happens on the third day. We buried him very late at night, on the *Daniſh Iſland.*

The 20th of *October*.

TO-DAY our boat was ſent to fetch water from the *Daniſh Iſland*, whither I went with it. We entered with the tide into a canal between the rice fields, nearer to the mouth of the river than in the above-mentioned burying-place. We fetched the water out of a pit at the bottom of a mountain; and nothing but the continual ſupply of water could make us believe that this was a ſpring; and even that might

might arife from the water coming down the hills. The inhabitants, who were here in their plantations, had purpofely ftirred the water to make it muddy, that we might not go higher up; for mifchievous people fometimes do them a good deal of mifchief by pulling up their potatoes, fugar-canes, &c. As I went on between their uninclofed fields, I was afked by them, what countrymen we were? and upon my anfwering, we are all of us *Soyamen* (for fo they call the *Swedes*), I met with no further oppofition; but a *Chinefe* told me, that fome *Englifhmen* had pulled up feveral roots in his garden the day before: he then accompanied me, and offered me fome potatoes; but I was more thirfty than hungry, and the water was fo wretched, though it was become clear, that when it was ufed for tea, it ftained cotton with blue fpots. From this we concluded it was a mineral water; but we wanted the neceffary materials to try it. It became milky with fugar of lead.

OXALIS *corniculata*, by the *Chinefe* called *Syn-mce*, grew near the fpring, and in other low and fhady places. The *corollæ* is as long again as the *calyx*: the *capfule* is pentagonal, oblong, with a point, and the whole plant is hairy.

RUELLIA

RUELLIA *crispa* grew under a tree on a high mountain. The *calyx* is double, perfiftent, and vifcous; the lower one is triphyllous, its *foliola* linear and ciliated; the upper one is quinquefid, with fegments as in the inferior one: neither of them are deciduous, but the flower is fo: the *corolla* is infundibuliform, cylindrical below, and inflated at top: the *faux* is bearded: the *limbus* is quinquefid: the *laciniæ* are almoft round, equal to each other, emarginated, and fomewhat reflected: the four *filaments* are pointed, and fet at the bottom of the cavity in the *corolla*: the two longer ones are woolly, and bend towards the incifions of the *limbus*: the *antheræ* are oblong, triangular, erected: the *piftillum* is longer than the *filaments*: the *germen* is oblong: the *ftylus* is filiform, and dentated at the top: the *ftigma* is long, fharp-pointed, and often bent. The plant is a *fuffrutex*, and has the appearance of our yellow cock's comb (*Rhinanthus crifta galli*) it is rough, and lies on the ground. The root is ramofe: the ftem is almoft round, knobby, naked below, woody, and ramofe: the leaves are alternate, lanceolated, oval, petiolated, undulated, green on the upper, but whitifh on the under fide. The

flowers

flowers grow at the top in globose *cymæ*, and are yellow: the *bracteæ* are lanceolated. It grows on open hills. The *Chinese* name is *Patt-fa*.

MONARDA *Chinensis* grew on a barren mountain. The *calyx* is double; the superior one is pentaphyllous, with leaves of equal breadth; the lower is diphyllous: the *corolla* is monopetalous: its tube is cylindrical, and longer than the *calyx*: the upper-lip is undivided, and small; but the lower is trilaciniated, inflected, and longer than the upper one: the *stamina* are two, with a single *pistillum*. Its yellow flowers are axillary, and very small. The stalk is fibrous. It grows on barren places.

LOBELIA *Zeylanica* flowered in the same place with the former. The *calyx* is quinquefid, expanded, hairy below, with oblong fringes of the length of the *corolla*, which is monopetalous and fastened to the *calyx*: its tube is cylindrical: the *limbus* quinquefid: the upper-lip is trifid, with oval, cuspidated, reflected, *laciniæ*: the lower-lip is bifid, its *laciniæ* are the same as those of the upper-lip: the five *filaments* are filiform, broad, of

the

the length of the tube, and come out of the bell-shaped *nectarium*; two of them are hairy below: the *antheræ* grow together into an oblong cylinder: the *pistillum* is of the length of the *filaments*: the *germen* is almost egg-shaped: the *stylus* is filiform: the *stigma* is bifid or bilabiated: the *capsule* is egg-shaped: the *seeds* are numerous, and very small. The plant grows in watry and shady places, and creeps: the *stalk* is round: the *leaves* are alternate, cordated, crenated, smooth, petiolated: the *flower-stalks*, or *peduncles*, are axillar, are the length of the leaves, and each bears only one flower: the flowers are blue.

EVOLVULUS *alsinoides* is a very small, but fine and scarce plant, which likewise was an inhabitant of a barren mountain; and at a distance looked like flax: the *calyx* is quinquefid, with sharp *segments*, which are shorter than the *corolla*; this is monopetalous and inflated: the five *filaments* are shorter than the *corolla*: the *antheræ* are oblong: the *germen* is single: the *stylus* quadrifid: the *stigmas* entire. The plant is of the length of a span, and looks like the common flax.

HEDYSARUM *triflorum*; the flower of this plant has eight *antheræ*, whereof one is single, but

but the other seven are connate, or grow together.

POLYGONUM *Chinense*, by the *Chinese* called *Ka-yong-moa*.

SOLIDAGO *Chinensis, caule procumbente, ramis alternis, foliis radicalibus linearibus.* It grows scarce one foot high.

POLYGALA *ciliata.*

VERBESINA *Chinensis*, by the *Chinese* called *Kaling-fa*.

CLEMATIS *Chinensis*. It has from three to six *pistilla:* the *styli* are plumose, reflected, and placed in a circle. I have seen no filaments. The shrub is one of the climbers, and very ramose.

COMMELINA *communis.*

COMMELINA *Chinensis*, or, as the *Chinese* call it, *Ka-tyaa*. The *petals* are all equal in size: the *stem* is knobby: the *leaves* are narrow, lanceolated, rough, alternate, and end in a *vagina*. Perhaps it is the same with the *Commelina nudiflora*.

ARTEMISIA *vulgaris* is the only *Swedish* plant in this country [c], though it varies in some measure from ours. The *Chinese* heal wounds with it; and to that purpose apply the fresh plant bruised. They call it *Gnai*.

BACCHARIS *Indica*, by the *Chinese* called *Kate-gnai*.

BUXOIDES *aculeata*, what the *Chinese* call *Sow-pann-ghipp*, is like our *box-tree*, but thorny. I did not see its parts of fructification.

ZANTHOXYLON *trifoliatum*. A tree which has not been observed before. The *Chinese* call it *Lack-fa*.

CONYZA *hirsuta*, of which the *Chinese* name is *Kang-gan-fa*.

KATOA is a long climbing plant, with round leaves and red flowers. It was without flowers when I saw it.

S'YOE-LOCK-TAO (*Dolichos scandens maximus*) had large black beans, which were said

---

[c] This is also an *English* plant, *mugwort*.

to be poisonous. The pods likewise grow black when the fruit ripens.

NAUCLEA *orientalis* grew on an hill, and was now in flower. I made the following remarks on it: the partial *calyces* are monophyllous, quadrifid, pilose on the margin: the *corolla* is infundibuliform: its tube is almost cylindrical: the *faux* is inflated and woolly: the *limbus* is quadrifid, and reflected: the four *filaments* are short, fastened in the *faux*: the *antheræ* are small, though longer than the *filaments*, and erected: the *stigma* is narrow, and bifid. The plant grows bushy, and is of the length of a span. The *root* creeps, and shoots many branches: the *stem* is quadrangular: the flowers form a *capitulum* or head: the *leaves* are oval, lanceolated, without incisions or foot-stalks, and opposite. The *Chinese* call it *Moy-fa*.

CASSYTHA *filiformis*. The description of the genus is to be met with in *Linnæi Gen. Plantarum*. The plant is scandent, filiform, rough, and commonly climbs on the *Euphorbia*. The little *branches* are in no order: the *flowers* grow in bunches like grapes: the *stipulæ* on the branches are oval and small.

In the *East Indies*, boats and vessels are neither tarred, nor their chinks caulked (filled up with tow); but they are made to keep out the water with a sort of cement, which is prepared in the following manner: the aforementioned plant is taken and beaten to a pulp; then some lime, both pounded and sifted, is kneaded amongst it, till it grows to a proper consistence. This cement secures their boats longer from springing leaks, than tarring; besides that it does not become fluid as tar does in hot countries. When a person's head is rubbed with the slime which is squeezed out of the *Cassytha*, it makes the hair grow the thicker. When the bruised stalks are put into milk, it curdles, and the whey is useful in agues. See *Rumph. Herbar. Amb.*

END OF VOL. I.

www.ingramcontent.com/pod-product-compliance
Lightning Source LLC
Chambersburg PA
CBHW020122020526
44111CB00049B/624